Don't Call Me "Mother"

Isolde Martin

First published by Busybird Publishing 2017
Copyright © 2017 Isolde Martin

ISBN
Print: 978-1-925585-75-9
EBook: 978-1-925585-76-6

Isolde Martin has asserted her right under the Copyright, Designs and Patents Act 1988 to be identified as the author of this work. The information in this book is based on the author's experiences and opinions. The publisher specifically disclaims responsibility for any adverse consequences, which may result from use of the information contained herein. Permission to use information has been sought by the author. Any breaches will be rectified in further editions of the book.

All rights reserved. No part of this publication may be reproduced, stored in or introduced into a retrieval system, or transmitted in any form, or by any means (electronic, mechanical, photocopying, recording or otherwise) without the prior written permission of the author. Any person who does any unauthorised act in relation to this publication may be liable to criminal prosecution and civil claims for damages. Enquiries should be made through the publisher.

Cover design: Busybird Publishing
Layout and typesetting: Busybird Publishing
Editor: Robert Frolla

Busybird Publishing
2/118 Para Road
Montmorency, Victoria
Australia 3094
www.busybird.com.au

Contents

The Year 1923	1
The School Years	15
It's a Young Life	40
The Young Have to Serve	98
Coming of Age	125
Time to Get Married	145
Holy Matrimony – A Niche for Life	184
Pride and Dignity	206
About the Author	237

The Year 1923

The year 1923 was one month old. It had come in with subfreezing temperatures. Even though this was to be expected in January in the lands on the northern foot of the Alps, the people living there each year found it a challenge to live through this frosty time. Of course, they also felt pride in their ability to withstand such harsh conditions, to have enough food through the winter and a warm place to return to from outdoor work, and to enjoy cozy evenings to play cards or tell stories in the only room of the house that was heated.

In this household that warm room, the Stube, functioned as both kitchen and living room. That was the architecture and the lifestyle of dairy farmers in that area at that time. The hall, the stairways, the upper floor gallery and all bedrooms were left to the winter cold. The sleepers, after they had become fully awake in the morning, often were greeted by pretty "ice flowers" on the windows. Then one needed to dress quickly or put on the clothes under the covers. As there was no warm water in the mornings, any washing was put off until it had been heated by way of cooking a meal on a huge wood burning stove.

On that day the only bedroom on the ground floor at the north side of this old house was warmed a little more than usual by the women who were standing around the only bed in it. One of them was scolding her daughter, who was in bed wincing with pain, for she was in labor. The other one, a mature woman with a seemingly short and stocky but sturdy body, was the midwife, Maria.

"That's okay," the mother hissed down at her daughter, Liz. "You deserve that pain. That's what happens to sinners doing such dirty things. Why did you give in to that irresponsible man?" In her anger, the mother had not considered that she had borne her thirteen children in the same physical pain.

Yes, why did Liz agree to a time in the barn with him? He was not particularly good-looking. But he talked sweet and had the means to raise a family. And Liz at her ripe age of twenty-nine desperately wanted to get married. Spinsterhood in this conservative community of farmers was not anything to look forward to. Her social value, that she knew for sure, would now slip to the bottom of the hierarchy. She would simply have to stay at home. Nobody would want to marry her now, with an illegitimate child. Oh yes, she would be tolerated by her family. After all, additional labor on a dairy farm was always needed. Later, after the death of her parents, one of her older brothers would inherit the farm and the blacksmith workshop. Should he get married she would have to take orders from his wife and work for next to nothing. Her prospects would indeed be dismal. So she had risked a little sex in order to better her chances to get married. It had not been even very enjoyable sex. He was a bit rough and it hurt. But his sweet talk had fooled her.

However, her calculation, if indeed it was one, did not materialize. After her partner for an hour of fun heard about Liz's pregnancy he retreated, denying any involvement. He had little to fear for proof of paternity. As a respectable husband and father of four it was easy for him to accuse Liz of lying. She obviously was a single woman of the loose kind. Why else would she work so far away from home? Liz knew that she must not even try. One time a sinner, always a sinner, so they thought. She was sure of that. Besides, it was better to keep her head down and hope that people would forget. Slim hope it was.

"Leave her alone now," the midwife interfered, trying to protect Liz's charge from mental pain in addition to her labor pains. She wanted the mother to leave so she could attend to the birthing process, to make sure that no complications arose. The social judgment passed over the young woman was already doing enough harm to her self-esteem, her feelings of guilt, her shame as a "loose woman" and her definition as a sinner as defined by the church. The midwife knew all of this because she was not the only one coming down with a pregnancy out of wedlock. Quite a few young beauties, such as her own mother, had suffered a similar fate after giving in to a happy hour as demanded by nature or by a promising man. The village priest had often times lectured sternly that such things are for married people only, and only then sexual activity was without sin. Otherwise, such activity had to be included in confession should there be any hope for forgiveness.

***

The time finally had arrived for the infant to be born into a family dismayed by the shame of this birth. The whole village knew about it, about this immoral daughter. Moreover, this birth happened in a house that was next door to a Catholic church, with only the graveyard and a small street separating the buildings. Every Sunday the church bells would call the people to mass, and every Sunday afternoon for prayers, and at least twice more on weekdays. Thus this sinner would not only be reminded of her despicable character by her mother, but also by the bells of the church.

Liz tried to give birth without crying out in a fruitless attempt to conceal the birth of her daughter. She did not quite succeed. Her muted cries of pain seemed to happen all by themselves. Yet, she would have liked to have screamed freely. She knew she was not entitled to that, for she was an immoral person.

"Here is your daughter," the midwife said, showing Liz the tiny infant. With curiosity the young mother raised her head, eyeing her baby like any mother would. But she also was not sure if this newborn was also a sinner now. Certainly it was not as valued as one born to a married couple. It would not have the same rights, the same opportunities, the same appreciation and maybe even not the same love. But love was exactly what Liz felt ambivalent about. She did feel love for her baby but it was mixed with feelings of rejection. In fact, she was very confused which feelings were allowed, feelings she was supposed to have towards her new daughter who was but a few minutes old.

She took her newborn from the midwife, and held her to her breast under the covers to shield the little one from the cold. She was a mother after all, protective and caring for the new life. Nature did not make the distinction between legitimate and illegitimate; people did. However, those maternal feelings did not rise above those other ones. The thoughts instilled into her brain by her elders – that this tiny human being in her arms was also the forbidden fruit of an immoral act – came back interfering with her motherly feelings.

"Take her back," she said, holding her daughter out to the midwife. Maria took the little bundle and put it into her cradle, rocking it to sleep.

Two nights and a day passed since Liz gave birth. The scolding had dwindled and then ceased. Liz's own mother, who initially had ignored the baby and refused to teach her daughter how to take care of her infant, showed signs of wavering in her resolve. She had already picked up the baby and inspected it. Liz knew that she was checking for physical signs in the baby's face that would refer either to the absent father's family or her own. This was no small matter, for it would be proportional to the acceptance of the new arrival in the family. This baby was and would remain illegitimate, and also would be a member of the family no matter what. It was simply fact. But that blow to the pride and honor of Liz's grandparents and siblings could be reduced by likeness of appearance. After all, then the baby girl could be identified as one of them, at least to the degree that she did not remind them of her unknown father, that good-for-nothing, irresponsible coward. He obviously had preferred anonymity and did not care for his daughter or her mother.

For the moment, nobody in Liz's family or in the village knew who had taken advantage of this loose young woman. And why should he not? She had probably seduced him, offered herself to him or was just simply not chaste enough the way the church taught and the sixth commandment demanded. Family and neighbors were sure to figure out who was the unlucky creator of this infant. For one thing, everybody knew where Liz had been working. It was that village about thirty kilometers west, the one that could only be reached by taking a left turn at the bottom of that hill. Did she not work there at the local inn? Of course, that was a house that had many patrons every day, an ideal place to engage in immoral behavior. With such discussions, the circle of candidates was narrowed down.

Like most dramatic and traumatic events in life this one also went away as the primary topic in people's conversations. Moreover, nature has equipped babies with much innocence and charm. Wide-eyed they look at everybody, with unconditional positive regard. Thus, the little baby girl gradually won over the hearts of the grandparents and, to varying degrees, her three uncles, who were unmarried and therefore still living at home, and her aunt. Grandmother now would hold little Rosa, change her diapers if her mother was outdoors working, rock her to sleep and keep watch over her. When Thekla, Rosa's aunt, came home for a visit, she played with Rosa and sang her the lullabies and baby songs that all children of that culture and time came to hear from their loved ones.

Thekla brought up another issue that nobody wanted to think about yet. Liz was very afraid of this.

"When is she going to be baptized?"

Liz felt immediate dread and remained silent. But the new grandmother shot back. "Don't know yet. Who do you think will want to be her godmother?"

That question sent a sharp pain through Liz's heart. She was afraid of the commotion and the rejections.

"I am not going to run around asking anybody," her mother announced firmly.

Thekla began to feel sorry for her sister.

"Mother, you should be holding your tongue a bit more. You had two kids out of wedlock yourself. Have you forgotten? You just were lucky that that man married you and became our father as well. Who was the godfather for your first one then?"

Thekla felt more and more angry at her own mother. But her words hit home. Her mother was momentarily at a loss of words. Daughters don't talk to their mothers like that! Her mother looked over to her husband for support. After all, he was part of her own sins. Why was he so silent? No word had come from him during the whole discussion. His wife urged him to respond. So he did, indeed.

"So what? Let the past be the past."

The rest of his feelings about babies born out of wedlock he kept to himself. Nobody knew that he felt it not to be a sin at all, that it was a nice thing to put a son or daughter into the world no matter what the circumstances were. He had his own feelings about morality and the sixth commandment. Since they were not congruent with the teachings of the church he kept silent. In those days and in that village you were better off to appear compliant.

But before she could collect her defensive words, Thekla presented the solution to the problem.

"I will go see the priest. And I will be her godmother and she will be baptized next Sunday like we all have been baptized."

Neither Liz nor the newly made grandmother had a comment to that, as they hoped that little Rosa would be baptized. They had heard of illegitimate babies that had to be baptized by the midwife. But this baby was accepted for baptism by this priest. Thekla never revealed anything about the conversation that took place between her and the parish priest. And nobody asked either. The baptism was not announced in the weekly church flyer. It happened as unobtrusively as Liz had hoped.

Despite such an important issue being positively, and slightly, resolved, the young mother could not shake off her feelings of guilt and shame. The latter, however, was not as firmly established in her heart as the former. For it alternated with her hate that she felt for the father of her child.

He was exonerated by society. A man, so the common understanding goes, has a very strong sex drive and thus at times succumbs to his desires. That would not happen if a woman would not be available or would firmly reject male advances. Liz was willing to adhere to this philosophy but was not quite successful. She was stuck with a child: she could no longer go to the dances in her village, she had lost her good marriage prospects, and she had to endure the punishment of public disgrace. But she did not utter a sound about her inner feelings to anyone. It would have been no use but instead would have opened the door for further wrath. Do I have to live like this now forever? she would ask herself. Will I never shake my image as a loose woman? Will I always be seen as the fallen woman, the second-class woman, unfit for marriage? She was desperate, angry, hateful and sad. She had no idea how to change her fate for the better.

Sleep eluded her, naturally. Of course, she nursed the baby, but she offered her breasts with mixed feelings. There was the pleasure of mothering her offspring, but her tiny infant was also the living proof of her downfall. Without her she would be the blond-haired beauty with the blue eyes. Her anguish grew and grew. Eventually it came to frighten her.

Fortunately, one day Liz knew what to do. She made a request to Thekla, who lived at home again for lack of employment.

"Before you go to bed tonight, come to my bedroom," she asked Thekla.

"Sure," Thekla answered, wondering about the unusual request.

Later that night, Thekla found the infant sleeping in her little crib and her mother was snug under the covers with only her head outside. Her beautiful blue eyes were tearful, her lips firmly pressed together.

"What is it?" Thekla asked her sister.

Motioning with her head to her sleeping daughter, Liz said, "Take her to your bedroom so that I don't do anything to her." Her sister's eyebrows shot up. Her face expressed incredulity.

"It is not that bad. Don't be ridiculous! It will blow over. We all love her."

"Yeah, sure." Liz's voice clearly conveyed her disbelief.

"I can do this now," Thekla said, "but I am not always going to be here. I will have to leave again."

Liz simply remained silent, not knowing an answer to that. Thekla took the child into her arms and went to her own bed upstairs. The next morning, little Rosa woke up in an environment she did not recognize. She started crying.

The men of those days adhered mostly to the understanding that babies belonged in the domain of women. This family was no exception to that cultural notion: that timeless rule stood fast. But this baby's uncles gradually, one after another, were drawn into the magic of new life in the form of their infant niece. The visible signs of this process were smiles and cooing in direction of the baby, or a little pat on her head or taking her tiny hands when walking by.

Kon, the youngest of her uncles, would even pick her up and carry her, lifting her up into the air with outstretched arms, hoping for a smile or a squeal of delight. As the baby's gross motor and social development progressed she showed signs of pleasure when Kon approached. Her little arms reached out for him – come to me, play with me. And thus, the foundation was laid for a trusting and affectionate relationship that would last for a lifetime.

But acceptance and surely love also came her way from her other uncles, even from the two who did not live on the farm anymore. There seemed to be a consensus that this child "is one of us", no matter what.

"What do you want, it's not her fault," Jakob said to the fully assembled family one winter evening. The importance of his opinion in terms of such children from immoral sisters was not to manifest itself until thirteen years later. For at that point he had become the owner of the farm. Although it was custom in those days that unmarried siblings could stay at their birthplace, it still might have been understood as a great sacrifice to let an illegitimate child and her mother stay forever. After all, there was a man somewhere ducking his responsibility. And why should he be left off free?

***

And so it was that little Rosa was sure of her acceptance into her mother's family. Nobody made any reference to her illegitimacy; nobody treated her as a burden. That was confirmed on a daily basis. The best was when her favorite uncle Kon picked her up and threw her into the air, catching her with a swinging motion. Rosa squealed with delight. She had developed trust in her uncles. They loved her just like that. She also knew what the do's and don'ts were. No special treatment for her either. The rules were clear. They have been in place for generations and derived from the local culture and the teachings of the church. Unexpectedly to some, her early childhood was a happy affair after all.

Rosa seemed to be a bit on the sensitive side, however. She cried easily, sometimes for no apparent reason. Other times the cause of her distress was obvious. This was especially so when her mother got dressed to bike to a store in the neighboring village. Little Rosa didn't just cry: it was more that she howled, almost to the point of a temper tantrum. The adults in the family felt puzzled and annoyed by the racket. It seemed out of proportion to the cause.

"Stop that!" her grandmother said sharply to her. "There is no reason for this. Your mother is only leaving for a few hours." Yet little Rosa's anxiety was high and could not be brushed away easily. She was just fearful that her mom would not return.

These were the small shopping trips to a fabric store, for it was Liz's chore to haul needed items home. For transportation she used a bicycle, which made for a tiresome trip up and down hills until she came into that village. It was located on the highest of the surrounding hills and therefore had a beautiful view all around. But Liz had no eye for the idyllic countryside. She had been given a sum of money from her mother with which to pay for the purchases. She always liked this little excursion for if she shopped smartly there might be some spending money left. In the past, she would often times be able to get a bright blue ribbon for her summer hat or anything else with that hue. It was a suitable color for her because it enhanced the blue of her eyes. But now that her daughter was four years old she opted in favor of a few candies for her.

It gave her pleasure to see the delight on her daughter's face when she handed Rosa the sweets. The problem was to hide the little bag of candies from the others, especially from her mother. She feared their reactions if they learned that her daughter used up some of the meager family resources. After all, her daughter should not have been. To be sure, Liz still felt ambivalent about her daughter. Often motherly love would get the upper hand with her feelings. So whenever she gave her daughter little treats she did it in secret and told Rosa: "Go outside and eat this in the sandbox. Do not tell anybody."

But it was actually no longer necessary to urge her daughter in secrecy in matters of extras. Rosa already had internalized that, together with a feeling that her mother must love her after all. How that behavior of hers related to the times when Liz pushed her away, little Rosa could not figure out. Actually at times she did not know for sure whether she was loved by her mother or not for she got confusing messages. It was not too long ago when she received a particularly puzzling and painful one as well.

On a rainy day, little Rosa stood in the door frame of the entrance to the house. She needed help to put on her little rubber boots and her raincoat to go outside. Her mother was just crossing the barnyard, walking towards the barn gates. Rosa had a strong voice for her small frame and called her mother with all her might.

"Mother, help me!"

Liz turned to look at her and put her finger over her mouth to signal not to scream like that. She came up to her daughter to get her properly bundled up against the heavy rain.

"Sit down on that first step," she told her daughter. And while Rosa put on her rubber boots, Liz instructed her, "Don't call me 'mother'." Her voice was almost a whisper. "Use my first name like the others do. Call me Liz."

Little Rosa just looked into her mother's face with big questioning, if not to say puzzled, eyes. She had heard her playmates use "mother". Was that not the right word to use for hers? She could not have described her feelings, but she could express them. Rosa started crying. Immediately her mother tried to comfort her.

"Don't cry! I am your mother. Just don't call me that."

In an extended family living under one roof, the pain of a little one is often diffused by the adults inadvertently. Since this was a dairy farm and blacksmith operation, her uncles were working outdoors most of the day or in the blacksmith's. Besides, the house was big, the barn even bigger. Together with the shed containing the chicken house, the firewood and the surrounding orchard, there was a lot of opportunity to spread out and things could easily be done without anyone else knowing.

Consequently none of the other family members knew about the conflicting messages that their little niece received from her mother. When Kon found little Rosa sitting on the front step crying, he asked what was the matter but did not really expect an answer. He just picked her up and carried her with him on his way to the wagon, which was already hitched up to an ox. He sat the girl safely onto the platform and off they went together. He covered her with an extra raincoat and talked to her, pointed out the water paddles and the little streams on the unpaved road and other things suitable to redirect her mind away from her cause of distress. It worked! Comfort settled into the little girl. She stretched out her arms to her uncle. He gladly took her and felt the pleasure of Rosa pressing her soft cheeks on his.

Uncle Stefan, when he was home on a visit, also gave Rosa that reassuring feeling. He loved her obviously too, for he played games with her that made her laugh a lot. He would place her on his knees, holding her with one hand in her back. With the other he squeezed the skin of her knee to make a fold.

"Look," he said, "that is a little calf's mouth." That made Rosa screech with delight.

"Do it again!" she demanded. And he did until she tired of the game and asked instead, "Do you love me?" Rosa, now five years old, sometimes needed reassurance.

Of course, there were other sources of affection and emotional comfort. No matter that those were of non-human kind. The farm was a lively and interesting place to live on. Little Rosa was taken along almost everywhere to the meadows that were sprinkled with colorful flowers like a Monet painting. She saw the grass being cut and dried to hay. That allowed for some fun hopping over the heaps or kicking them apart or playing hide and seek. She was taken to the wheat harvest in hot summer days and could ride home on top of the laden wagon. Kon lifted her up and took her down with strong protective hands.

A trip to the forest, be it winter or summer, made little Rosa jump with pleasant anticipation. It smelled so nicely from the pine needles and moss. The latter could be used to build a soft bed to lie down on, even if you got a bit wet on your behind. There were so many sounds from birds and so many blueberries, raspberries and mushrooms to collect. And there were the thickets, those where the witches might hide and where Hansel and Gretel hid, as it said in the fairytale.

But it was the animals on the farm that little Rosa favored. There were the baby calves, the rose-colored piglets, the little ducklings, and the fussy yellow geese that she saw working their way out of the eggs. All of them she wanted to hold and pet. She knew no fear. However, it was the cats that held still the longest for petting. The tiny ones, still with closed eyes, she felt a bit apprehensive about since a mama cat was disturbingly vigilant. But ones they no longer nursed, they played rambunctiously with Rosa.

Oftentimes, she needed to be guided and instructed to be gentle with the young. She learned that they would go to sleep on her lap! That means they liked her. Matter of fact and most important, she knew that they loved her. When Rosa had a fever and needed to stay in bed she could take one of the cats into her bed. That made for entertainment and for that all-important feeling of an emotional bond.

"A cat can take the fever away," Rosa was told. So she kept still, at least for a while, listening to the comforting purr of the cat under her covers.

So after the disaster of her illegitimate birth and with only one parent, little Rosa had settled comfortably into a life on a Bavarian farm. She enjoyed the full protection of her grandparents, and her hesitant, ambivalent but loving mother. Besides that, she was blessed with uncles Kon, Anselm, Jakob, Stefan, and Ferdinand. Ferdinand came home every Sunday for the day as he worked on another farm. Stefan and his wife lived so far north that they had to take a four-hour train ride to get there. But Stefan always made her laugh. Soon she would learn that she needed that protective umbrella of her family because quite a few inhabitants of her village adhered to the common thinking about girls born out of wedlock. They were the product of sin, weren't they?

For the most part little Rosa was happy with her life. She had plenty of playmates. In every house located around the farm there were at least two her age. The children were allowed to freely go in and out of each other's homes, play in the orchards that surrounded almost each home, or come to her to have a go in her pile of sand under the walnut tree. Parents were not afraid for their four- or five-year olds for there were also enough adults, family members or hired farm helpers who watched the children. Traffic through the village street consisted mostly of horse-drawn vehicles, bikers, or walkers.

Only when the conversation of those little ones came to their fathers little Rosa got quiet. She tried to retreat, hide, or, better yet, become invisible. For one time five-year-old Alois from across the street said to her:

"You don't have a father! My mom said he did not want your mom!"

Rosa was confronted with such a statement the first time. She stared at Alois. She was taken by surprise and could not think of a response. Her heart was pounding. Best thing was to look down and play on, as if she had not heard. But Maria had stopped with her sand artwork and asked:

"Why don't you have a father?"

Little Rosa started crying and ran into the house to seek comfort from her grandmother. She was in there preparing the evening meal. Liz's chores kept her mostly out of the house, in the barn, in the vegetable garden or in the field. Sometimes it took time to find her. Moreover, she did not interrupt her work for long to comfort her daughter. Usually her brothers were watching and Liz felt, like so often still, the full weight of her guilt and shame. Spending too much time with Rosa was a luxury she could not afford, for she should not be here in the first place, or so her thinking went. On that day, however, Liz was inside. She gave her daughter a quick hug and said empty words to her:

"Don't worry. Just tell them to shut up."

No-one saw the tearful blue eyes of her expressing guilt and longing when she thought she had to send her daughter away too fast. With her grandmother, Rosa could afford a bit more time for comforting and drying tears. Sometimes little Rosa ran first to her mother and then to her grandmother. But more and more she went straight to grandmother.

Of course, her grandmother was also "mother". Little Rosa had learned to call her mother by her first name. In fact, it was burned into her young memory and feelings. It was to remain there for the rest of her life. But the time would come when her mature mind would call up the issue again. For now she was not entirely left without the magic word that she heard so often from her playmates. On a daily basis, she heard her uncles and Liz call Grandmother by that name: Mother. She was everybody's mother in the house. As a matter of fact, little Rosa also learned that grandfather was Father. So she used the same names, mother and father, for her grandparents as all the other family members did. Nobody corrected her. She had a mother and father after all, just like the other kids.

The School Years

Thus, having the peculiarities of her existence, her illegitimacy, the absence of a father, the oddity of her mother called Liz and her grandmother called mother stored in safe, non-threatening places in her young, developing mind, Rosa had spent a largely happy early childhood. She had developed into a physically strong six-year-old girl with thick, heavy plaits of a brunette hue; green, vigilant eyes; and a pleasant demeanor. She was of a most inquisitive mind and could laugh with a chuckle that sounded like the water rushing over rocks in the many creeks in that landscape.

She was shy and preferred to avoid visitors, lest they were neighbors she had known since birth. They would perhaps pat her on her head but did otherwise not pay too much attention to her. But she did not only live on a farm: her family also ran a blacksmith workshop, working with everything that a farmer needed made of iron. This included putting horse shoes on their heavy horses. Although she loved to watch the activities in that shop or see the horses, she felt very uncomfortable when the farmers or their farmhands wanted to play around with her or even to tease her. Should someone be mindless enough to ask her where her Daddy was, she looked up and then ran out of the shop.

With her small peers, however, she turned out to be quite assertive. For one thing, she dared to talk back to them if they bothered her. And she did that vehemently if need be. The local grade school was only a two-minute walk away from her house, right to the east of the church. During their recess, the kids would play on the square in front of her house, where the farmers always parked their horse-drawn wagons when they had to visit the blacksmith workshop. That was the custom since the school had been established the previous century. So every weekday – six days that was – first graders as well as seventh graders, and all other grades in between, would be there for her to watch or mingle with them. She liked that. And that was good because come September 1929 she herself would be a first grader and play on that square in front of her house during break.

That was only a few months away now. She was eagerly awaiting her first school day. Yet there was also a feeling of trepidation mixed in. The teacher was known to be a no-nonsense guy, but fair. What exactly was "fair"? And the priest would be there twice a week to teach the Bible in class for an hour. She had been in church on Sundays with Liz or Mother-Grandmother often and had heard him shout from the pulpit. Although she never knew why he yelled so loudly she always felt uncomfortable then.

***

Rosa did not get a whole lot of new clothes throughout the year – only what was needed. Nothing was for show, nothing for vanity at all. Money was tight. Her mother had more the do-it-yourself attitude in terms of a wardrobe. That had long since been conveyed to the little girl that should not have been. But getting ready to start school was different. It was important to not stick out like one was poor.

Rosa was elated. She would get new clothing just like all the other first graders. She would get two new dresses, two new aprons, new shoes and blue ribbons to be tied at the end of her long, beautiful plaits. The other girls would be envious and they had no reason to tease her for being dressed in hand-me-downs. School was going to be fun.

The first school day had arrived. Rosa felt a mixture of excitement and anxiety. With her new dress, her new shoes and her plaits being tied with blue ribbons, she spun around the Stube to make her skirt fly.

"You are a pretty girl," her grandmother remarked with a rare smile.

Her mother looked at her daughter silently. Her heart was thumping in her chest, caused by her concerns about the things her child might experience in school. Would the teacher and the priest treat her differently because of her illegitimate birth? Would the children tease her? Sure, she was not the only child who had an unknown father and an unwed mother, but that did not matter, for they were all considered children of lesser importance and status. She knew this from her own school days.

She was pleased that her own mother had helped her to sew a few new outfits for her daughter. That way she surely was not going to be different from the other kids. On the contrary, there were first graders who did come from parents so poor that they had to make do with the best hand-me-downs they had. But then, was it not too ostentatious for Rosa to appear like a rich girl, as if she had a father with means to afford such luxury as a new outfit for school? On the other hand, this dress might conceal her social birth defect, at least for today. And that was worth a lot.

In those days, it was custom for the kids from the village to walk the few minutes to the school house and to the only classroom by themselves. The children from the farms located farther away, some as much as forty-five minutes walking time, were brought by their mothers. So Rosa was sent off with a "be good" from her family, alone. And that was it.

She ran to the school and waited in front of the door until the teacher opened it. Quickly all the other kids who lived in the village gathered around the entrance. Rosa was in the middle of it. Her eyes were nervously scanning her playmates for reassurance and then the children from the farms around for signs of sneering. However, nobody focused on anything else than the moment when they were let in and the things that would happen thereafter. And when that door finally opened widely and the teacher told them to walk quietly upstairs to the classroom, she did that with a light heart and full of eager anticipation. She had taken the first hurdle.

The room had a row of benches where seat and table were one piece. On the left side were those desks that seated two. On the right side, the window side, were the overly long desks seating four pupils in one row. These were the places for the lower grades. Rosa already knew that from all the talk about school while she had been amongst the children during break and from the grown-ups who had went to school before her. But she did not want to sit in the front row. The teacher would be right in front of her and all the kids would be behind her. She would be exposed to all of the people in the room. No, she wanted to be less visible, almost a bit hidden.

She made a dash for the second row of benches seating four and flopped down in the first place next to the window. At least she had four kids between her and the teacher. But her sanctuary did not last for any time at all. With a booming voice, the nearly bald teacher commanded the kids to be quiet. He will not tolerate any talking while in class, unless asked, so he told in a loud voice. Now, as for the seating, he will now place the kids as he sees fit. Rosa's heart started to thump. When the teacher stopped in his activity of rearranging the seating order and looked over his first graders she silently exhaled a sigh of relief. I can stay here, she thought. But then, like through an acoustic fog, she heard him tell Alois to exchange places with Rosa because he was too tall for the first row and Rosa too small for the second. While Alois took his brand new little slate and his sweater, Rosa still sat and looked on with big eyes, as if she waited to see whether it was meant for sure.

"Go take your stuff and come here. Get going, or did you not hear me?"

Rosa knew the teacher's word had to be obeyed. There was no question about that. Trying to swallow her tears of disappointment and her fear to sit in the front row, she stood up and walked away from her favorite place. When Alois came towards her, having his back to the teacher, he grimaced at Rosa in a triumphant way. That infuriated Rosa. She would not let Alois get away with that, that much she knew instantly. In the afternoon, when the village kids would meet to play hide and seek or maybe a ball game, she would make him lose the game. That was easy, for she could run very fast. She would outrun him.

But before she could get such sweet revenge she had to face the question she feared the most. It came as a surprise, for six-year-olds do not anticipate what the teacher might ask them the first day of school. ABC-students, as first graders used to be called in those days, considered the likelihood of being hit with a ruler over their fingers, or having to stand in a corner of the classroom, facing the wall. To name their parents was, of course, a frequently asked question on their first school day. Not that the teacher needed the information from the children. He had a list of parents' names and the matching child written next to theirs. Rather, it was a way of getting the new kids to talk, to see how they behaved, perhaps to categorize them. There were only four children in front of Rosa. Each rattled off the names of their parents, some with a whispering voice, some with more volume to theirs. Each child had to stand up to pronounce the name of their father and mother. This was considered respectful behavior to the teacher. Hanging heads, downcast eyes with only quick glances at their teacher's face, pulled-in shoulders and stuttering indicated a degree of anxiety the new pupils felt.

With a pounding heart and a flushed face, Rosa dreaded the thought of introducing herself. Nobody had told her how to answer this question before she came to school. What was she supposed to do? But she did not have time to consider the options. Her turn came too quickly. Without a second thought she named her grandparents as her parents. After all, everybody in the family, including her, called them Mother or Father respectively. This was not lying; it was true! Rosa was not reprimanded by her teacher, who knew about her illegitimate existence.

"Is Liz also your mother?" the teacher probed. Rosa only nodded. But Alois, the playmate, shouted out what he knew with all good intentions to help Rosa.

"She does not have a father!" he said. The teacher pointed at Alois with a thin switch, cut from a willow tree.

"You keep quiet! You were not asked!" he boomed in a threatening voice. Rosa's eyes began to flood with tears but she held them back defiantly.

"You sit down," the teacher said to her.

And so began the first class of the first day. The pupils settled down. There was no whispering and no snickering anymore but anxious, tension-ridden silence. With big eyes the kids stared at the teacher, waiting to be told what to do next. Rosa sat almost motionless in her seat. She still could feel her heartbeat, but it was not nearly as wild as before. In fact, she was eager to learn the alphabet. She had been told that this was going to happen the first day of school. That would suit her just fine. Since she had been taught a few letters by Kon already, she had nothing to fear in terms of embarrassment. She was eager to show off what she knew, for that could compensate for her handicap as a fatherless child. She would shine as a smart student and that way be regarded with respect. The other children would like her and that was important.

After four hours, at noon, the first day of school was over. Rosa packed her slate into her schoolbag and stood in line at the classroom door like everyone else. The teacher required them to say goodbye in chorus, as well as answer in chorus. Then he told them to walk quietly down the stairs, and he opened the door. Downstairs, in front of the big front door they stood again until the teacher opened it too. Outside the mothers received their children, at least those who had a long way to walk home, perhaps even through patches of forest. For in those days the people walked or, if they were better off, used bikes. But the kids who lived right in the village, in spitting distance, as it was said, bolted from the front door. Rosa crossed the graveyard as a shortcut. She was home in no time at all. Her uncles saw her coming.

"Did you get hit?" Jakob asked.

"Was it good?" Kon asked.

"Yep," she replied with a grin. She had done it; she was a first grader now! Pride and relief stood written on her face. Later, in the house, Liz nervously waited for Rosa.

"Did they ask you about your parents?" her mother asked, carefully avoiding the word "father". Rosa felt heat rising into her face. But truthfully she answered her, "I said Mother and Father were my parents. That is true."

Without a word Liz put her hand on her daughter's hair and ruffled it a little as a gentle gesture. Rosa knew she had done well and was loved.

The next day at eight in the morning she would be back in school, from now on six days a week for the next seven academic years. However, at seven in the morning, mass was being celebrated in the village church for all the school children. This was no big challenge for six-year-old Rosa. Her mother, her grandparents and her uncles all had to rise before then to tend to the dairy cows. Although she could sleep in until 6.30, the concept of waking up early was already established in her mind. And September, after all, was still a month of warm temperatures.

Since the children were taken to church services by their mothers or grandmothers before the children entered first grade, that mass with Rosa's classmates was nothing unusual save the fact that from now on they had to kneel way in front, in the much smaller children's pews. All the grown-ups could see them and watch their behavior. That was uncomfortable for Rosa. It made her tense to know all the eyes in her back, including her mother's. She had to make sure that they found no fault in her behavior. So she watched the other girls to her left and right with shifting eyes. She simply would do like them, then she would be alright.

Eventually, when the organ started playing, Rosa relaxed. Uneventfully mass proceeded and finished. All the children left and pushed their way through amongst the adults to the main door. Once outside, Rosa started running with the other kids towards the school in a matter of another minute.

All the kids from first to seventh grade, all in one room, sat instantly still when the priest entered the classroom. They knew of his reputation as a stern and also punitive teacher. Indeed, after prayer, he went to the teacher's desk and picked up the switch laying there. Rosa, like most the kids, sat motionless, eyes wide with fear.

Two times a week the parish priest came into the classroom from eight to nine for Bible studies or to teach catechism following mass. Thus, it was better for the kids to attend church service. For the parents knew this man to watch which kids were made to attend services.

That was a good time during summer months. Parents and children from remote farms could walk during the cool hours of the morning. Most who lived on farms far outside the village followed the shortcut paths across meadows and through forests. These trails were well trampled down by their ancestors before them and cut the walking time by half. The morning air also was pleasant, and the grass sparkled with dew drops. Sometimes the forest animals were in the meadows browsing. Flowers of all colors swayed in the breeze all over and made the hilly landscape look like it had been carpeted. As for the winter, things were an entirely different matter. Not that the snow-covered silence would not be beautiful. No, but it was so very cold at 6.30 in the morning. By the time the little walkers reached church their toes and their tender young fingers were tingling from the cold, despite wearing gloves. It was hard, but it was the custom to attend mass at least once or twice during the week before classes started.

Rosa did not particularly like to attend mass. She had been taken by her grandmother already at a much younger age and therefore knew how difficult it was to keep physically and verbally still for so long. Now she felt triumphant, as she had only a very short dash to reach the church. Also, what with most of her classmates around her, holding still had more of a competitive purpose and thus would not be so difficult. She was going to see who was failing and not get a picture from the priest for good behavior when he came to teach "religion hour". To be sure Alois, over on the right side where the boys knelt, would not be able to refrain from looking backwards or whispering too much with Sepp next to him. But Rosa was going to get a picture, which she then could show him in the afternoon when they met for play with all the other village kids.

Only part of the allotted hour did the priest spend with the first graders, for he had another six grades to teach. Dressed in a black suit he walked back and forth in front of his students, all the while swinging and pointing with the switch. He asked the names of the six-year-olds. They had to answer standing, as was the custom with their teacher as well. Some shot up and almost shouted their name, others stood shyly with hanging shoulders and head, whispering. Rosa anxiously awaited her turn, like most children, although she had no problem to just say her name. In that respect she was no different than all the other school mates. Everybody had a name, but not everybody had a father. For his name, luckily, the priest had not asked. He was quite curious otherwise.

"How many of you pray at home?" he wanted to know. All hands went up.

"Who can say a prayer?" he inquired. A few were raising their hands. Rosa certainly could recite prayers, but she did not volunteer. She wanted to go unnoticed.

"Can you say a prayer?" the priest asked, pointing at her with his switch.

"Yes," she said. She stood up and recited an evening prayer.

The priest seemed satisfied. But Rosa, being very vigilant, had an uneasy feeling for she was the only one having been called upon specifically.

Finally, the first hour of religious studies was over. It ended with a prayer. It had not been so bad, after all. Nobody was scolded, nobody had to stand in the corner and the switch had just been a stick to point with. For the rest of the day it was the teacher's turn. Rosa was looking forward to that.

Under the protective umbrella of her mother, her uncles and her grandparents Rosa lost her apprehension and her initial fear of school. Moreover, she was a keen student and enjoyed learning everything. She was the first of her class to read fluently, and was only challenged by her playmate Alois. Arithmetic was almost no effort for her but great fun. It was the best because homework was done quickly, if there was any at all. The teacher began to notice her. Amazing, that girl, he thought; it must be her uncles who cause such an academic performance, for there is no father around.

He was not entirely wrong. Kon was not helping her with learning. But almost every day, when Rosa came home from school he would tease her gently with, "Look, we got new baby chicks while you were in school." Or, "Ha, you were in school what with such nice weather?" or "Did you have to recite that poem?"

Rosa was intuitively aware of the positive nature of these remarks. She knew her uncle liked her and was proud of his smart niece. This kind of attention Rosa enjoyed. She learned that there was praise in a successful performance and that she wanted to be noticed like that. The family was happy with her, approved of her. That was the way to go!

But one day, Rosa's generally comfortable feeling about herself received a bad blow. She was walking home from school. Under the walnut tree in front of the blacksmith workshop stood her uncle Jakob, who was talking to a customer when he suddenly interrupted himself and pointed excitedly to the street exclaiming:

"Look, there goes your father!"

Rosa saw two men walking by on the street. At first she wanted to run to them, but then she did not know which one was her father. Jakob had pointed at both. Neither man turned his head to look to the walnut tree or the little girl in front of it staring at them. They walked by as if they had not seen anybody. Intuitively she knew that she was not welcome and that kept her from running. Instead, disappointment and hurt slowly rose to the surface of her feelings. He had ignored her; he did not want her. He must not love her. She let go of her tears. Jakob swept her up into his arms.

"Stop crying, that idiot is not worth it. You are our girl," he said roughly.

**

For the next four years, Rosa's life routine was set by school and church. Every day she would dash off to the only classroom that the school had and in which one teacher taught seven grades of about seventy pupils. She still greatly enjoyed learning, for it came easy to her. Neither reading and writing nor arithmetic or religion required her to study hard. Her comprehension and her memory were excellent. She was also one of the best in sports, which consisted of playing ball games mostly. Her inquisitiveness seemed insatiable. Almost every subject seemed to be her favorite. Only music caused her distress.

One hour per week of singing was on the curriculum agenda. All the folk songs needed to be taught to all students, for it was required in those days. Since Rosa had not been blessed with a voice to hold a tune, she disliked that hour of the week. Otherwise she had learned quickly that excellence in academic subjects caused the teacher to like and her peers to respect her. And that was a good feeling for her, it was a feeling she needed to keep. For being important was something she could not do without. And being overlooked and disregarded or, heaven forbid, to be looked down upon was not an option she could afford. Forget singing!

***

Rosa's and her mother's endurance regarding that particular sin and the issue of legitimacy would not rest. Things in village life and habits came up to raise the issue again.

So it was with the religious holiday of Corpus Christi. This was a day of great excitement for little girls more so than for anybody else. Religious figures were carried through the meadows, fields and forests. There was a prestigious job to be given to early school-age girls to carry a pole, four to a figure, to lower the quite heavy statue on when the procession stopped to pray. Girls could wear white dresses and a wreath in their hair. Rosa and her mother held their breaths to see who was selected. Somehow Rosa was not chosen. They both thought the reason for that exclusion was obvious. By crying together in Liz's bedroom, Rosa and Liz were thus together in one unit of mother and daughter. No, she did not want to be called mother, but as a mother she functioned when circumstances called for it. Actually, for that reason Rosa felt good and bad at the same time.

Yet, Rosa's need for recognition and equality received ample positive feedback from her family. When she was only in the third grade, she was entrusted with small jobs. Sometimes she was sent to the village store to fetch bread, sugar, yeast or other items needed in the kitchen. Other times her grandfather would send her for one cigar for him, which was a real honor to be sure. On Sundays, she might have to fetch a bottle of beer from the local pub, next door to the store. Since she was quick with numbers she even received the coins needed for the purchases. Proudly Rosa put the change back into the open hand of the recipient to whom it was due. The smile or the pats on her head that she received for the task well executed gave her a warm, satisfied feeling. Of course, the feeling did not last forever and thus needed to be regained time and again. However, she was to experience proof of her equal standing in her family another way as well.

She was ten years old now and basically a healthy child. Of course, there was the usual cold or flu every winter. Sometimes there were so many pupils sick at one time that lone voices in the classroom seemed to echo. But in the fall that year it was not the flu that caused a number of students to be absent. Since no adults seemed to be concerned, including the teacher, Rosa was not either. Faithfully she was sent to school. One afternoon she did not feel quite right, had a headache and red spots on her upper thighs and arms. In the evening they seemed to have multiplied. Now her mother stared with a frown at her daughter's skin and called her own mother. Rosa's grandmother put her knitting aside and came to have a look.

"Put her to bed," she said. "She has got the measles."

"No, no, it is not evening yet, I don't want to go to bed," Rosa protested. But her grandmother was in charge and adamant. She had been through measles with her own children several times, not to mention her own suffering as a kid. Rosa was put to bed and sternly told, with a raised finger, to stay under the covers. To make sure that the little patient understood the danger of leaving bed, her grandmother threatened her with other diseases that could develop and bring her near death. Rosa's fever rose quickly so that she did not have any desire to get up.

The next morning her body was covered even worse with red little patches. The family agreed to call the doctor. With his orders, grandmother and mother shared the nursing, which involved keeping the young patient in bed, applying cold wraps around her legs to reduce the fever, and offering plenty to drink. After four days and nights of worrying about Rosa and tending to her, the red patches seemed less shiny and her body temperature dropped. However, on the fifth day Rosa started to complain about pain in both her ears.

That night she did not stop whining from ear pain. Her mother, who always took care of her during the night, boiled chamomile tea to have a source of heat. She soaked two pads in it and put them on her daughter's ears and kept them there by tying a bandana around her head. For a while it seemed to reduce the pain, but her ears did not improve. The doctor was called again.

"Did you get out of bed?" he asked Rosa. He did not receive an answer, for Rosa could not talk or shake her head from pain.

"This is a bad middle ear infection," he said to Grandmother. "She has got pus inside and that needs to come out."

For one more week Rosa had to stay in bed while feeling weak and miserable. Her hair was falling out and collected on her pillow.

As the fever and the pain radiating from both her ears were causing havoc, as well as her immune system fighting both diseases, she was a bundle of misery and easy to keep down in bed. She did not ask for much but for the presence of her mother or grandmother. Either presence was reassuring to the patient. Of course, both had to tend to their usual work on the farm. But they looked after their charge as much as necessary to take care of her needs and to ensure her recovery. Thus, Rosa had to spend considerable time by herself in her bed. This time, for reasons Rosa did not understand, cats were not allowed in her bed. During those spells of loneliness, Kon would often come for a brief visit. Rosa liked that a lot. How come he always came exactly then when she had to stay by herself for so long and felt lonesome? He cheered her up and his funny comments delighted her. Sometimes he told her a short story, which made the time go by quicker. He was her favorite uncle for sure.

When Rosa finally had recovered enough to go back to school she was more than ready. Being at home had felt more boring every day. She wanted to be with her peers. The only thing was that her hair loss was severe and it had not grown back enough yet to hide her thin, if not to say, bald spots. She was afraid of the teasing she was sure to get. To her surprise there were still quite a few empty seats. Alois was not there either. Did he have the measles? She did not dare to ask the teacher but she would find out during break.

"You are back," the teacher commented. "I hope you are fully recovered."

"Yes," Rosa said simply.

***

"Take out your sketch pad and your color pencils. We are going to draw a tree today, a family tree," the teacher instructed his fourth grade pupils one day.

Rosa's eyes went to the teacher as if she could learn from his face what exactly he had in mind. This was going to be one of the first history lessons of many more to come over the next four years. After all, a family also has a history. Thus a family tree served as a tool of introduction to the study of the past. Rosa had always liked to read stories that started with the four words "once upon a time". Those were stories of the past. With curiosity about this project she was laying out the required tools on her desk. She had a family, a loving one at that, and a large one, of that she was sure. Following the teacher's instructions she drew a mighty tree with strong branches culminating in a large crown.

Next, the teacher demonstrated on the board how to draw little rectangular boxes hanging from the branches.

"These need to be large enough to write names into them," the pupils were told. "In the lowest two boxes on the left and on the right sides you write the names of your grandparents," the teacher instructed.

Rosa started with her mother's parents. She looked at her work and found it satisfactory. Without a thought she moved her hand with the green color pencil to the other box and stopped. Her heart started to beat strongly and she felt her face getting hot. She looked at her classmate's paper next to her, to see what she was doing. Oh God, she is already filling in her second grandmother's name.

The hand that held the green color pencil started to sweat. As a matter of fact, she felt hot all over, and she began to feel dizzy. Sitting rigid, she stared at her paper not knowing what to do.

"And up here you put your mother's name and on this side your father's name," the teacher pushed on.

Rosa's desperation was complete. This time she could not please her teacher. He might not like her today. Briefly she considered bolting from the room. But that, so she knew, would attract punishment for sure. Feeling trapped, finally, tears started to roll down her cheeks. But no sound escaped her. Suddenly the teacher stood next to her pointing with his index finger at the two boxes she could not fill in.

"You don't need to put anything there," he said in a very quiet voice. Slowly the comprehension reached Rosa's upset mind. He said I don't have to fill it in? He did! Her symptoms of anxiety started to recede. Her fear of not being able to fulfill a required task diminished. Yet, another thought, even worse than the first task, rose as if it was a revelation: she did not have a father's name to fill in! It was a fact that would not go away but would instead come up as a stumbling block again. That she knew suddenly with clarity.

Rosa's mind left the task at hand. Why did she not have a father? He must not have wanted her. Why? She felt certain of her mother's love for her, even though she could not address her with that magic word that could heal all wounds. Her mother was good. Perhaps then she herself was the reason for her fatherless existence. She already knew that she was not as important as other kids with fathers. They did not have to hide when they got an extra sweet from their mother. They even could call their mothers by that magical name. She was not important enough. It was that family tree project that had pointed out her deficit very clearly in the middle of her class. Thank heavens that the teacher solved her problem; yet, despite the subtle support from him, she still had felt humiliation. The ugly truth had caught up with her again. It was very hard to have to do a family tree when you could not fill in all the boxes.

She felt anger towards her teacher for confronting her with such a project, anger that she had to hide inside her. That feeling revisited her when she was in bed that evening. It took her a while to fall asleep, unlike most other nights when she had no trouble drifting off into dreamland. Another feeling, that the young fourth grader was not aware of, had taken root in her mind. It was the fear of sudden, unexpected situations or calls that pointed out her fatherless, immoral existence. In that regard, Rosa now started to become a master of anticipation. Briefly she even considered to question her mother. Perhaps she knew why her father rejected her. However, she quickly discarded that option, believing that her mother would not give her an answer.

Rosa never did forget that history lesson. Having a family and knowing who its members were became increasingly important to her. She observed and learned about her classmates' families from abundant gossip among adults. To learn that some of her fellow pupils also were of illegitimate birth astounded and pleased her. She was not alone with that secret. Yet a bitter feeling remained because she and her mother were abandoned by that same important man. Moreover, she believed that her mother did not want to be reminded of that subject either, just like she did not want to be called "Mother".

***

As Rosa grew older and entered the upper grades she developed a fierce interest in the relationships of important, well-known people. That interest and need of hers expanded into a quest for understanding historical figures and their impact throughout history. She was the best in all her history classes throughout her school years, and also excelled in other subject areas. Mathematics, German language, literature and geography came easy to her. Throughout her life she would recite phrases, paragraphs, anecdotes, or poems. She worked diligently to gain her teacher's praise. And indeed, repeatedly he would point out her superior work. She experienced recognition and admiration from her friends, besides their teasing, of course.

The latter did occur regularly in day-to-day life. It was just the thing children did. But for Rosa it meant pain. In her last years of school the annual nativity play came around just before Christmas recess. And, as she had hoped for in sixth grade, the previous year, she wanted to get the prestigious part of Mary. Alois would play Joseph and that would be nice. But another girl was selected both times, one who had been born into a proper family with married parents. Rosa did get a minor part, yes, one with very little or no dialogue. People would not notice her much that way. But then, on the other hand, that was a safe place to be in case she forgot her line. She felt ambivalent.

In such a state of inner conflict Rosa completed her seven school years. She had learned and integrated that excelling intellectually, academically and in tasks, where she was often rewarded by positive attention and by the feeling of being important, admired, maybe even envied. But on the other hand, she knew she also wanted to stay away from being a leader of any sort. That way, if things went wrong, she would not be the one who had to stand scrutiny, and to be held responsible. Rosa could not afford running the risk of failure, disappointing important people and possible humiliation. One must always strive for high status to be positively regarded.

The last day of school ended rather unceremoniously but within the customary frame. Without being specially addressed, the class of 1936, together with the six grades behind them, attended mass in their village church. In the classroom, after church services, their teacher wished his near seventy students a safe summer break. For the seventh graders leaving school he had a few more subjects to cover that seemed pertinent to him. After all, he did this every year at the last day of the academic year. He warned his class that now they were going out into the real world. Those of them, he said, who were from at least a medium-sized farm had their work waiting for them. Since he did not want to use the term "poor", he called the rest "the others". They needed to learn a trade or, at least, would have to find a place where they could work as day laborers or farm help to make a living. That will be hard, he reassured them. The girls did not need to worry much. Their destination was to find a husband and raise children. "Of course, some are usually left over," he said with a malicious grin, and recommended they consider a trade, such as tailoring. After such advice they were handed their last grade report, which doubled as a diploma, and were sent on their way into said new life of work.

However, the school years were not completely over yet. No commotions of "goodbye forever" scenes were necessary. They would stay in the village, work on their farms, or go to a place of apprenticeship every day and return home every evening. At least every Sunday most of them would come to church. Most importantly, pupils were required to attend vocational school once a week for the next three years. Their togetherness of sorts would continue Sundays after church services. And it would be an increasingly flirtatious atmosphere amongst them. Rosa was aware that at some time during the coming years she and her classmates would have to learn ballroom dancing. That was the custom and it was unthinkable not to know the steps for all those different dances. And Alois would be there, too. She knew she and Alois would seek each other out as partners, as though drawn by magic.

Rosa took the end of her regular school years with a light heart and with pleasure. She would not have to attend class everyday and would have more freedom for herself. More importantly, she felt more than she knew that some underlying, ever present tension was lifted from her soul. Now her classmates would not be able to tease her or otherwise embarrass her about her not having a father. That was liberating! Not that they would have bothered her about it all the time, but she never knew when they would. That required vigilance on her part to either mentally hide or let them have it.

Besides these issues, her life would not change drastically after graduation. As far as apprenticeship for vocational training was concerned, nobody had approached her about this. Her mother had told her that she would stay on the farm and learn what was appropriate for a female. She was needed right here in this family business. Her uncles and her grandparents had not mentioned anything different. At the age of thirteen Rosa was glad about this arrangement because she was a bit afraid of leaving home. What she did not know was that her mother did not want her to leave, work in another village and be exposed to the dangers that lurked there. She did not want her daughter to have a chance to fall like she did. Liz had had a peaceful life on that farm, after all. Her sin surely was never forgotten but it was not referred to either, neither by her family nor by the other villagers. She alone carried that burden throughout her life. In time she became increasingly important for her family by way of running such a large household and vegetable garden, and by taking care of her siblings and her daughter. She had overcome her desire for marriage and accepted her spinsterhood. Life left her to live in peace, and she was content with that. For her daughter, however, she had a sinless and married life in mind. Now she needed to be especially vigilant.

***

Graduating was no big shakeup in Rosa's life. Another issue, however, that happened during her last year of school, had caused her considerable confusion. It was something she had not worked out yet.

During summer recess before starting seventh grade, in 1935, her aunt Thekla had come home for a visit from Munich where she worked. Rosa liked her and was happy about this visit. Thekla had always treated her with kindness and acceptance. But this visit had turned sour. Her grandmother's face looked very angry and she had tears in her eyes. Her aunt seemed to have none of her usual cheerfulness, for she kept her head down. Rosa even had heard her crying at night. What was going on?

One time, when Rosa came into the kitchen, Grandmother was badly scolding her aunt. She was a sinner, Grandmother said, she should be ashamed of herself. Did she not know the sixth commandment? What were the people going to say when her second daughter also was pregnant out of wedlock?

"You have to have your baby in Munich, not here," she told her daughter. "I won't have another child from an unmarried daughter of mine here."

So that was it! Rosa ran outside, not knowing where to go. She felt that not only had she an immoral mother but also an immoral aunt! Was she from a bad family then? But she liked her aunt and loved her mother. Why did they do such shameful things? Rosa was not quite sure what that shameful thing they did actually was. Nobody had told her. But she knew for sure that having a baby before marriage was deplorable.

Sitting on the log behind the barn, she thought about the things she had just heard. Slowly it became clear to her that she was not going to be the only one in this family without a father. Whether that was better or worse for her she did not know. Of course, she was not going to be alone in her predicament anymore, and that actually was a relief. But what about coming from a family with two bad members? There was no telling which of these two facts had a greater impact on her feelings and self image. After all, she loved all her family members and they loved her; that much was sure. So how can they be bad at the same time? It did not make sense to her. And nobody talked to her for clarity.

It was more than a year until Rosa understood that the birth of this little baby boy meant that she now had a cousin. After all, that shameful birth in Munich in January 1936 was hushed up in her family, unlike her own birth. Yet she did not know that one day her grandparents had received a letter informing them about their new grandson. Only the whispers between family members allowed her a vague idea what the hush-hush was about.

However, in that cold month of February 1936 Rosa had to deal with the loss of a loved one first. Her cousin was more of an abstract concept at that time and could be put aside in her mind. That was convenient and necessary, for the sudden and unexpected death of her grandfather shocked and frightened her deeply. It also challenged her fragile identity. Like with her grandmother she had come to call her grandfather Father. That's what everyone in the family did and no-one had told her differently. In as much she had not been completely without a father, he had provided a stand-in for her. And he had loved her. Now he had left her with a blank space in her self-understanding that gave rise to a scary, diffuse feeling. She was very sad about her loss. It dropped her into the painful hole of mourning a man who had not only shown her love, but had also been an emotional and social crutch for her.

In late September, when the harvest had been brought in and everybody could take a deep breath in satisfaction of the successful completion of the season's task, a monumental thing happened. Her aunt came for a visit with her baby boy in her arms. Moreover, to Rosa's great surprise, the father of the boy came with them! He even talked to her grandparents, reassuring them that he would marry their daughter as soon as he could get divorced.

Divorce – what is that? Rosa's head was spinning from confusion and unanswered questions. She headed for the log behind the barn. There she tried to sort out the unheard-of and almost unbelievable facts. This baby boy was going to have a father! Why had her father not married her mother? Perhaps her little new cousin was different from her – a more important kid than she herself was? Had she not been important enough for her father to claim her as his daughter? Or was it her mother that was not worth it for her father, or both? In any case, it was obvious to Rosa that there was somehow a difference between her infant cousin and her.

One day, when the father of her new cousin came around the western corner of the barn she wiped her tears away and turned her head. He came slowly but unmistakably toward her. He smiled at her in a way that made her feel comfortable.

"So, young lady, what are you doing alone out here?" He sat down next to her. "You like your new cousin?" he asked.

Even though she could have said that she felt threatened by him as well as reassured, for some strange reason she remained silent. It was difficult to put her thoughts into words. They were so many, too many to sort them into some sort of order. She had a number of questions about this new situation. But she had learned that it was better not to ask as the answers were usually not satisfying to her or she was simply dismissed. Also, her mother always snapped back that she was too young to understand. So she remained silent and felt shy. What did this man want from her? Why did he come?

"One day we might need a babysitter for him, Rosa. I hope you will come to us for that."

Rosa did not know what to make of this. They did not live here but in Munich, so that was the end of that! Briefly it was silent between them. Then the man reached into his trouser pocket and pulled out a necklace. He held it out to Rosa and asked her if she found it pretty. She stared at it. It consisted of honey golden elongated pearls, some smaller than others. There was enough sun to make them sparkle a little. She found the necklace beautiful. Never had she received such a gift, even though she was already thirteen years old.

"Here, take it, it is yours," the man said. Rosa did not reach for it but looked at him questioningly. He put the necklace into her hands. She held it, and looked at it and again at him. Reassuringly he repeated:

"It is yours. Let me hang it around your neck."

Rosa finally comprehended that this was a little gift to her, and held still. Once the necklace touched her chest and neck she felt different, bigger, important, and, yes, loved. This man likes me, she thought. He likes me! Off she ran to her mother and grandmother and whoever else might be there to show off, leaving the father of the baby boy sitting on the log. She was to keep this necklace for almost all her life.

Because of the necklace's beauty Rosa had forgotten about the invitation to be a babysitter to this new baby boy. Thus she had not had time to fret over it, be scared of leaving the village or consider the mere fact that she had been found worthy of the offer. However, during supper the issue came back into her mind.

The baby's father brought it up by asking her mother and her grandparents to let her travel with them to Munich and stay for a short visit. That request, spread over the dinner table, with everybody sitting around it, including her uncles, had the impact akin to a small bomb exploding. Spoons stopped in mid air; the eating stopped, silence reigned. The first one to speak was Rosa's mother: "No!" Next, Grandmother asked, "What for?" Kon wanted to know, "What is she going to do there? She is only going to get lost." Anselm stated flatly: "We need her here! She is young, she can go later. I have never been to Munich either and have survived."

Rosa remained silent and looked from one speaker to the other. As she followed the verbal exchange between her family members in disbelief, she was only dimly aware of her pounding heart. Fear was the cause of it – fear to leave familiar ground and going into the unknown, fear of those strange city people. What would they think of her? Would they even like her? Simultaneously, excitement combined with curiosity about that city mixed with her fear, battling inside her.

Ferdinand, the baby's father, had expected these reactions. He took them with a quiet smile. Calmly he tried to convince the family to let Rosa go, at least when her work and school allowed for it. He explained that she was old enough to put her nose into the wind outside this village, that it would be beneficial for her and her future, for her "to have been somewhere far away". His most convincing argument, that he was at work during the day, he had saved for last. He did not want for his bride to be alone so much with a small child, he explained. Rosa would be a big help to her aunt even if it was only for a short time. And she would be well protected in their house. Finally, it was agreed to let her go but for no longer than a week. After that decision had been made, at last Rosa was asked if she wanted to go. She quietly nodded in agreement.

That night, unlike any other night, Rosa took a while to fall asleep. Anxiety had a firm grip on her. She had never been on a train before and had never seen the big city. Any lifestyle outside of her village was alien to her. She was also afraid of all the unknown people she might meet. Anticipating and imagining all this newness made her thoughts go into overdrive. But eventually, in a state of exhaustion and proclivity, she did fall asleep. The next day Rosa was going to leave her comfort zone.

Rosa spent the next night in a bed in an apartment in Munich. Again she had problems falling asleep. Her mind was unable to stop the memory in her head: she was still riding the train; she was still walking with her aunt, carrying her tiny cousin and with his father through the Munich main train station. She felt dizzy from all the people rushing by who did not look at her at all and from the lights everywhere. But it was not a bad feeling overall, just a bit too much stimulation. She was actually looking forward to the next day, albeit with a bit of trepidation.

That next day was the first day of the routine for the next week. She was up early, just like what they all did on the farm. And besides, she heard the baby screaming. Shyly she went into the kitchen. Her aunt was feeding little Hans. She herself was hungry too.

"Sit down, have some breakfast. It is all on the table," her aunt invited her. That was a comfortable start to the day, away from home, the first time in her young life.

Her biggest surprise that first morning was the discovery that the apartment was on the fourth floor. One could see over all the tree tops in the street below and out into the park on the other side. She wanted to run out into the grass as she did at home as a matter of routine – get up, eat breakfast, go to school or run outside. But here, she could not do that; she was afraid of going outside. And besides, she was four floors up. Could one just run down those stairs? People might see her! How was she to cross that road with oncoming cars that never seemed to stop coming?

But it worked out okay. Later in the morning her aunt took her and little Hans with her to do the daily small item shopping: fresh milk, fresh bread, and other odds and ends for the household. Rosa stayed very close to her aunt. She was bashful when the people from the various stores, or the neighbors who also were out shopping, asked her aunt who the young girl was. "This is my niece," her aunt answered to each one of them. I am a niece, Rosa thought. And my aunt tells everybody that I am her niece. Almost like she was proud of me!

Eventually Rosa began to like the routine. She loved to see all the shops and hear the sounds of the big city. Her suspicious vigilance and her fear of being judged by the city people diminished. To her surprise nobody had asked about her father either. Every afternoon, after little Hans had taken his nap, they would go out for fun and recreation. Rosa felt proud to push the baby pram. It made her feel important and that felt real nice in turn.

One time even, when her aunt had to go downstairs to the nearby pharmacy, she was alone and therefore responsible for little Hans. By now she felt confident to rise to the task. When her aunt did not return within the expected time she was not afraid. She opened the window, put the baby on the window sill, gave him his baby rattle, put both her arms around his body to hold him and watched the street below. When the baby dropped his rattle it fell into the room, luckily. Rosa turned loose of her small charge, made two steps away and retrieved the rattle. But from the sidewalk below her aunt saw her baby son sitting alone on the fourth floor window sill. She shouted like mad for Rosa. When Rosa heard the blood-curdling scream she dashed to grab little Hans and pulled him into the room so violently that the boy also screamed. Rosa knew she had made a bad blunder. She had failed and she felt terribly guilty. Mortified, she stood and listened to a stern lecture from her aunt. Was she going to be sent home now, alone on the train? Will her aunt tell her mom? When nothing of that kind happened, Rosa felt puzzled at first, but gradually she understood that it had blown over. Her aunt did not even seem to be angry any longer. The remaining days were just as much fun as before. But her confidence in herself had received a blow that did not go away for the rest of her days in Munich.

At the end that little dip in her self-esteem was balanced out by her courage to travel home by herself. Her aunt had put her on the right train that would arrive at her train station an hour later. Rosa was aware that she would be the only one amongst her peers who had been in the big city and, on top of it, took a train ride by herself. She could do that!

Thus, her school years had still ended with a big bang. Now her apprenticeship years would start. That required her to go to school only once a week in the same classroom that she had just graduated from and with the same classmates. Life was not bad at all.

It's a Young Life

In the fall of 1936 and the following winter Rosa was involved in the day-to-day operation of the farm. Her work was almost entirely outdoors, which she liked. The picking of apples and pears was done by her favorite uncle, Kon. Working with him as his assistant was great fun to her. But the preservation of the pears and apples required her to stay indoors stirring in a pot endlessly until her mother finally found it enough. Rosa preferred to work outdoors in almost any weather or temperature. She also loved to take care of the animals, all of them: the cows, the piglets, the chickens, the ducks and the geese.

But the main task that she was gradually introduced to was the daily milking, feeding and caretaking of the dairy cows. Rosa almost had a personal relationship with every one of them. Since in those days the dairy cows were kept inside a stable for the cold months of the year, they needed to be tended to more when they gave birth, so Rosa had to raise, feed, bathe and clean the young. Rosa was allowed to take the little calves to their mothers for nursing. This was actually difficult because the little ones were so jumpy and unruly. This, however, made her laugh a lot. Some of them she had watched being born. With each one of the newborns a bond developed between the calf and its human caretaker. Rosa felt easy and carefree with her little charges.

Finally, it was time to learn the strenuous task of milking by hand. Rosa called up all her strength. This, she knew, was her opportunity to prove her worth to her family. The job was very tough on her hands. The first few times their strength vanished quickly and pain crept up her arms before she could finish squeezing one udder empty. But that did not matter to her two teachers, her mother and Kon. Twice a day this job had to be done with or without sore muscles in her hands and arms. Sometimes Kon would take pity and finish the job for her. But he also knew that Rosa had to get through the initial pains, despite the tears of frustration. And, indeed, after a few weeks had passed, Rosa complained no more. Instead, a good feeling of accomplishment and success filled her soul.

There were always a number of cats in the part of the stable where the feed was kept. Rosa knew that they came for the warmth and the milk, which she would pour into their dishes right after she finished milking the first cow. Later, when the work was done and the family was enjoying the evening in the Stube, the cats would also be there. One of them would always curl up in Rosa's lap, which required Rosa to hold up her knitting a little higher than she normally would. But that was okay, because the purring of that furry creature was soothing and reassuring to Rosa. Cats did not question her origins, her worth or her talents; they accepted her petting and caretaking as it was. It was a special infatuation, a special connection she felt for that species.

For the next two years Rosa was required to learn all the other different tasks a farmhand had to do in those days. Most of them revolved around the dairy business. But there was also grain to be planted and harvested; potatoes, turnips and other such vegetables had to be grown and processed. In addition, a large garden specifically for the kitchen with vegetables, berries, and herbs needed to be tended all summer. This work and the preservation of various kinds of fruits lasted into fall. Versatility was definitely called for. Rosa had no problem with that as she liked her work. She was a very good worker and easy to teach. Only with indoors work was she often unhappy. But she was lucky; nobody asked her to stay to learn to cook beyond occasional help when there was too much to do overall. Cooking was done by her grandmother, with Liz's assistance. Rosa was not in the least bit interested in that particular daily task.

In the evenings, however, indoors was cozy. Often there was an hour of card playing, which was a rather lively family activity. In addition, Rosa did engage in those crafts that only females had to do. She actually showed great aptitude for knitting and sewing. At the age of fourteen she could produce her own winter sweaters. Those skills would serve her well in the coming years and, indeed, throughout her life.

In those days it was not custom to pay family members for their work on a farm. An attitude akin to subsistence life still reigned. Anyone who lived in the household was given chores to do as a matter of course. If you are living with us you have to contribute to making a living. Food, shelter, clothing and, if necessary, medical expenses were just as consequently carried by the household unit. Why then would any family member need money? Rosa was very much a product of that philosophy. At this age, she went to school once a week, she went to church and she worked on the farm. That was all inclusive. All others around her lived the same way. None of her school mates had more money in their pockets than was necessary to buy a few candies in the village store or to drop a few coins into that red velvet collection pouch with the bell attached at church. And yet, gradually she realized that those few of her female school mates, who had entered an apprenticeship as seamstresses or as future midwives, did have purchasing power that went a bit further than just a bag of candies. They could afford a few ribbons for their hair or pretty pictures for the poesy albums that were circulating among friends and school mates. Small items to be sure, but Rosa had to ask for such extra pennies, which resulted in uncomfortable questioning as to the need and justification of spending extra money.

So one day, when Rosa's courage was up, she approached her mother about becoming a seamstress.

"Well, you do not need to go somewhere else to learn what you already can do," her mother snapped. But Rosa did not give up in her plea.

"But Vroni and Mal are doing it. I could earn a little when I am finished with apprentice time," she tried to reason. But it was to no avail.

"No, we need you here," her mother retorted firmly without meeting her daughter's eyes. By now Rosa's green eyes began to tear up and her lips were pulled downward at the corners. But she had another trump card up her sleeve.

"You had gone away for a while when you were young! Why can't I go?"

Her mother had turned away from Rosa, pretending to pick something up from the floor.

"No, Rosa," her mother answered firmly. "You are needed here. You are not going anywhere."

Rosa knew this was the final word. She turned and went to her place behind the barn where nobody could hear or see her cry. Nor could she see her mother trying to prevent her own tears from overpowering her resolve.

It was not easy for a mother to have to deny the desires of spreading the wings of independence that kids crave. But Liz's own suffering from the wrath of shame and humiliation showered upon her because of her pregnancy made her determined to protect her daughter from that – and from the embarrassment of a lifetime in spinsterhood. Liz, however, did not contemplate to explain this to her daughter. She knew for a fact that young girls alone out there in the world were taken advantage of. Rosa was not going to have that happen to her. And Liz would not suffer again through such hidden ostracism from some if her daughter came home pregnant. She was almost totally sure that this would happen. Quickly the people would say that the daughter had inherited the lack of morals from her mother.

One can remember what happened the last Christmas in school: Rosa wanted to play Mary in the annual Nativity play, but she was denied that and as a result came home crying.

"The teacher said to me I can't have the part of Mary. Why did he say that, Liz?"

"He doesn't know what he is doing!" Liz answered in an effort to console her daughter and thus avoiding the real issue. She was certain what the issue was that kids born as a result of sin couldn't play the Mother of God. The girl who got the part was of proper birth and had a well-to-do father on top of that.

***

Rosa had started to question if she was needed that much on the farm as she had been told by her mother. Yet, Liz's reassurances served her insatiable need for recognition and value to others. She was not just an accidental, unwanted member of this family. No, she had her place in this house. She worked hard and conscientiously and was at least content with that. When Anselm once spontaneously told her, "You are not lazy, Rosa," a feeling of pride and success filled her anxious soul. The time when her industriousness would be of even greater importance, and of still greater value, was approaching. It would point out that she was a determining factor in the smooth operation of the farm. She would actually now be invaluable. It happened soon after Thekla married Ferdinand, the father of little Hans. It was 1938.

Thekla and Ferdinand's wedding was merely a formality in a city far enough away that it took a train about three hours to get there. Nobody from the family made that trip. It was January and bitter cold. That winter weather was not the only reason, Rosa knew, for the non-attendees. They did not know how to feel about that marriage. After all, Ferdinand had had the audacity to go to court and ask for a divorce from his wife to marry Thekla. That was unheard of! The church certainly did not approve of this and would not remarry a divorced man. So there was nothing else but a signing of papers, no wedding in church in a long, white dress with a train. Rosa secretly regretted that there was no church ceremony. She so wanted to carry the bridal train of her aunt. And to think she would wear a light blue, long dress for everybody to see her. But she kept that thought to herself. Perhaps girls of illegitimate birth would not be allowed to carry trains?

All this was talked about heatedly within the family. Rosa's head was spinning with all the words and odd terms that flew back and forth between her grandmother, mother and uncles. But she understood clearly that little Hans, now two years old, would have his father and his mother together. He would not have to be embarrassed about his birth like she had to be. He could answer who and where his father was. Rosa felt a pinch of jealousy. But when her aunt came to visit with the little guy she was full of joy – joy to have a legitimate cousin, joy to be allowed to push him around in his open buggy in the village. This cousin was not something to hide or be ashamed of. She showed him to her school mates. It felt like she was a bit more legitimate herself. Not only that – when Thekla and little Hans went back home she was going with them to spend a week. This time it would be an even longer train ride. She would see the great river Danube as well. Who else in her village had been traveling so far? Rosa felt entirely special.

Her life of all but sixteen years went on uneventful after that. Of course, there were the various special days during a year, where the village, like any other village in Bavaria, celebrated something. There was the Volksfest and the Kathrein Dance in the fall. Alois' family next door every year in October built a huge swing in their barn where all the village youth then met to have fun. Christmas time seemed to lead from one special event to another culminating in the Christmas play at the theater room in the local inn. It was a good life.

In August 1939 Rosa became aware that the people in the village talked often about politics. She was not interested in that, but it did puzzle her that the adults seemed to be worried. One day in September Anselm came home from an evening at the pub where he often went after work. Usually he was a bit cheerful when he returned from there. But that night he looked worried. He stood with eyebrows raised in the middle of the Stube. The other people in the pub had claimed that the army had crossed the border into Poland.

"Have you heard that?" he asked his brothers.

Kon sat up straight and stared at him. Their suntanned skins that both men had acquired over the summer had turned a grayish hue. The fear in their wide open eyes seemed to match their tense demeanor. Liz and Grandmother stopped their handiwork, stared at Anselm and asked in unison:

"What?" and then, "No, I don't believe what those drunk guys say in the pub!"

"Rosa, turn on the radio," Jakob commanded. Rosa did as she was told. Anselm's diffuse anxiety had settled in her stomach. Tension was vibrating in her family. She knew clearly what "war" meant from the history lessons in school. But why should a distant war make any difference to them?

The next morning it was clear that there was shooting going on at the Poland border. It was a subject that Rosa heard the grown-ups talking about in hushed and whispering ways. That frightened her even more. Sure, everybody went on with the day's work, but it was not the same as the day before. There was a strange, eerie silence hanging over the day. The faces of all her family members expressed worry. And worst of all, her grandmother, the pillar of strength in the family, seemed to have been crying. Suddenly Rosa remembered that Hans, the one uncle she never met, had been shot and killed in France during a previous war. Understanding her grandmother better she now felt her heart pounding all day, but she tried to play cool and asked nothing. She was afraid of the answers. Whenever Rosa saw tears in her family she felt a strange kind of guilt as if she was responsible for the distress.

Despite the tense, gloomy atmosphere that hung over the days and over the village, life went on as usual. The rest of the harvest had to be brought in; the threshing of the grain had to be done. Apples and pears had to be picked and stored carefully or preserved by drying to make them last through the long winter months.

Also the festivals, due at this time of the year, were properly celebrated like all the years before. The gloomy feeling that had taken a firm grip on the village people retreated that way. Although at sixteen Rosa was not yet allowed to attend the Kathrein Dance at the local pub, her age group met at Alois' barn right by the large swing. It was a very cheerful meeting place then for the youth of the village. Custom required that one boy and one girl stood on the swing, facing each other, trying to go the highest by way of competition. Rosa loved to swing with Alois. He fought her out for it. A pleasant tension vibrated through her swinging with him. They were a great and daring team when the other former school mates stood watching and cheered them on.

Of course, always the next day after such a festival, lots of gossip was exchanged in the families. But this fall it was mixed with the issue of an ongoing battle in Poland. Not all families were in possession of a radio. So during such gatherings stories were told by some about the things happening and then they were carried on by word of mouth. Rosa overheard her family talking off and on during their meals or while working outdoors. It just would not go away. On the contrary, the tension seemed to mount.

The first terrifying blow of the war reached Rosa's family when one day, in January 1940, the postman brought a letter and handed it to Anselm. He was in the blacksmith workshop when he opened it. After he read the letter Anselm put his hammer down and came into the Stube to inform his mother and his brothers that he had been drafted into the army. Rosa had never seen him white in the face. Moreover, Kon and Jakob looked just the same. Liz exclaimed:

"Mother of God, help us!"

Grandmother simply sat down and started crying without a word. She knew what it could mean, for she remembered her firstborn son who had to leave for the previous war and never came back. There was not even a grave she could visit.

Rosa's heart was beating wildly. Fear had taken hold of her, although she did not know what she was afraid of. Naming a date, Anselm said he had to be in Berlin that day, checking into the army base there at 1700 hours precisely. His eyes were huge as he spoke. He seemed terrified. In his young life he had never left this village, and had never been on a train before. Certainly he had never been in a big city the size of Berlin. How was he going to negotiate a city so big and use its transportation system and, moreover, be there at five pm sharp?

The day of Anselm's departure came all too soon. It was a cold January morning. Rosa stood in the Stube and watched her mother and grandmother. Like the adults she tried to fight her anxiety and the tears burning in her eyes. She felt nauseated.

"Liz, is he coming back?" she asked.

"Of course," her mother replied with false conviction, remembering how her oldest brother who once left and was never seen again. Rosa did not feel comforted by that answer.

"I have to go," Anselm said, and ended all commotion. He was scared to death and did not want to let it be seen. He grabbed his meager bag and stormed out the door. Kon stared at him, white-faced. Jakob turned away and went into the blacksmith workshop without a word. All too fresh were his father's tears burned into his memory when the letter came saying that his firstborn had fallen in 1917 in France. It was the only time that Jakob saw him cry. He picked up a hammer with a trembling hand, and started to work in a desperate attempt to enforce normalcy. The clear sound of his furious hammering on the anvil seemed a mockery, considering the situation. Now he had to handle the whole workshop by himself.

"Be careful and write," the mother shouted after her son. Then she went into the kitchen and sobbed uncontrollably.

Rosa stayed close to Liz and watched tears rolling out of her beautiful blue eyes.

"Is he coming back?" Rosa asked again.

"What do I know? He is going into a war!" Liz snapped at her daughter. That answer was quite devastating to Rosa. This was a man who had also accepted her despite her shameful birth. She did not know why she felt that she had lost him. It felt that with Anselm leaving love and protection went away with him. She felt very nauseated again.

After Anselm's departure an underlying tone of anxiety prevailed in the family. It was present from sunrise to bedtime, during meals and during work. Everybody tried to put on a normal face as if to force the dreadful thoughts out of their minds. These were not the days where a soldier picked up a phone and called family to reassure them of his arrival or wellbeing. No, letter-writing time was assigned. Eventually, after what seemed an eternity a note arrived, written on dirty brown paper. It read:

I am well, still in Berlin. Will probably go to the front soon. I will write again when I can.

"O dear Mother of God," Grandmother sighed.

"What front is he going to? When? Is it dangerous there?" Rosa wanted to know. She did not receive an answer. But the white faces of her family members around her made her feel even worse than before that message arrived.

"He is so young!" Jakob mumbled.

Under this blanket of anxiety life went on. Animals had to be taken care of, cows to be milked and the product had to be marketed. There was no time for depression. Rosa's youth seemed to help her come to terms with the situation.

When she met her school mates for the weekly classes or when they met for a game of card playing on winter evenings, it seemed almost normal like before. Besides, she learned from her peers that other families also had one son already in the army. Even Alois' family had to let his older brother go.

Just when Rosa had seemingly adjusted to this new situation the next blow jolted her out of her fragile inner peace. In February Kon was also drafted into the army. He was to be stationed for training in a small city at the Danube, about two hours by train away.

"No!" Grandmother wailed. "Are they going to take them all – all my sons? The first one in the last war was not enough!" Her knees gave way and she sank to the floor sobbing.

***

Rosa would often go sledding with some of her school mates. It was the depth of winter when there was not too much to do during the afternoons until it was time to tend to the cows. As always, those winter months were great fun for her when the snow was covering everything at least ankle-deep. Snowball fights were a must and resulted in lots of laughter. Sled rides, besides the wonderful feeling of dashing downhill, were a challenge to see who was going to go with whom on one sled. They were a great excuse to approach the opposite sex under the cover of a socially well-accepted activity for a long time. After all, the person sitting behind had to hold on to the one in front. Rosa liked it best when Alois asked to go with her. When the shades of the leafless trees grew longer or when the church bells tolled four times Rosa had to go home. Most others had the same curfew.

One day she was accompanied by Maria and Alois, as all three had to go in the same direction. Rosa's fingers and toes were hurting from the cold, but she did not pay any attention. Stumbling, sliding, and laughing, they reached the point where they had to separate to go to their respective homes. Now Rosa started running to reach the warm Stube. She took off her boots, gloves, scarf, cap and coat, and threw all of them in direction of the wardrobe and entered the room.

Almost at once Rosa noticed a different atmosphere. Grandmother, who was cooking the evening meal, and Jakob did not greet her with a teasing comment today.

"You are back, good," was Grandmother's only acknowledgement of her presence. Jakob said nothing at all. Rosa stood still and looked from one to the other. Grandmother had red eyes. Jakob looked on stoically. Rosa felt a bad feeling rise in her and her stomach, although hungry, made her feel nauseated.

"What's the matter, Mother?" she asked. There was no answer from her.

"Uncle Jakob, what happened?"

"Kon's marching order has come in. He has to leave tomorrow!" he exclaimed through clenched teeth.

Rosa was feeling weak and her heart was pounding madly.

"Uncle Kon has to go tomorrow?" Rosa whispered.

She stood stock still as if she had been frozen to the living room floor. Then she stormed out and ran into the cow stable where Kon did his daily chores. She ran right into him and threw her arms around his waist. He stumbled and just managed to get his fork out of the way. Rosa clung to him and screamed:

"No, you are not going, are you? Don't go, don't go!"

Kon was glad that she had her face buried in his sweater. He did not want her to see his tears because he was a man and must not cry. But he did not know how to react to such a desperate niece. He had always looked out for her, took her with him when she was small, let her ride on the wagon, and protected her. He was her other father. Now he had to leave to go into the most dangerous of all callings that life could have. He was frightened, but he wouldn't let Rosa know this. She was already terrified. So they just stood and cried, each in his or her own way, until there were no more tears. What could he say to her? He had to go. But in the end he did think of something.

"You have to do part of my chores while I am away. You and your mother need to take care of the animals. You are very much needed, Rosa. She can't do it alone. You have to be strong. This house and this family has to rely on you very much now."

Rosa nodded emphatically. She was afraid to talk for fear of losing control and starting to shout her frustration out. Her grief and her fear were immense. Her mentor and her teacher, her support and her protection, her safe harbor in the male world, the person closest to resembling a father, was leaving.

***

Rosa was seventeen years old now. For the next few weeks she worked like she was possessed. She did all her chores plus heavy physical work that normally was understood to be a man's job. Together with her mother she milked, cleaned the stable as well as the animals, and carried huge forks full of hay from the barn to the cows' stable. She filled the heavy metal milk containers with fresh milk mornings and evenings. These containers could only be lifted with the help of her mother. They needed to be put on a special wheelbarrow and rolled out to the street where at seven in the morning at the latest a milk truck would come to pick them up to take them to the dairy company. To have those milk containers ready Rosa needed to get up at five, the same time her mother and grandmother got up. Up until now sometimes she had been allowed to sleep until six. But now she had to take over from Kon as promised. Without her input Liz would not get the work done in time. Rosa adjusted quickly to this challenge even though she found it very hard to leave the warmth of her bed and step out into a very cold, unheated bedroom to get dressed.

She felt her worth, her value for her family. It was a good feeling. It was the feeling with which she coped and balanced her ever present fear about the safety of her uncles. That worry was enhanced by her awareness of the somber mood that had settled over the remaining family at home. Sometimes she desperately wished some laughing, joking, and teasing would come back. Often she felt sick in her stomach and could not eat properly. But then Grandmother would soothe her, urging her to eat a bit more and not to worry. After all, she had to do heavy work and that required strength.

Rosa turned out to be tough on herself. She was reliable in completing the tasks assigned to her. Moreover, she soon could plan her work to be done at a given day by herself. She was a big help and did a man's job. Praise was not often coming her way. That was not a habit. What was particularly appreciated, when she was told by Jakob, was the absence of complaints when bad weather and freezing temperatures made work especially tough. No, she did not complain. In fact she liked the challenge, for she could prove herself to her family. These feelings resonated in Rosa's body posture. One could see pride in her gait. Her eyes looked up, not so much downcast than before. And yet, on occasion, one could also see her change back to her shy ways. It was like there were two sides to her. And Rosa, one could see, had adjusted to the new situation on the farm. Not that the worry about her uncles would not be a constant companion in her and her family's life. But she had at least found a balance. Happy moments were possible.

The annual three main Carnival days – Fasching Sunday, Rose Monday and Shrove Tuesday – provided an opportunity for such happy times. At seventeen she had come of age and like her peers she was excited to attend the customary Carnival ball. No-one asked for being eighteen anymore. Moreover, she had already learned a few of the dances and loved it. On Sunday it would be the big ball and she was allowed to attend. After all, her friends and school mates were also going to be there. When they met during the one day of school per week they had been discussing the masks each one would wear in a heated and teasing manner, accompanied with a lot of laughter.

"Rosa, what are you going to wear?" Anna was bending over with laughter.

"Don't know yet," Rosa replied. "Maybe I will be the Sleeping Beauty or Snow White."

"Shit, are you waiting for Prince Toni?" Toni asked.

"Shut up!" Alois shouted.

"No, I think she should be Gretel and Toni can go as Hansel then," Anna said laughingly.

"Or better yet," she suggested, "Rosa can be the witch." Anna and several others broke into another spell of laughter.

"She should be Rapunzel. She has beautiful long braids." Alois said, looking at Rosa. Rosa's face turned red.

"Listen to that!" Anna said with raised eyebrows.

"Shut up!" Alois repeated.

The customary masks to be worn, if any at all, were of the threatening, scary, ugly kind. At the end of Carnival, the legend said, the winter needed to be driven away to make room for spring. Therefore the masks needed to be hideous enough to accomplish that. Rosa was not sure about such a mask for herself. Actually, they were going out of style. Some of her female friends were adamant about not wearing something so ugly over their faces. They wanted to be pretty for the dances. Yet a mask of the angry kind, Rosa considered, felt good to her. Besides, behind it, you could look everywhere, see everything without being seen. But then for the dances such a monstrous thing on your face was not good at all. She could not come to a decision on her own. Finally, she walked three houses down to see Mal.

"No, I am not going to wear one," Mal said firmly.

Well then, Rosa would not wear a mask either. What about putting on some lipstick? She did not have one, but she thought Mal would probably let her use hers. Before the dance Rosa would go to her house first anyway to pick up her and her sister. They would go there together, for no girl in her right mind would show up single at a dance. There was time enough to put on some lipstick then.

Rosa's feelings of excitement as well as anxiety already started Sunday afternoon. Would she be pretty enough? What if the guys did not ask her for a dance? That would be so humiliating. Some of her male classmates had never paid any attention to her unless they were teasing her. Others, however, seemed okay with her. But then

Mal was not pretty and she went to the ball. The only way to avoid being hurt would be not to go. But she could not possibly do that. Go she must. So after a lot of mental anguish it was time to put on her shoes, her coat, her hat and scarf. Heading out the door to go to Mal's house, Rosa yelled over her shoulder into the Stube, "I am going."

Her mother's head jolted up from her embroidery.

"You behave well. I don't want to hear anything. Be back by midnight! And watch those boys."

Her mother's voice was not unkind but firm, almost alarmed. Rosa did not know why she should watch her male school mates. Like most teenagers she forgot her mother's words as soon as she had closed the door behind her.

The young ladies already heard the music from the dance floor when they approached the building by slipping and sliding through the snow and over the sheet of ice right in front of the steps up to the hallway of the inn. Rosa almost bolted before they entered the dance hall. Mal's sister, however, was older and had been at dances before. With a firm grip she guided Rosa and Mal into the room and to a table. Shyly Rosa looked around. It was not full yet. But within a short time the place was humming like a beehive, and when the music played one had to shout. Other girls joined them at their table. They talked, broke out in loud, nervous laughter, pointed at somebody and laughed again. Rosa did not participate in the excited conversation. Instead she sat hunched over and let her eyes scan the scenery. Who was going to be the first to be asked to dance? Hopefully I am not last or left over, Rosa thought. But what if I don't remember the steps? Georg came to pick up Mal. Her sister was already out there on the dance floor. Thank God there were some of the other girls still sitting there. Rosa's hands were sweating. She started to dig in her purse looking for nothing. Then she heard her name. She looked up and saw Thomas. Not him, shot through her mind. But then she was glad to be rescued from her seat.

"I was not sure you would have a dance with me," Thomas said. What made him think that? I am glad he's asked me. Why would I refuse him? Rosa asked herself, slightly puzzled. It was a fast polka that she danced with him to. Suddenly she had no more fear, no more worries; she loved the music and the dance. Thomas led her well. When the music stopped they all applauded and he brought her back to her seat.

"You are a good dancer, Rosa," Thomas said, and promised to come for her again. Rosa had been rescued from being left sitting at the table. Everything was going to be alright. She felt elated and cheerful. And Thomas did come again and again. After a few dances Rosa became aware that most of her classmates were present except Alois. Did he not come at all? While she was scanning the room Bert approached the table and motioned to Rosa to dance with him. He was a few years older than Rosa and came from one of the largest farms. Rosa asked back, pointing at herself:

"Do you mean me?"

"Yes, come on," he said impatiently.

"Look at that," Mal exclaimed, astounded. "Him and her?" was the last thing Rosa heard walking toward Bert. He was the son of a rich farmer, a sought-after candidate for marriage.

"I was watching you with Thomas," Bert explained. "You are a good dancer."

Rosa was not used to two compliments within the space of two dances. She blushed and looked down. This was a waltz, one of those long ones. Bert was a superb dancer. Rosa moved effortless in his arms. She looked into his eyes, her own shining. This was heavenly. He was even better than Thomas.

"I was right, you are the best dancer," Bert said when the music finally stopped. They were both out of breath, yet it had been just so effortless and wonderful.

"Save the next dances for me, Rosa," Bert demanded. Rosa gladly agreed to do so.

Rosa felt light and relaxed. All her pre-ball anxieties had vanished and had been replaced by deep satisfaction. Not only was she not left sitting at the table watching her friends dance away, but she also was desired by one of the best dancers in the village, the son of a farmer who had status and prestige. He had chosen her, the girl without a father. As the evening progressed her peers took note of her and Bert. Some complimented her including Mal. She, however, also dropped a bit of poison that made Rosa flinch:

"Don't let it go to your head, Rosa."

No, she wouldn't, she knew her place. It just felt so different tonight with Bert and all. But Thomas added some fuel to that fire.

"Isn't he a number too big for you?" Bert was aware of that social hick-hack.

"Don't pay any attention to them," was his advice. "They are just jealous because they can't dance like us."

And the music and dancing had its soul-lifting effect on Rosa again. It was during another waltz when suddenly Alois clapped his hands next to them. That was the sign for Bert to release Rosa for him, a custom that had to be adhered to. Rosa went into Alois' arms and followed his lead. She noticed the difference immediately. Alois was not the dancer Bert was. She regretted it only for a moment. It was Alois. He was here after all.

"I came several times to your table for you. But I was always too late. What are you dancing with him for all the time?"

"Well, he just came for me," Rosa defended herself weakly. Alois did not leave Rosa's side anymore than necessary that evening. Rosa was dancing on a different cloud now, one that felt hot and cold simultaneously. Bert had not looked at her the way Alois did. She also had not felt the touch of Bert's hands the way Alois' hands made her feel. It was wonderful. When Mal reminded her that it was time to leave for home by midnight, Rosa regretted the end of that ball and the dances with Alois.

"I will walk you home," Alois offered. Rosa nodded in agreement.

It was freezing cold outside. Coming from the heated excitement of the dance floor out into cold made Rosa shiver. Alois put his arm around her to keep her warm. Rosa was startled but did not protest, and then snuggled into his arm. In front of her house Alois kissed her on her mouth so quickly that Rosa was stunned. But he already had walked a few steps in direction of his own home.

Rosa turned to go in. Her lips felt strange, an unknown feeling. She would have to think about this. Was that actually a sin?

Her mother was still awake and heard her come in.

"How was it? Good girl that you came home now. Did you behave yourself?"

"Yes, of course," Rosa whispered.

***

On Ash Wednesday the pre-Easter fasting time started. It was a somber time, still winterish with freezing temperatures, although they were not quite as low anymore. There were no more cheerful dances or other festivities. In addition, once a day Jakob wanted to hear news from the radio that made the voice of the speaker so dull. It was very important to him. The German troops were expanding eastward, he said. He looked very worried – not for himself, for he was older and had only one eye left and thus had not too much to fear in terms of being drafted. But his two brothers must be out somewhere. Rosa was frightened more and more.

"Mother," she asked her grandmother, "are you worried, too?"

"Oh, not too much," she lied in trying to keep up appearance.

Yet, truth be told, Grandmother was very concerned inside. Most other families in the village had one male member in the army already. Rosa knew that as well from her peers and was not pacified by her grandmother's attempt to protect her. Rosa worried about her two uncles, especially Kon. She did not know where they were. When Easter arrived and fasting time ended her mood did not really lift a lot. It was like she and many other people around her were walking with a heavy load on their shoulders. One day after the Easter holidays that changed at bit for the better. Youth was youth and asked for the right to be young – and behave like it.

***

Her friend and school mate Lisa came by one afternoon. She had good news.

"We are going to have real dancing lessons in our Stube, Rosa. You have to come too. Mal will also come; you both can walk to us together. Probably Alois will walk with you." Rosa had heard his name clearly. There had not been much contact with him since that night at the ballroom, only an occasional passing when their path would happen to cross.

"I have to ask," Rosa said with obvious excitement. "But I will come. When is it?"

"Sundays in the afternoon. We will stop in time to get home to tend the animals."

"Who is teaching us?"

"My brothers and I," Lisa answered.

They were older and had already been taught the local dances by their older peers some years before. It was their turn now to pass on the skills. These were important to have, for both men and women. Many festivities culminated in the ballroom, even when they started out in church with a mass in the morning. The social hierarchy of the village was reflected in ballroom etiquette. Who could dance with whom in what order followed well-established social rules. Evading or violating these made the culprit the target of gossip. For the young those balls served as an acceptable way to establish amorous connections, to flirt, and maybe even to find the mate for matrimony. That's the way it had been for generations. And Rosa, like anybody else, was not going to be left out.

Those dancing lessons, of course, by way of preparation, provided such a forum as well, albeit in a much less formal way. Rosa loved them. There was a lot of joking and teasing accompanied with a lot of laughter. Bert was seeking her out to demonstrate the steps for the waltz, the tango, and all the local Bavarian dances. She was easy to lead, Bert said, and her feet were quick. Rosa was very proud to be selected in such a manner. For Bert was a champion dancer and demanded an equally skilled partner. They were the best pair. She wished that Alois would be that caliber dancer, and he was a good dancer, but just could not match Bert's excellence. But when he walked back to the village late in the afternoon, with her and Mal together, those dancing skills did not matter anymore. He would warm Rosa's hands in his as they walked through the snow, and he made sure she did not slide and fall. That was so wonderful that for some reason it made her almost tremble.

Spring had arrived, the snow had melted and the temperatures had climbed up above freezing levels. The fields had dried off enough so that it was time for planting the different kinds of grains, potatoes and turnips. Liz took Rosa with her to the fields to teach her how the business of planting crops worked. It was tiring work to keep the oxen going and the sowing machine in a straight line. Particularly the turn at the end of the field was difficult. Rosa learned quickly, though. She had a way with her oxen; only the machine was a problem. When Liz was satisfied with Rosa's work she left her to the task and walked home. Her own mother still did the cooking and other household chores. Of course, she had grown older and weaker and the work was hard on her. Liz needed to help to get the main meal of the day ready for the three women and Jakob. Before it was served, however, she would walk back to the field to see that Rosa had done the job right and to help her home with the oxen and the heavy sowing machine. When the animals sensed that they were to go home they tended to become rambunctious, walking faster and faster on the main road. It took some experience to keep them in line.

Liz did not particularly praise her daughter for her work. That was just not her way. However, she would say, "Yeah, this field is finished."

That statement to Rosa was as good as praise. She felt very proud as she walked home for lunch alongside her mother.

The planting season was hard work for most families because nearly every one of them was missing a young man or two on the farm. The army had taken them away. There was not much time for social gatherings with such demanding chores. The villagers met mostly in church or by way of passing on the street or out on the fields that were adjacent. It was a somber time.

Rosa's family, or whoever was left at home, had already discussed their concerns of bringing in the harvests with young Rosa and Liz. Grandmother could not help anymore with such heavy lifting and all. Jakob was not exactly in his youth anymore either. However, since he had only one eye he could occasionally be rendered temporarily blind if any dust or dirt got into it. But they would make it, of course! Rosa was aware that she had the strength and resilience of her youth and that the family counted on her.

Despite that chance of proving her worth she was often overcome with dread. She tended to wake up early before it was time to get up at five. Frequently, scary dreams would wake her up and keep her frightened for a while longer. Then she would think about her uncles Kon and Anselm in the army. For two months they had not received a note from either. Their mother prayed for their safety every time she led the prayer before lunch.

In turn, however, that raised Rosa's anxiety every time. Alois was teasing her because of it. He called her a frightened rabbit. Rosa was mad at him for that and told him that he better be worried about his own brother. But her friend denied all fear and tried to convince her that their relatives were not in harm's way. Rosa felt belittled then. She was not scared for nothing. Jakob had said that it was a war and they were being shot at.

"Do you have to go to war, too?" Rosa asked Alois.

"Me? No, I am needed at home and I am only eighteen," he said flatly. "Are you coming to the Maitanz the weekend after next?" Alois asked, abruptly changing the subject.

"I have not asked yet," Rosa answered. "Do you want me to come?" she asked coquettishly and blushed simultaneously. Alois stepped closer and took her arm.

"You come, Rosa, promise!" he tried to impress on her.

"I'll ask," she said and walked away.

She felt hot and uncomfortable, but she had to get away from Alois. His eyes seemed to burn into hers. He is barely a year older than me, she thought, he has no right to be so bossy. But then it made her happy that he wanted her to come to the Maitanz so badly. She intended to come, but she needed a new dress – one for the summer, with a wide skirt that would flutter out from dancing those fast polkas and waltzes.

"You have such a dress from last year. It is still good," Liz argued with her daughter.

"It is too small. I grew out of it," Rosa tried to convince her mother.

"Don't be silly, you did not grow a lot."

"Liz, I did, it is too tight around the chest." Rosa blushed. It was true.

"So what? It is not enough to throw away a perfectly good dress. It still looks pretty. You want to stand out? Be modest, Rosa!"

"Mother," Rosa turned to Grandmother for help. She smiled quietly, looked at her own daughter and then said to Rosa, "Give me your hand!"

Rosa stretched out her hand towards her grandmother. She put a few heavy coins into Rosa's palm and closed her fingers over them.

"Go find a matching fabric and make a new top that fits to that beautifully wide skirt," she said.

For the next week Rosa was very busy after her chores were done. She put her excellent seamstress skills to work. She separated the skirt from the top and sewed the new top on that she had just finished sewing. With a few meters of color-matching lace, she had produced a dress as good as new. Now she was looking forward to the ball even more.

***

When Mal and Rosa entered the dance hall everybody was already there. The music was loud and inviting. As soon as both sat down with other girls from the village Thomas was already asking Rosa for a dance.

"Rosa, he has got a crush on you," the girls exclaimed. But Thomas already had taken her away. Several other young men took her to the dance floor next. Rosa hardly got a rest in between dances. Every time she was brought back to her table she secretly took her shoes off under it. Above the table she joined the chatter between the girls. That is, she listened more because the excited whispers of her female companions did not leave any gap of silence, except when the music started up again. Then the girls quietened and looked around. Who would come and ask them to dance? It was very embarrassing to not be called upon. In that time of quiet Rosa could not help but overhear the boys at the next table. They also seemed to discuss amongst themselves which girl they were going to take to the floor this time. She saw Schorsch shaking his head at Thomas.

"No, I don't think I want to ask her. I mean, what should I do with her? You don't know anything about her other side of the family. Who is her father anyhow?"

Rosa's face paled. It was like somebody had poured cold water over her. She felt sick in her stomach almost instantly. Then her mind began to work. They don't like me, they don't want me. I want out of here! Frantically she put on her shoes, got up and turned around to bolt for the door. Right in front of her stood Alois.

"Sorry I am so late," he said. "Where are you going?"

"I don't know," Rosa stuttered.

"Come on," he said taking her by her arm. "I have not had one dance with you yet."

Rosa followed him like a lamb. How come he wants to dance with me? Does he like me?

She questioned her worth with Alois only briefly. When he put his arm around her a feeling of defiance and triumph came over her. Alois, after all, was well-liked and well-regarded by most. She knew that Mal also would like to dance with him. Rosa pushed her thoughts aside. She had to concentrate on the dance steps to make Alois like dancing with her. With him it was like dancing on clouds anyway. She felt the warmth of his hand in her back. It made her feel weak, proud and important at the same time. The night went on and Alois did not let her dance with anybody else. He hardly left her side. At one point, though, Rosa missed Bert as a partner. She liked to dance the complicated dances with Bert for the sheer joy of the movement. Did he not want her as a partner anymore? Where was he?

"Where is Bert?" Rosa asked Alois.

"Don't you know? He has been drafted into the army. Don't know where he is at." Alois answered. Rosa stared at him. The second time this night her heart had started to pound heavily. Alois looked at her suspiciously.

"What?" he asked.

"No, nobody told me," Rosa said. "Him too?"

For the next dance Thomas had to be very quick, faster than Alois. So before the music started he stepped up to the table where Rosa and the other girls sat sipping their lemonade and chatting excitely.

"Alois, please let me have this dance with Rosa," Thomas asked with a strange glint in his eyes. His familiar grin had been replaced by a serious expression on his face. Alois stepped back without a word to Thomas.

"He has nothing to worry about. I spoke to him," Thomas said. "Please, Rosa."

Rosa was puzzled by Thomas' behavior. Something made her follow him to the dance floor. It was already a late hour; the dancers had spent most of their energy and the orchestra played slower tunes. Thomas led her lightly.

"You are a good dancer, Rosa," Thomas complimented her. She did not answer as she was not in the habit of receiving compliments, nor did she know what to do with them. The following silence between them was not unusual.

"This will be our last dance for a while, Rosa," Thomas said. Her heart started pounding harder immediately. Her feet stumbled. She looked into his face. Oh my God, him too, she thought. Weirdly, she suddenly realized that Thomas was no longer the boy, who was older than her, that she had always seen in him. He was a young man.

"I have to go," was all he offered as an explanation. His face was rigid.

"You and Bert together?" Rosa asked with alarm.

After a quick and chaste hug, and a kiss on the cheek, he was gone.

Rosa was looking for Alois when she found him sitting at a table with his friends and school mates in the far corner. Obviously he had been watching her and Thomas, for he stood up immediately when he saw her searching the crowd. He approached her, reaching for her hand. It was not proper to take her into his youthful arms just like that and with everybody watching. A dance, however, was justification for that.

"Do you also have to leave?" Rosa asked anxiously.

"No, I told you I am needed at home and I am too young," Alois replied, trying to sound convincing. Lately he had begun to feel less secure of his statement. But he could not afford to doubt it or let Rosa in on his doubts.

"I want to go home," she said.

"Me too. I'll walk you home. Get your coat and I'll meet you outside the door."

"Be careful," the girls said to her when she picked up her coat. They laughed mischievously. "Your mother will be watching. Make sure you don't have to go to confession."

Rosa swirled off and rushed out the door. Bitches!

Alois took her hand and Rosa drew it back like she had been burned.

"Rosa, don't pay any attention to them," Alois said tensely to her. When they were out on the street in the dark night Rosa did not resist when Alois put his arm around her. It was so nice, so exciting and so comfortable.

He stopped under the walnut tree in front of her house and put both arms around her, drawing her closer to him. Questioningly he looked into her eyes and then kissed her. Rosa felt unable to resist or consider the possibility of this being a sin. It was wonderful.

"Good night," Alois said gently.

"You are not going to go, Alois?" she asked one more time to assure her shaken mind.

"No," Alois said and walked on to his home. Not yet anyway, he thought. Immediately he distracted himself to ban the fear that had settled in his mind. Rosa's shy response to his kiss served that purpose very well. Different from the first time, he thought and smiled.

Rosa, however, was bothered by ambivalence as she entered her house. There was great happiness and satisfaction that she felt about Alois and his kiss. And that feeling was mutual. But did her mother not warn her about boys? Rosa did not understand why they were to be regarded with so much caution as if there was something dangerous about them. When she went to her first dance she harbored a lot of anxiety that her having no father would keep the dancers away. One did! But others did not seem to care about the circumstances of her conception. And Alois was a son from a family who had status in the village and he liked her, danced with her, preoccupied her thoughts and walked her home, every time! With him she threw her mother's concerns to the wind.

Those feelings about Alois also seemed to keep her occasional nightmares at bay. She had never had a great problem falling asleep or sleeping through the night. But since Kon and Anselm had to join the army, that had changed. Sometimes she had trouble falling asleep or she woke up from a bad dream in the middle of the night. Then she started to worry about them. Grandmother said that they are still being trained and not on the front.

Since Jakob needed to listen to the news every evening and morning she could not help but hear more then what was said. It was clear that there was shooting going on and there was something called infantry that advanced, the speaker said. Advanced? That surely meant more danger in her mind. But Alois was reassuring, something Grandmother and Liz were not, and he made her feel strangely calm, even just thinking about him had that effect on her. That way she could fall asleep again.

***

Eventually summer had arrived and with it the need for cutting the grass on the meadows to dry it to hay and bring that into the barn. As usual, it was very hard labor for the three of them. Swinging a scythe into the wet grass for a few hours exhausted Jakob. He often had to stop and rest. Liz lasted longer, but always had to quit when it was time to start cooking lunch, the main meal of the day. Rosa did not even have to be told to finish mowing the rest of the meadow; it was understood.

Swing after swing she walked through the grass in a rhythmic way as she had learned from her mother. Oh, she did feel her sore muscles the next morning, but the work did not exhaust her. She was strong and she was carried by the wings of pride knowing that she was a most important link in the operation of the farm. The thing was, though, that these comfortable feelings did not last. It required repeated efforts to regain them, and that was the exhausting thing for her. Hence her trepidation thinking about July and August when all the fields of various grains, wheat, barley, oat, and rye had to be cut and bound into bundles. Not to think of bringing them all home on wagons loaded high, pulled by two oxen. What with her uncle Jakob's limitations… would she be able to last through these weeks to come? If only one of her uncles was here. She was determined to keep up her end of the tasks with all the might of her seventeen years. What would they think if she faltered? Alois also had to do double duty, Mal did, almost all of her peers did, and so would she.

Life did show some mercy, one that neither of them three left on the farm had reckoned with. One afternoon Jakob was sitting just outside the barn, hammering the little dents out of a scythe to make it razor sharp again, when Rosa heard him yell:

"Hey, where are you coming from?" Rosa turned around to see who was coming.

With her mouth agape and squinting into the street she saw a man walking into the yard. His clothes were not very well kept and all too loose. Then she recognized his grin and she started running towards Kon.

"Kon!" He caught her in his arms, held her and let her cry. After a while he did what was custom. He pushed her gently away at arm's length, wiped her tears away and dried his own, as men did not cry.

"Stop it, silly, it is all okay."

Liz had appeared in the door frame, drying her hands on her apron. Jakob stood there, his one eye staring widely at his younger brother.

"How come you are here? I thought you were in the infantry somewhere east."

"Many soldiers from farms have been sent home during harvest time," Kon explained.

He looked thinner than when he left in the depth of winter. His eyes seemed tired. Of course, he had walked the five miles from the train station to his home.

"Come in and have a snack before we have to tend to the cows," Liz said in a motherly way. When Kon entered the Stube, his mother had been sitting on the sofa. Her hands were covering her face.

"Mother, I am here," Kon said. She took her youngest son's hands into hers, put them into her lap, still not looking up, tears dropping silently. Rosa stood right next to both watching the scene. Her fingers were holding on to Kon's dirty sleeve.

Two days later a similar scene happened, when one late afternoon Anselm walked into the Stube. Everyone was sitting at the table having a snack. It took only a few seconds of speechlessness before the commotion of his welcoming set in. Grandmother ran her hands up and down her son's chest as if she was checking if he was for real. Rosa stood next to her and received a pat on her head. She liked that a lot. Like Kon he also seemed to have lost weight. It was upsetting to notice that for he always had been the strongest one, the one who did not even get a head cold in winter.

"You are here to help us harvest, too?" Uncle Jakob was asking with hope. It had been very tough for him so far, to help with the farm work and tend his blacksmith work simultaneously. Exactly during harvest time the other farmers needed work done from him more than the rest of the year.

"Yep, that's what I have been sent home for."

After the sensation that both brothers had come home had spent itself, relief settled over everybody alike. They were going to make it! And they both were back without a scratch.

Soon Kon and Anselm both were swinging their scythes next to each other on the field. It was as it used to be before they were called into the army – yet not quite. Anselm did not smile at all, did not tease Rosa anymore, and talked very little. In the evenings, they still sat outside on the front steps watching the swallows catch flies in the sky, watching the summer sun set. Soon after Kon told stories from his army training. Anselm listened mostly in silence. It was not until eight years later that he would reveal what had made him so silent that summer at home. He already had his marching orders after his return to his caserne in Berlin, eastward, into the frontlines of war. Inside he was scared spitless. Rosa had felt his terror. She often sat close to him as if she had switched favorite uncles. She had asked her grandmother to get her own diffuse feelings clarified.

"Mother, why does he not talk?"

"Oh, perhaps he just enjoys some peace and quiet," she answered with her head turned away. Her explanation did not satisfy Rosa, though it would have to do for now.

After most of the dried wheat and rye plants had been brought into the barn, the time was approaching when both uncles had to leave again. That's when they both, as if in unison, started to ask about their school mates.

Neither man had seen more than one or two of them from each class during church services. If they were there they would have attended Sunday church as sure as two and two equals four. As they dropped one name after another during the last few lunches and suppers, they learned that nearly all of their classmates had been drafted. Both Kon and Anselm received such news with a stony, expressionless face.

Grandmother would catch her sons repeatedly looking thoughtfully at Rosa. She was the youngest and strongest left at home. This seventeen-year-old girl was the hope of the family that they were going to be able to keep up the operation of their farm for an unknown period of time. How good that they had her!

Rosa, listening to the adults of her family sending two- and three-word sentences across the table, slowly began to comprehend reality. Most farms had lost their best workers, being sons, fathers, or farm helpers, to the army. It was the women, older men and those still very young who had to take over and do all the work previously done with more people. How was that supposed to work for her? Was she strong enough to replace two strong men? What if she turned out to be too weak? Surges of anxiety and self-doubt came over her like avalanches. She had to do the job. Her family counted on her. So she listened to the instructions from Kon with concentration.

After the end of a hot day he would sit with her behind the barn on a log and instruct her how best to tackle the tasks of fall. There were seven trees from which the apples had to be picked and properly stored to last through most of the winter. But the pears could only be stored for a short time. They tended to spoil and thus had to be preserved.

"You are the youngest, so don't get dizzy up there in them trees. You are the only one who can be up on that ladder. Always hold on with one hand, and don't lean out so far. Rather, have somebody move the ladder."

He went meticulously through the job of applying the plow to uproot the potatoes and bring them to the surface.

"Liz knows how to hitch up the two oxen; learn it from her. And be patient with the oxen. Let them walk their own speed and let them rest after two or three rows. Do not hit them, or you will spoil them, Rosa."

"I will not do that! I can work with them."

"I know," her uncle reassured her.

"But how are we going to do the threshing of the wheat and all?

The sacks of grain are so heavy and we do not have enough people." Rosa was afraid of that day.

"Don't worry, Rosa. The neighbors will help you, as much as they may ask you for help." Kon succeeded to calm her.

"Do I have to bring the wheat to the mill then?"

"Yes, why not? You know the animals and where the mill is, and the miller knows you."

That was a different matter. Rosa felt she could handle that four-kilometer trip to the mill. And besides, she had to lead her oxen and the wagon through the main street of the village. That was good because everybody could see how she did a man's job. Alois would be impressed for sure.

Soon the day of Kon's departure had arrived. He had to leave early in the morning to catch a train that would bring him to his unit. His face appeared to be set in stone. Quickly he downed a cup of grain coffee, and tried to have a slice of bread but did not finish it. Everybody seemed very busy. Grandmother cupped her son's face with both her hands and said, "Come back!" Jakob slapped Kon on the back and turned away. Rosa threw her arms around her uncle and pressed her face onto his chest.

"Where are you going? When are you coming back?" she howled, letting her tears stream freely.

"I am going to France," he said. "Don't worry, I'll come back. I will write, too."

Rosa went outside with him, holding on to his arm. Anselm stepped out of the blacksmith workshop with an equally expressionless, tense face.

"Get going," he said. "Be careful."

Two days later almost the exact same scene happened when Anselm had to return to his unit as well.

"Where are you going? When are you coming back?" Rosa's eyes were swimming in tears.

"That is not up to me," he said harshly. It must have been Rosa's terrified but hopeful face that made him add:

"France is not so cold. I will be lucky. I'll write," he promised, tenderly touching Rosa's head. He picked up his bag and rushed out the door.

"Come on now," Liz called her daughter. "We have to hurry to milk the cows and get the milk out on the bench or the milk wagon will be there before us."

Rosa turned around to her as if coming out of a nightmare. Slowly she recognized that the time had returned to put in her full strength. Yes, I will milk half of them now, she thought.

***

Somehow the day passed. Liz worked closely alongside her daughter to correct and instruct how the work had to be done properly. In turn, Rosa paid close attention to her mother's teachings. After all, she had done this for years; she was efficient and industrious and, moreover, she was the boss now. She was not overly harsh. Actually, she was kind and had some patience. Yet, no smile crossed her face. Rather it seemed to express tension, sadness, and worry. This was much how Rosa felt herself. But neither woman addressed that issue. Work had to be done: that was the priority. Who had time to talk about feelings and who would even admit to having any? That was just not the habit in this family, or in this community, for that matter. The milk containers had to be cleaned for the evening milking, and the pigs had to be let out of their nighttime quarters. That alone was work for two, for the pigs ran and jumped like crazy once they were out in the open. It was a chore to get them to go into their enclosure in the garden. Fodder for the evening meal had to be prepared for all animals such as the cows, the oxen, the chickens, the geese, the ducks, the cats and the dog. Oh, and the doves, Rosa remembered.

Anselm was gone. These were his doves; he had bred them. They were the kind that found their way back home when taken far away and set free. It was Rosa's job to take care of them until Anselm came back. She would do a good job of it – he would be proud of her. He had a special tune that he whistled to get the doves to come when he threw wheat or some other grain out for them. Rosa knew the tune and she could whistle as well. And she would do it even though it was said that Mary, the mother of Jesus, always cried when girls whistled. How else would I get the doves to come, Rosa thought defiantly. And I have to stay there until they fly away with a bulging sack protruding from their neck. Or else, the chicken would come and drive the doves away.

"Rosa, pay attention!" Liz almost shouted. "Mother wants you to go into the garden and pull out three radishes for supper. Hurry up! Bring them into the kitchen to her and help her." Only now Rosa realized that tears were rolling down her cheeks. Hastily she wiped them away with her hands. It was not lost on her that her mother's voice had become scratchy.

There they sat, Jakob, Grandmother and Liz, silently eating fresh radishes, sliced and salted, freshly baked bread in their own oven with some butter on it. Self-made yoghurt prepared as a drink refreshed them. Apples, the variety that started to ripen early, were the dessert. Rosa always loved these kinds of suppers, but today the mood around the table was somber. Kon's and Anselm's absence had left a huge, painful, scary void.

"Eat up, Rosa," Liz rushed her daughter. "We have to go milking and feed the animals. And the stable needs to be cleaned before we can put in fresh straw."

"Let her finish eating in peace," Jakob reprimanded his sister. Rosa looked at him gratefully. He is sticking up for me, she realized.

At eight, after the evening news, Rosa went to bed. She had worked a thirteen-hour day and fell asleep almost instantly.

***

The last days of August with their warm temperatures were enjoyable days. Most of the harvest was safely in the barn. At the same time potatoes and apples, the next crops to be brought in, were not quite ripe yet. With the heaviest field work completed, only the daily routine of tending the animals, the vegetable garden and the household chores seemed easy by comparison. The nights were still reasonably warm. And with the August sun still strong during the day there was an afternoon at the pond behind the western forest.

Even though Rosa's peers liked the idea of pond time a lot, she was wavering between eagerness and apprehension. Nobody had taught her how to swim, which made her fearful of both the water and the teasing. Worse, she did not own a proper bathing suit. If she wanted to come along she had to wear the hand-me-down swimsuit from her aunt. That one was tight on her because her aunt was thin as a rail. But it was her only choice to come along, short of letting her underwear do the job. And that was completely out of the question.

Mal had an older sister to borrow her swimwear from. She did not mind. But then, everybody else had a sibling and was used to wearing clothes that were not new. Everybody knew that. But Rosa had no siblings, which also everybody knew. But it was important to appear properly outfitted. She was not going to be different from her friends. And most importantly, Alois always came along and always stayed close to her both in the water and out on the meadow.

He always pried her hands loose from the bushes along the pond banks. Holding both her hands he would take her into the deeper water where she lost touch with the muddy floor. Then he turned her on her back and held a supporting, reassuring hand under her back. That way he floated her all around the pond, swimming calmly beside her.

Whenever they reached the most western end of the pond they felt the very mushy, muddy ground again and would step in amongst the reeds. There Alois always held her close to him. Rosa could feel his wet chest and his strong wet arms on her skin. Then she let her head sink onto his shoulder and close her eyes. She could feel his as well as her own heart pounding. Gently he kissed her wet, trembling lips. More privacy, sadly, was not afforded to them. Their friends were shouting their names with urgency and concern in their voices. Rosa was not the only female who could not swim. And everybody looked out for everybody.

"Come," Alois said gently, "we need to go back."

"Alois, turn her loose! She will never learn to swim if you drag her over the water," Mal yelled at them across the pond.

"She is swimming on her back. I am only watching her," Alois yelled back. Everybody laughed.

When it was time to leave, all the girls ran together into the forest and changed clothes behind the bushes. Everyone was careful not to get caught by the thorns of the blackberry vines. The boys changed out in the open by the pond. They all had been taught the art of redressing by the pond without revealing anything.

Soon the noisy, teasing, laughing group of young folks walked down the path to their village. Returning home Rosa had to rush to put on her garments that were only used for working in the cow stable. For a few hours in the circle of her school mates and friends, the carelessness and cheerfulness of youth had taken her thoughts away from hard work and the worries about those family members who were somewhere in France or in Russia in harm's way.

***

Fall had arrived, and September indicated the start of cooler temperatures. Some of the apples were ready to be picked. Rosa had to climb the ladder high into the tree. She did not mind. That was easy work. Better yet, after these early ripening apples were picked there was the potato harvest to be done. For that one it always had to be sunny and dry. On such dry, warm, lovely fall days, after the potatoes were safely stored for winter, children, youth, and seniors would gather again on a potato field and burn the crisp, crackling vines. Usually that was a lot of fun and Rosa was very much looking forward to that event. Why else would anybody be eager to walk, back bent, bucket-carrying, forward over freshly plowed soil to collect potatoes? Some of the fields of her peers' families were adjacent. So they could either make one gigantic fire or several slightly smaller ones on different days. Using the latter method the danger that the large fire would go out of control was reduced and the fun could last for more than one time only. It was always a big spectacle for the village. Potatoes that had been missed during gathering were dropped into the flames to broil them, and white cabbage was ripped out of a field nearby, stripped of its outer leaves and eaten raw. If the winds were favorable the younger children would fly their kites while being instructed and helped by the village teens.

When the sun started to sink lower on late afternoons the boys stopped feeding the fire. Rosa had exhausted herself with playing tack, running with the kid's kites, collecting potatoes for broiling, and laughing and having a good time. Several people were already sitting by the fire using a stick to fish for a potato in the glowing coals. Rosa did the same. Her eyes were scanning the people around the circle. They like me, she thought, feeling at home with them. Where is he actually? Alois, did you not come? Such little happenings were always an opportunity to be together with him besides work. And perhaps, who knows, there might be a quick kiss when nobody was looking.

In fact, Alois had asked her to meet Sunday afternoons or evenings for a little, after work was done. But how could she get away without Liz noticing her absence and on her return to ask where she had been? What would she say then? If her mother would find out that she had lied to her or that she had been with a male, either would be very bad, of that she was sure. She was, however, not as clear about herself. She knew she hesitated to meet Alois alone after sundown. She wanted to but then she did not. Rosa felt hot and cold interchangeably when thinking about him. It was strange, and it frightened her.

And then she saw him approaching. He emerged from the smoke that was blown to the other side of the fire place. He is coming to me, she noticed. Her face blushed but in the shine of the coals nobody noticed. Calmly Alois sat down next to her. He took her stick and poked it into an almost black lump of a potato in the coal. Then he pulled it towards him and blew onto it.

"Here," he said, "you can peel it now." He would not dare to put his arm around her with all these people watching. Still he paid close attention to her.

***

Each morning, like the last time at the pond, there was the hazy presence of the first fall fogs hanging over the meadows and forests. The grass grew slowly. Still it looked pretty with all the flowers of autumn sprinkling the valleys and hills with colors like in an Impressionist painting. That was the time when everybody who owned a cow opened the stable doors to let them out into the pastures for the afternoon. In those days farm lands were not fenced in with an electric fence. Everybody knew where their own property started and ended and where their neighbor's began. It has been this way for generations. Thus, somebody had to stay out with the animals to keep them from meandering off into the neighbor's meadows.

This was the job of the youngest family member. It has been Rosa's job since she graduated from school. For the months of late September, October and November, or at least until it started to freeze, she would take her little three-legged stool and her knitting and lead her animals to one of the pastures of her farm. It was easy work for her but also quite boring. If she was herding the cows to the meadow in the western valley then it usually was a good time with Mal. Her family's pastures were adjacent and they could get together to gossip. Here, they could also discuss all things female without the fear of being overheard.

Mal knew a lot about female things that Rosa's mother would not tell her. In Rosa's family such talk was taboo. Mal also somehow came into possession of love stories that she would lend Rosa. Suddenly this job of minding the grazing cows was ideal, for she could read those forbidden romances without her grandmother or Liz catching her. She hid the little booklet in her knitting bag.

But one day, Rosa was lucky to have avoided an incident. It was a blue sky afternoon and the autumn sun was still comfortably warm. Rosa decided it was too warm to knit socks, so she pulled out her reading. She forgot to watch her charges until Lisa hollered at her from her adjacent pasture to the west.

"Rosa, one of your cows is in the clover!"

But Rosa read intensely and did not hear her. Lisa knew that cows can get badly bloated from too much clover and they must be chased out of it. She tried again:

"Rosa, get your head out of your romance story and run that cow out of the clover field!"

Rosa's head jerked up this time. She grabbed her stick and ran downhill, jumped over the little creek and ran towards the cow. The cow started moving back before Rosa could even get close. Out of breath, Rosa went over to Lisa.

"Thanks for that, Lisa."

"What are you reading those love stories all the time for? You have a real one and don't need to read them," Lisa scolded with a meaningful look. Rosa blushed instantly.

"Oh, look at you! It is true then, you and Alois?"

"Of course not, shut up!"

"You would like that, ha? I don't really care. Just don't get pregnant like your mother did."

Rosa stared at Lisa motionless, as if she was frozen to the ground. Stars danced in front of her eyes. Without thinking she grabbed her stick and waved it in the air.

"You slut," she screamed at Lisa. Lisa jumped back and hollered:

"Are you crazy? I just tried to warn you! Calm down!"

Rosa was fighting back tears. Lisa stepped closer and put her arm around her friend. But she did not calm down so fast.

"You don't even know how to get pregnant!"

"You don't know how to either," Lisa shot back.

"Well, when I asked Liz she said I don't need to know. She will tell me when the time is right. And your mother, did you ask her?"

"Yes, but she said that she does not want to talk about such things. It might be a sin to do that. But she will tell me, she promised, before I get married."

"I say we should ask Mal, Lisa."

"Does she know? How does she know?"

"Oh, look at that cow. She is in the clover again. I have to run."

Secretly Rosa thanked the cow for providing a good reason to get out of that conversation. It was embarrassing. But I do want to find out. We really should ask Mal, Rosa thought.

By late October the fall fogs came in earlier in the afternoon. It was not much fun watching the livestock. Rosa's fingers got cold and moist, and the yarn for her knitting did not slip easily anymore. Sometimes the autumn winds were so strong that she preferred to hunker down behind the trunk of the old pear tree that stood at the edge of their property. These were the afternoons that made Rosa long for the church bell to toll at five o'clock.

Later, in November, when it was still colder and foggier, she was often called back early. Liz would appear at the gate to their orchard and wave and holler down the meadow, to the valley, until Rosa heard or saw her. Usually by that time the cows had started grazing uphill to stand then in front of the gate, waiting to be let in. They are not stupid, Rosa thought about her charges. It was almost like solidarity taking place. She loved her animals.

***

"Rosa, today, after lunch, you have to help me carry the chrysanthemums to the graveyard and fix up our grave for All Saints' Day," Grandmother said.

"And what about my cows?" Rosa asked.

"Liz will watch them until we are finished. Then you go and take over."

"Sure," Rosa answered, making no attempt to hide her pleasure about this change of chores. Watching the cows on the meadow had become unpleasant. Now, one day before the first of November, the grass was mostly wet. One could not sit on it anymore. The temperature had dropped, which made for cold fingers and toes. Neither reading nor knitting was comfortable. But to decorate the grave with flowers, pine cones, Tannenbaum twigs and moss was a pleasant thing to do. Many women would be at the graveyard the next two days applying their skills in floristry. Along with them would come many female school mates. It was always nice to get together so casually and visit, exchanging things that mothers don't need to know.

Last year, during that social get together at the graveyard, Rosa found out that she was not the only one finding blood in her underwear. It had happened the first time the previous fall. At first she was really scared and did not know what to make of it. But after about two days it stopped again and Rosa put it out of her mind only to find it returned about three weeks later. It came in irregular intervals, for she could not tell when. Every time considerable cramps went along with it. She was really frightened by them, and finally told Liz about her problem. Liz blushed, which made Rosa blush in turn.

"Don't worry about it. All women have that," Liz reassured her.

"Oh, you too?" Rosa asked, blushing, even though Mal had already secretly informed her in that matter and in a convoluted way. Perhaps this is a sin, Rosa thought.

"Yep, listen," Liz cut her short. "When it hurts then you use a hot water bottle over your stomach. But don't let the men see you with it. Don't talk about it with them either. And during those cursed days you must not get wet. Don't get into a rain and you can't wash your hair. If you do you can get crazy." Hearing these rules of behavior Rosa's fear changed. That is something dirty, she thought.

"But why do we have that?" she asked Liz.

"It is dirty blood that comes out and it has something to do with getting pregnant. Now quit asking."

Then Liz showed her how to use napkins to protect her clothing. Rosa had a lot more questions about that connection to pregnancy. But she was told that she did not need to know more and that she will find out soon enough. Even her grandmother refused to talk about it. When she met with her female school mates there were occasional whispers about their experiences with that curse and their mothers. But nobody was really talking sense and that was that. One did not talk about that thing.

All Saints' Day came in with light frost in tow. Rosa left the warmth of her down filled bed reluctantly. She had to help milk and feed the cows. The milk cans had to be on a platform next to the main road through the village by seven o'clock. She dressed in a hurry and without checking the weather. She did not need to take a look. The morning fog was a given by now, and since none of the bedrooms were heated she always knew from the room temperature how warm to dress.

I will have to wear my winter coat for the ceremony at the graveyard in the afternoon, she decided, though not certain. I will see what the others are going to wear and I will go to Mal's house and ask her. Rosa was always careful to watch her people. She did not want to be so different, or stick out the wrong way.

What was otherwise so nice about All Saints' Day was the

congregation of all the villagers. That was a day when the whole family was expected to be at the family grave. Relatives living elsewhere had to travel to show up for that hour in the afternoon at their family grave. Anyone missing would be gossiped about. Mostly people would wear dark colors, although black was a must the next afternoon.

Rosa liked to stand in the middle, with Grandmother and Liz on one side and her uncles on the other. This year, however, Rosa felt some unease. Mother was crying and Jakob had a tense expression on his face. No wonder, Kon and Anselm were not with them. Worse, they had not received any Feldposts from them either. Rosa looked around after the priest had walked by sprinkling holy water on graves. The people standing there he sprinkled by accident. Alois' family's grave was one row in front of hers. She could see Alois and his older brother Georg next to him. Between them was little Sepp, who was fourteen years old.

"Liz, why is Alois' mother crying?" Rosa whispered to her mother.

"Because Georg has been called up into the army. Be quiet now!" Rosa caught her breath in fear. She felt terrible for Georg but was also glad that it was not Alois who had to leave. But she could not be quiet now.

"Liz, Peter's mother is dressed in pitch black and she is also crying."

"Be quiet," her mother hissed. A moment later she still provided an answer.

"Peter's father has been killed in France," she said, her blue eyes swimming in tears. She had known Peter ever since she went to school with him. Rosa stared at Peter. *Dear Mother of Jesus, he does not have a father anymore!* Rosa's heart filled with empathy. *But he at least once had a father, unlike me,* she thought.

***

Since that All Saints' Day Rosa did not feel the same. She was in a subdued mood often times. Usually at this time of the year people were in a light, upbeat state of mind. After all, the harvest was completed and the threshing had been done. Everything they needed for humans and animals was stored safely and would last through the long winter months. The daily workload would be a lot lighter now. This satisfaction of a difficult job successfully completed was marked annually by the same celebrations. There was Thanksgiving Day, a festive mass that would be celebrated in church, and the best meal of the year followed at home. This year, however, that highlight was overshadowed by worries for Kon and Anselm.

Then there was the Kirchweihfest, which was actually a religious holiday. In addition, as for every year, Alois' father, with the help of his two younger sons, put up the ropes for that Kirchweih swing. Tradition could not just be suspended. The youth of the whole village wanted to come. Even this sad year, come afternoon, the Gillmer yard was full of laughter and shouting. For a few hours sorrow and worries were put aside. Rosa was aware that Georg and Peter did not show up.

"I have to go home now for the evening milking," Rosa announced, speaking to no-one in particular. A small chorus of "me too, me too" was the resonance. Jackets and bags were suddenly picked from the floor and a general "bye bye" sounded through the barn.

"See you at the Kathrein Dance?" *Who said that?* Rosa, already outside, turned around. A hand had gripped her arm. As she looked into Alois' questioning eyes she felt her face turning red. Worse, Alois grinned at her.

"Oh, I don't know," Rosa replied. Like a flash the memory of the Maitanz experience came to her mind. *Bert and Thomas won't be there. What if nobody will ask me for a dance?* she wondered. But she did not want to share this with Alois. He might think she was scared. Under no circumstances would she remind him about Schorsch's refusal to dance with her – like when he said that her unknown father was a problem. Perhaps Alois might also eventually not like that issue about her.

"Why not?" he asked her.

"Don't know," she evaded a truthful answer. But Alois was not to be put off.

"I'll pick you up," he said resolutely. *Oh, no, not that,* Rosa thought, *that would look like we are a pair.*

"Well, I will ask Liz and Mother. And then I'll come with Mal. But you are going to be there for sure?"

"What do you think, Rosa? I want to dance with you and I won't let you dance with any other guy for half the night!" Alois' eyes met Rosa's blue-green ones. Blushing, Rosa turned quickly and left for home. She went straight into the warm Stube.

"Ah, it must have been exhausting on the swing," Jakob remarked. "You are all red in the face."

Rosa grinned but noticed with anger that the blushing in her face did not stop. Cleverly she used the question that she had asked frequently the last three weeks or so, to divert the attention away from her person.

"Did we get a letter from Uncle Kon or Uncle Anselm?"

"Yes, it is there on the table," Liz answered. Rosa dashed to it and immediately recognized Kon's handwriting, although it looked a bit jittery. It was not a long letter. But he did confirm that he was safe in France. Sadly, he would not be home for Christmas.

"And Uncle Anselm?" Rosa asked.

"Probably the same since he is in France as well." Grandmother said that with a sigh.

"No," Rosa wailed in disappointment.

"Rosa, be glad they are safe and not hurt," Grandmother reprimanded her. "Think about Peter's father, God bless his soul!"

Rosa understood and turned to change into her stable clothing. She did her chores together with Liz. After that she went to bed immediately. She had had enough excitement for the day. *I will ask about the Kathrein Dance tomorrow*, she decided.

The next day when the family gathered for lunch, Rosa found the courage to ask for permission to attend the Kathrein Dance.

"Do you have to be at every dance there is?" Liz asked. Rosa stayed silent and poked at her food on her plate.

"Well, why should she not go?" Grandmother asked.

"Because it is not the right time with Anselm and Kon gone," Liz stated.

She did not reveal that she simply did not feel comfortable to let her daughter mingle with all these men all the time.

"Let her go," Jakob decided with authority in his voice. He had a suspicion, a fear, that this could be the last Kathrein Dance for a while. But he kept this to himself.

"But you are going to go with Mal," her mother demanded.

Rosa looked at Jakob gratefully. *He helped me*, she noticed.

Alois kept his word. He asked Rosa for the dances as they came and she forgot the worries she had had. Instead she felt safe with and proud of Alois, as she knew that there were other girls who wanted him to dance with them. His arm around her felt so reassuring and somehow loving. She had to be careful that no sin developed out of this, although she did not quite know how that could be.

"I have to dance with Lisa and Mal at least once," Alois said apologetically to Rosa, "lest they get angry at me and you." Oh yes, Rosa did not want that. She had no right to be possessive with Alois.

It was a nice atmosphere at the dance, yet somehow not quite the same than before. The absence of Bert and Thomas made a gaping hole in the group and everybody knew somebody, it seemed, who had to leave next. Alois also had stated that he was worried about his brother Georg joining the army in January. Peter also was absent. To be sure they all were older. But would the boys from Rosa's class be drafted next? And Alois? And now, Rosa had learned that another friend, Regine, had been called up for Social Service. She also had to leave in March to work in a factory.

"Is that true?" Rosa asked Mal and Lisa.

"Yes, it is. All girls have to go to Arbeitsdienst," Mal said with vigor and fear in her eyes.

"When?"

"When we are old enough. Perhaps next year they will call us in."

A subdued mood settled over the friends.

"I am tired," Rosa said to Alois during the next dance, a slow waltz.

"I will walk you home," he answered agreeably.

"Look at those two!" Lisa exclaimed as she saw them walking out the door. Alois and Rosa pretended not to hear and walked on. In front of Rosa's gate, under the leafless walnut tree, Alois pulled Rosa into his arms, holding her tight to him. A clear, star-sprinkled autumn sky was sparkling above them. But they had no sense for that kind of romance tonight. Erotic feelings mingled with the fear of the war. They held on to and kissed each other as if to store those emotions for the future.

***

Alois and Rosa were not the only people with an elevated anxiety level and a subdued mood in the village. They, like others, kept up the activities common for the winters in Bavaria. There were the Christmas tree auctions that drew crowds. People bid for the bottles of wine and schnaps, for the cakes baked by the women of the community, and for other things Bavarian or Alpine. Furthermore, people staged a nativity play, like every year; they decorated their homes; and they went to midnight mass on Christmas Eve and sang "Silent Night, Holy Night" in church on Christmas Day.

But the enthusiasm to celebrate seemed curbed by the news about fallen fathers and husbands that came in regular intervals. The same news reached them from the neighboring villages. It seemed that each Sunday mass one more woman came dressed in black. Rosa mourned with her community. Thankfully she did have enough work – the work of a man, really – to keep her from dwelling too much on her rising anxiety about her uncles. Still, neither Kon nor Anselm had sent a Feldpost letter. Sometimes during lunch Grandmother, Liz and Jakob mentioned that it would be high time to hear from them. Nothing more was said than that. Rather, the meal was finished in silence. Moreover, Rosa had been taught to not discuss anything about the war with anybody unless it was positive. But better yet, they said, just don't talk about it outside the family. Since Rosa had often been told to "be quiet" while growing up, she was puzzled but had no great problem obeying. However, she still had one ally who she confided her fears to: Alois.

Occasionally they met in the deep, snow-covered forest on Sunday afternoons. Then she did not hold back to share her thoughts and fears with Alois. He seemed to share her concerns but still always managed to calm her. She no longer considered the possibility of sin in connection with him. How could it be? He was her support and she loved to meet him. As a matter of fact, what she felt for him must be the love her female friends always whisper about. Alois held her tight in his arms, keeping her warm and kissed her lips repeatedly despite the freezing temperatures. It felt right, not wrong – how could this be a sin? She did not even mention this issue to the priest during confession. Still, one does not meet a man in secret. Often they left the forest using different trails home, which reduced the problem to be seen together.

One day in April 1941, after Sunday mass, Rosa's godmother Helene walked into their warm Stube. She was dressed completely in black. Rosa's heart did an involuntary jump.

"Oh Mother of God!" Mother and Liz exclaimed together.

Helene could not answer in her effort to stop her tears from flowing down her cheeks.

"Is it your father?"

"No, my brother," she whispered.

For a moment there was stunned silence. This time it had hit home.

"No, I don't believe it!" Mother retorted. This was her nephew, the cheerful one, twenty-two years old.

"Oh Mother of God!"

Rosa had turned white in her face with her eyes being huge from terror.

"Where are Kon and Anselm?" She shouted her question as if she held her family responsible for not knowing. But shock had set in and had everybody in a firm grip. Nobody answered her. Rosa started crying and ran to her refuge behind the barn. *It is Sunday. After lunch I will meet Alois*, she tried to comfort herself.

Rosa's agony found some temporary relief a few weeks later. The first Feldpost from Kon arrived. It came from France again. He reassured them that he was relatively safe as he had to take care of the military horses. The comrades he had lost had been "further to the front".

Almost within days of receiving Kon's letter Anselm's Feldpost arrived from the Balkans.

"Shit!" Jakob said. Anselm had been transferred to the unit in those mountains early April. He wrote that it was a bad assignment, for it was a partisan war. That was the worst, he wrote, for you had to be ready to be shot at from any direction any time.

"He should not write that!" Jakob fretted fearfully and looked at his mother.

Rosa did not care. She only heard that they both were alive and unhurt.

***

It was the first Sunday in March 1941, during Sunday mass, when Rosa noticed that Renate was not at her usual place. In those days people's senses had been sharpened to a state of vigilance and alarm as there have been such absences, at least of men, before. And Rosa knew what that had meant. She was alarmed and gave Lisa a nudge.

"Renate is not here today." Lisa scanned the pews in front of her and even turned her head to look back. This was usually frowned upon by the congregation and the priest. She did not care. These were different times.

"Has she left for her year of Social Service? She must have gone," she whispered to Rosa with an expression of surprise and disbelief written on her face. Rosa's eyes widened for the same reason.

"You mean she has left without saying goodbye? Why would she do that?"

"I would do the same," Lisa whispered back. "Nothing to celebrate."

"Why not? She is not at the front. She gets to see another place and it is not so dangerous there."

"Be quiet now," Lisa hissed.

Rosa could not pay attention to the priest celebrating mass at all. She went through the motions, but her mind was on the issue of the Social Service year. Renate was eighteen years old. *Do I have to go when I am eighteen next January?*

At that moment Rosa knew that her call would be coming sometime next year. Realizing that certainty, the blood seemed to flow down to her knees. A slight dizziness engulfed her. Her stomach felt sick and she hoped she would not have to leave church before mass was over.

Where might they send me? But an even more frightening thought surfaced: *they don't know about my sinful birth and that I don't have a father! They will all ask!* Rosa felt terror rising. It was clear that she had to be exempt from Social Service. She was needed at home. And maybe they don't want any woman with only a mother and no father. She was going to ask Jakob to fight for her with those arguments.

He had spoken up for her in a protective way before. Rosa calmed down, but she could hardly wait to get out of church to speak to her uncle.

Of course, her small family was one source of comfort and anxiety control for Rosa. Actually, and strangely so, she now felt more secure about herself – like she had been liberated. She knew she was part of the reason that the farm worked smoothly. A wonderfully soothing feeling had settled inside her as she felt needed and confident in her agrarian knowledge. The subtle underlying feeling, once a constant in her life, that she should not have been born, seemed to have disappeared. She felt important. The circumstance of her birth did not concern her too much anymore. Except, of course, if she should have to go to a new place where she was unknown.

She also had Alois to fill her need for comfort. Each Sunday afternoon they would meet somewhere out in the field, the forest or the meadow. There were benches in hidden places they could sit and be together. They were careful to keep those dates a secret from everybody. They left their homes separately and returned one at a time. Sometimes Alois had to take quite a detour to come back into the village from a different direction than Rosa did. Rainy Sundays were a problem for them as they needed to find a dry place for an hour or two. Rosa sometimes could not meet for lack of a good reason that would make her mother understand her desire to go for a walk. It was a real challenge when it was cold, windy and raining. But most times they found a way to meet, and then Rosa would fly into Alois' arms everytime. She loved it when he held her tight to him for a long time.

At first he always kissed her in a hesitant, probing way. And Rosa loved that touch of his lips and the feeling of weakness that overcame her every time. But lately his kisses usually changed quickly, became more intense, more probing and demanding. It excited and scared Rosa to feel his tongue, yet she could not withdraw. That happened, however, when he held her so close that her breasts were crushed against his chest and when she felt his thighs perfectly aligned with hers. Then she jumped back without thinking.

"Rosa," Alois whispered then. She did not understand what he meant by that but did not ask. They were both catching their breaths, smoothing out their clothes and finally walked on. Next Sunday afternoon they would meet again.

Wrapped up in her own struggle for emotional well-being Rosa did not notice that Alois was not as confident, strong, and fearless as he appeared to be. He loved Rosa and would calm her at any cost, but he was worried about his older brother in the battlefield and about his friends Bert and Thomas. He figured that one day he would get the same letter calling him into the army that had taken them away. He tried to deny to himself his growing terror. What about Rosa then? He avoided the subject with her entirely.

Rosa and Alois continued their Sunday afternoon meetings under the cover of nature in the fields. But they had to be more careful with selecting their meeting places and the times they met. Already Liz had asked her where she spent those couple of hours every Sunday afternoon. Rosa's heart picked up a beat.

"Sometimes I go to Resi and Berta, sometimes I go to Mal," she answered, being uncomfortably aware that she was lying. That was a sin. To undo that sin and to hide her real aim from her mother she now had to visit Alois' sisters, whereas he had already left before to go to their place. Unfortunately, that reduced the time for her with Alois. But what else could they do? It had become complicated.

Soon the times they had available for their dates were also narrowed down by the circumstances of those early war years. Berta, Alois' older sister, was called up for Social Service, which would start just after harvest time. Since she had worked in the stables with the cows and in the field, Alois had to take over her part. Sometimes he looked tired, or came late to church. This was before Rosa started to worry about her grandmother.

"Mother is not feeling well. She's not cooking a lot anymore. Liz has to do that. And I need to help with the household chores as well," she complained to Alois. He knew that this meant that his darling Rosa had to put in still more hours in the field and dairy work. Of course, Jakob helped, but he had to tend to the blacksmith workshop as well. Everybody worked hard, long days.

On hot summer days bringing in the harvest, particularly the loading of the wagons, was exhausting work. Often times thunderstorms were on the horizon, and these pushed the people to hassle even more. Luckily it was custom for the people after such a day to go down into the valley and dive into the cooling waters of the river. Rosa went with her peers with great anticipation. Alois would be there legitimately. They did not have to make a date or lie to anyone.

There were great splashing and shouting and ball games in the water. Rosa let Alois touch her underwater, lift her up and teach her swimming by floating her on his hands. Mal and her boyfriend, Josef, did the same. It was not a sin; it was all right. More than that, it felt wonderful. It made her close her eyes and just feel the light pressure of his hands. And his eyes – they always had a strange glistening in them that made Rosa look away only to return her gaze again. She had this strange feeling of wanting to hold him, to feel his whole body on hers. But she did not dare; that surely must be sinful like the sixth commandment suggested. Although she had never been quite clear what that commandment actually meant for her. Neither the priest nor Liz had been explaining it well. It was almost a taboo subject.

So the summer turned into fall. The usual, customary celebrations were approaching. Jakob had his ear on the radio once a day and reported what he heard. The German troops were deep in Russia now, in apparently a victorious way. But he did not like the tune for he saw too many black-dressed women in church. When he went to the pub on Sunday afternoon he heard of fallen husbands and fathers from the neighboring villages. Somehow the radio was wrong, he felt. The mood amongst the farmers was no longer ready for rambunctious card playing and drinking beer; no, it was somber. But life went on in a pretend fashion. Everybody had one farmhand missing by now and for those left it meant to put the nose to the grindstone and plow on.

That notion in Rosa's family was particularly backbreaking as Grandmother's health had worsened. She had developed strange pus-filled bumps on her chest and breasts. As much as she tried to cook the meals for the family, she could not hide her spells of weakness. Liz would then have to take over for her. Rosa had to finish the chores outdoors and the tending of the cows alone. Often her arms ached from milking ten cows and putting the little calves to their mothers to drink. But she did not complain. In fact, she still welcomed the opportunity to display her strength and reliability. That sometimes got her praise from Liz and her Jakob. However, Rosa watched with silent trepidation the decline of her grandmother's health. She was worried about Grandmother. Every time Rosa walked by her she squeezed her grandmother's pale hands.

***

There was no Katrein's Dance that fall. Not that this would have been decided in an official grand style. No, there was nobody who organized it; there was nobody who found it appropriate, nobody who had a whole lot of fun with it. Rosa and her peers decided to meet anyway at Lisa's home where they once went for dancing lessons. But even there the right mood did not come up. Oh, they were joking around, laughing and even dancing a little. But the absence of Bert, Thomas, Renate and a few more was keenly felt. There was a social hole in their community. It was not right that Bert, Thomas, Renate and the others would be in harm's way, and here at home they had a good time.

Even Alois, the cheerful, positive guy, seemed to have lost his humor. He looked pale. Sometimes he fiercely squeezed Rosa's hand under the table. It actually hurt her. She was puzzled and concerned about him. Was he sick perhaps? But once when she asked him on the way back home he pulled her very close and said that he was fine. Rosa let herself be soothed, but still was not entirely convinced by his answer.

It was difficult to come up with Christmas presents in those days. But for Alois, Rosa had already been working on it while she was watching the cows in the meadow the whole of October and part of November. She had knitted a pair of gloves for him using double thread yarn because he always seemed to freeze his fingers working out in the snow. With a different color she had worked a snow star on the top side of each glove. They were going to keep his hands warm and they looked good. She could not wait to see his face when he saw them.

On Christmas Eve they met out in the snow-covered forest. It had to be a short date because each family had a lot of things to do before Christmas. Alois pulled Rosa under a pine tree with deeply overhanging snow-laden branches. He kissed her fiercely. He never let go of her. He put a small flat package into Rosa's pocket.

"What is it?" Rosa asked curiously. "Can I open it now?"

"No, do it at home," Alois' eyes were begging her. "It is just our class picture from our last year in school," he explained. "But I wrote something on the back, and I want you to read that undisturbed. Please, Rosa."

Again, Rosa was puzzled and concerned. He was acting strange. But she was also eager to hand him her gloves.

"Look at it," she encouraged him.

Alois stared at the beautiful gloves, and then felt them gently. Suddenly he pulled Rosa back into his arms, held her fiercely, kissed her and mumbled between kisses:

"Rosa, oh Rosa, my girl, my Rosa." She felt her cheek getting wet, not from his kisses but from his tears. He loved her, Rosa knew. Her gift had shown him what she felt for him as well. This time, they both walked home together, Alois keeping his arm around her. It did not matter anymore whether anybody saw them or not.

When New Year's Eve came around Rosa waited for Alois to contact her. Somewhere she and her friends and classmates were going to have a little celebration. When she did not hear from him, Rosa went to his house pretending to visit his sister Resi.

"Where is Alois?" she asked casually after a while.

"Alois?" Resi called out astounded. "Did nobody tell you?"

"Tell me what?" Rosa asked, clearly alarmed.

"He has been called into the army. He left yesterday morning for Berlin."

Her face had turned white like a sheet. Her heart was racing like crazy and she had difficulties to swallow. Not a further word came across her lips. Slowly the tears started to fill her eyes and began to roll down her cheeks. When she became aware of her tears she jumped up and bolted for the door. Without stopping she ran home and immediately went behind her barn and sat on a log, ignoring the snow on it. Then she remembered his gift. She ran inside to her bed for she had hidden it in her bedside table. With trembling hands she opened it and read his message on the back of the picture again. It had double significance and meaning now: *I love you, Rosa. Wait for me!*

Nobody seemed to be in the mood to celebrate anything. Rosa did not care. She was devastated. Alois left without saying goodbye to her. Why did he do that? But instinctively she knew that he was avoiding the pain of separation for an unknown time. And, truth be told, Rosa was a little relieved. It would have been terrible to separate from him. But she was worried because she could not tell him that she loved him too.

The next few days she developed a much bigger fear. *Will he be safe?* All those thoughts went around in her mind like a windmill that could not be stopped. It had become difficult for her to fall asleep at night. She could not calm down night or day, it seemed. Often she felt sick after eating or she did not have any appetite in the first place. On Sundays she went to Alois' farm to visit Resi. It felt a bit better there, as if he was closer. Her hopes to learn about his whereabouts were always disappointing, however, Sunday after Sunday. All Resi knew was that he had to report to Berlin and then probably was sent to Russia.

One day after lunch when the dishes had been done and Liz asked her daughter to come to the barn to help cut straw and hay, Grandmother called Rosa back.

"Go ahead to the barn, Liz," Grandmother told her. "I want to have Rosa with me a little. She will be along shortly." Liz nodded knowingly to her mother and left.

"Come," Grandmother said, taking Rosa's hand and pulling her down to the sofa.

"It's because of Alois, isn't it?" she approached the subject directly. Rosa blushed but nodded her head. Tears were collecting in her eyes.

"I know," Grandmother said gently. "We all need to be strong now, Rosa. We have a farm to run and we cannot do anything about the war."

"Mother, what is going to happen to him? And Uncle Kon and Uncle Anselm, and Bert and Thomas and..."

"No, no, Rosa, stop that. I fret about them as well. But you have to keep it down. We need to focus on our work and that helps to get the worries out of your mind. Anselm wrote in his last Feldpost that it is very cold in Russia and they need warm clothes. They need gloves and socks knitted with double thread. Do you want to help me with that and then we can send them to them? And you can make some for Alois as well."

Grandmother looked questioningly at her grandchild and saw how Rosa's eyes looked up with a sparkle in them. That would be at least something she could do. Yes, this felt better.

"But what if they get hurt, Mother?" Rosa asked.

"Well, then they are taken to the field hospital or they are sent home," she answered.

"Home, really?" Rosa almost shouted. *Well, maybe them getting hurt, well not too badly, would be a good thing*, she thought. But she already had heard of so many deaths in this and the other villages surrounding them. Jakob always brought home that news from the pub. Fear always washed across Rosa instantly.

"Will they come back? Do you think Alois will come back?" Rosa's eyes were pleading for the reassurance the wanted.

"I can't say, Rosa," Grandmother answered. "Maybe we just need to pray for them. And we need to be strong. And don't complain to anybody about this, Rosa," she added.

"Why not?" Rosa was thinking talking to Alois' sister every Sunday.

"Because they don't like it. Say only good things or nothing. That way you don't get into trouble. Now, go help Liz."

While still a bit puzzled Rosa left for the barn. Well, she will not complain then, she could do that. She could talk to Mother – that will have to do. But she was just so exhausted all the time; even talking made her tired.

Moreover, Grandmother's health deteriorated. She did not get up in the morning anymore and needed a lot of care. It was around the time to cut the grass for making hay, so they desperately needed another hand on the farm. Jakob suggested asking Thekla to come for help. Rosa liked the idea a lot. She had not seen her beloved aunt and her baby cousin Hans in probably two years.

***

By mid June Thekla and her now five-year-old son had arrived. Rosa got a tight hug from her aunt, which made her feel that she was still liked as before. But little Hans looked different than the picture Rosa had in her memory. He was taller and a bit shy around her. He was not what she remembered, especially not the timid boy hiding behind his mother. Rosa hesitated to approach him. What if he turned away from her entirely? But her aunt broke the spell.

"Come on you two, don't be so shy. Give Rosa a hug, son." After that Rosa took her cousin's hand and took him outside with her to show him the ducks on the pond. It was the beginning of an affectionate relationship that lasted for a lifetime. Rosa was aware that this cousin, a close relative of hers, had a proper father who also liked her.

Thekla took over the cooking for the family and the nursing of her mother. Her husband finally had found a job again. Unfortunately it was in Dresden. He could not come home often at all. Still, life had become a little easier for them. Rosa took Hans almost everywhere she went. And the little boy liked it; he liked to be out in the sun or the rain, in the meadows and in the forest. He was a happy kid.

The only sorrow they all shared was Kon and Anselm's absence, and the lack of information about their conditions and the worsening health of Grandmother. She hardly ate anything anymore and she seemed to be in constant pain. The pills the doctor had left to suppress it made her very sleepy on top of that. It was difficult to awaken her for a sip or two to drink or to ask her what she might need.

But support came from an unexpected corner. June was about to give way to July. Rosa, Liz and Jakob knew that the three of them would have to bring in the rye, the wheat, the barley and the oats. It would be hard work again. Then one day Jakob saw a soldier walking towards him as he stood just outside the door to the blacksmith workshop.

"What? Anselm?"

"Yep," Anselm said with a slight grin, realizing that his brother was very surprised to see him.

"Did you not get my Feldpost?" Anselm asked him.

"No, we did not!"

"Oh, well, I wrote that when I had been given home leave. Let's go inside."

"Wait, Anselm," Jakob stopped him. "I have to tell you something. Mother is very ill. She may not recognize you," he tried to prepare his brother quickly.

Anselm's already unsmiling face dropped further. He stood stock still without another sound or question coming from him. Then he turned slowly and walked into the house. He was greeted in an intense way, despite the surprise. The family was still inside as they had just finished cleaning up after lunch. Hans ran to his mother. Rosa felt like yelling in happiness to see one of her uncles, but was also full of sadness like everybody in the family. She came with him when he went to his mother's bed.

"Mother, it is me, Anselm," he called quietly with a choking voice. He had seen immediately that she was close to her last hour. Too often had he looked death in the eye out there in Russia. His mother slowly turned her head.

"Mother, do you recognize me?" he asked.

"Yes, I recognize you son," his mother answered slowly in a barely audible voice. Then she closed her eyes and never opened them again.

Rosa remembered the two days before the funeral almost fondly. Like the rest of the family she was in a state of grief, which stayed all day from their waking up to falling asleep. Grandmother's coffin was put up in the entrance area, which was a cool part of the house. By way of day-to-day life everybody had to pass by there often. Rosa, although she was uncomfortable about it, stood there repeatedly looking at her grandmother and holding a mental dialogue with her. She was the woman she had called Mother! She had always been attentive to her. She even had been her ally when Liz would be too strict. *She loved me*, Rosa would think over and over again, like a refrain. When the funeral day came Rosa felt acutely what she had lost with her grandmother's death. She did not have any grandparents any more.

The tears of pain trickled down her face almost all day. Yet she felt content, for she had told her grandmother in the coffin that she had loved her too, and that she would be a good girl. She had to, because Grandmother and also Grandfather had loved her and that was all that mattered.

After the funeral there was not much quiet time to dwell on the void that Grandmother's passing away had left. The grass of three meadows needed to be cut and the hay to be brought in. The barley was ripening and soon needed to be harvested. Thekla and little Hans had left for the city by the Danube again, which had now been their home for a number of years. So the family was short on manpower. Two weeks later Anselm had to go back to his unit at the Russian front again and Rosa, Liz and Jakob were the only ones left to get all the work done. In the end, the people left in the village would help each other, successively completing the harvest work for each farmer. It was great solidarity. Not only did work make them stick together, but each family had a loved one, sometimes more than one, about whom they worried or for whom they mourned.

Jakob seemed to listen to his little radio more and more often. At times he brought his ear to it very closely as he had the volume turned down low. Usually he did not speak about the news he heard. At most they could see him shake his head, or hear him mumble to himself, "Are they crazy?" That comment, however, alerted Rosa.

"What, what is it?" But Jakob did not answer other than to implore Rosa to never talk about it to anyone. This left her with a lot of anxiety about Alois and her two uncles.

The family's routine and fragile peace of sorts experienced an additional blow. In late August 1942 a letter arrived from the Kreisamt. It was addressed to Rosa, but Jakob had already opened and read it. The next day at lunch time, when the three of them were together, he told Rosa and Liz the news.

Rosa had been called up for Social Service, beginning on the first day of October.

She was to report to a small city by the Isar river, a two-hour train ride north-east. There the young girls were sent to the surrounding farmers to help with whatever work needed to be done. Priority would be given to those dairy farmers who had the fewest farmhands available.

Both Rosa and Liz had turned white like a sheet.

***

"They can't pull her off here," Jakob complained during lunch. "How are we supposed to run our farm with me being in the workshop alone already?"

Liz, however, fretted not only about that fact but Rosa having to go out into a world that she had experienced as deceitful and false. So far she had been able to keep her daughter under her watchful eyes. But now she could not think of a way to reverse that calling, lest she be branded as someone resistant to the cause and the leadership. That attitude, she had been told, could land her in prison. So she kept quiet on the surface. When she was alone with her daughter she implored her to stay away from any man, to be vigilant with them and not to trust them. She also impressed upon Rosa to do her work well and not to ask too many questions or, God forbid, disagree with the bosses. She was just supposed to keep her mouth shut and do her job.

Rosa felt a bit puzzled at the vehemence with which her mother talked. The blue of her eyes seemed to be more vivid. But her mother's worries were the least of hers. In fact, Rosa was quite frightened to go so far away from her home, to so unfamiliar a place, and hopefully the other girls would be nice to her, like her and take her in. And if they ask her about her home, her parents, or… would they want to know about her father? In that case she would just tell them that he was on the front in Russia. That was easy and very plausible, no problem now.

Still, at night Rosa took an unusually long time to fall asleep. Fear had a firm grip on her. How was it going to be there in that camp? She could not escape into Alois' arms out in the forest. He would have calmed her down. She missed him terribly. And worst of all, how was she going to tell him where she was? Perhaps she could ask his sisters Berta and Resi to send him a message from her with the next Feldpost.

"We have not received any letter from him lately," Berta said to Rosa when Rosa came to ask for that favor.

"Nope, zip, we are not sure where he is now," Resi added. "We assume he is still in Russia with his unit close to the Volga River. But last time he wrote he said they had to march a little further north. He did not say where to, but probably he is not allowed to write that."

"You don't know where he is?" Rosa asked with huge eyes staring at both her friends. "But then I can't get a message to him," she wailed.

Berta looked at her questioningly.

"You don't get that upset about Georg. You don't even ask about him," she remarked significantly. Rosa blushed instantly. She had overdone it; she had let her feelings show.

"Well, just tell Alois that I won't be home for a year when he writes next time or when he comes home for the harvest next time," Rosa said, dashing out the door.

On 29 September 1942 Rosa was standing with her mother at the train station waiting for the train that would take her to Straubing, the place she was going to be at for one year, as far as she had been told. Not a word was exchanged between them. Rosa felt panic rising, alternating with eager anticipation to step out into the big world, something she always had wanted. This time mother had to let her go.

Liz's mind was filled with anxiety. She kept herself calm by recalling that Rosa would be coming home for Christmas, which was just three months away. And if they needed extra help Thekla had agreed to come. She did not live far away from Rosa's new place of work. Perhaps she could keep an eye on her in her stead.

When the train finally thundered in, blowing steam and a white cloud into the air, Rosa's panic skyrocketed. She turned to her mother, stretching her arms out for her and said:

"Mother!"

Liz hugged her daughter shyly and mumbled, "Don't worry, Rosa, you are strong. You can do it."

She had to push her daughter gently into the wagon. Rosa was four months shy of her twentieth birthday, when she left to do her duty that was required of her by her country.

The Young Have to Serve

The wagon Rosa entered had but a few travelers already seated in it. She chose a bench that was still unoccupied, yet she was not sure whether she could sit there or if it was reserved for someone important. Since there was nobody to ask, she finally grabbed her small suitcase and lifted it up into the overhead luggage net. In a small handbag, one of Liz's, she had enough money to buy a drink if necessary. But Liz had packed a sandwich and a small thermos bottle of tea. She had just had lunch and was not hungry at all. But in one or two hours she might want to have a snack. It would be best to eat and drink the tea just before she arrived as she did not know when, what, or even if she would have dinner that night.

The train stopped frequently along the route picking up more and more passengers. Eventually the train was full. Rosa felt squeezed in and got increasingly frightened. Across from her two young women her age had taken the last free seats. They both sat on the one seat. She wished they would not look at her so much. Rosa pretended to study the landscape flying by. But to no avail, one of the girls, the taller, blondish one, tapped her on her shoulder. Rosa's heart began to pound. *What does she want?* Shyly she looked at her. To her surprise she found herself looking into sparkling, kind eyes.

"We are both going to Straubing for Social Service. Are you also going there?" she asked while the other girl suddenly was sitting stock still, watching Rosa.

"Yes," was all Rosa could utter with a scratchy voice.

"So we are going to the same place. Do you also have to be at the barracks at five pm?"

"Yes."

"What's your name?"

Rosa froze. *How much is this girl going to ask?*

"Rosa."

"I am Frieda and this is Else," the blondish girl introduced herself and her companion. "We are going to be picked up, you know. So the three of us can get into one… With what vehicle are they going to get us?" she interrupted herself.

"Probably with a horse-drawn wagon," Rosa said with a still nervous voice, repeating what Jakob had suggested.

"Oh no, I have never been on such a thing. I am so afraid of animals," Frieda exclaimed.

Rosa stared at her. Where did this girl come from? She was not from a city, was she? Oh yes, she was a city girl from Westphalia, an industrial area in the so-called "coal pot". It was a densely populated area with several cities close together. It was a place one could love or hate.

Frieda was of a gregarious nature with a sanguine character. She loved and helped everybody and consequently was popular amongst her peers. This city girl and this country girl, Rosa, were destined to become close friends, at least from the latter's point of view. It was launched before they even arrived at the compound where their barracks home was going to be for the next year.

How can one be afraid of animals? Rosa thought, and she quickly realized her chance to get the first person to like her.

A woman in an all brown uniform awaited the new recruits at the train station. "I am going to be your group leader," she announced in a loud voice. Rosa stood still like Frieda and all the other girls trying to ignore the anxiety that threatened to rise. It was already seated in her stomach and felt like a stone. She quickly glanced into Frieda's face, which looked calm.

Two well-fed horses were hitched to a wagon that probably seated twenty people. On each side there was a bench as long as the wagon. Two steps in the back of it were supposed to help the girls to climb up. It still required big steps.

"Now, I want you to row up behind those steps two of you at a time. Leave your bags over there. Another wagon will bring them to the barracks."

A subdued commotion resulted from the turning feet on gravel and quiet mumbling between strangers who had met just minutes ago. Pairs formed quickly. Frieda, however, stood still motionless staring at the horses and the open wagon where she was supposed to ride on. Rosa touched her arm and said, "Come on, Frieda."

They looked at each other, one invitingly, the other with relief. Without a word Frieda reached for Rosa's hand and let herself be taken to climb up on that despicable vehicle. They both sat next to each other without letting go of their hands. Rosa felt Frieda's hand to be moist and she squeezed it reassuringly from time to time.

The horses were trudging along at a steady pace. Frieda's hand relaxed a bit. She even withdrew it from Rosa's just before they came to the gate and had to disembark. During the twenty-minute ride Rosa's heart had been pounding with anxiety. She scanned the faces of the other young women sitting across or even next to her. Some looked down as if they were checking the wagon floor; others took in the landscape with wide-open eyes. Some girls met Rosa's eyes straight on. She did not like those. A quick glance at Frieda next to her gave her a reassuring feeling. Frieda's only worry seemed to be the horses. By the time they all could disembark Rosa grew attached to her very new friend. It was the start of a mutually beneficial relationship.

After their arrival the woman in the brown uniform led her charges into the dining hall and told everybody to sit down where they happened to stand. Rosa and Frieda took seats next to each other, waiting for things to come. There was only a humming tone audible in the room but Rosa could feel the tension. Soon the woman in uniform clapped her hands and shouted to them to be quiet and listen.

"I will be your group leader for the duration of your service time. It is my duty to assign you to your work places, to watch over you and to write reports. All inquiries, all problems you might have, personal or at your assigned work place, you can and should bring to me. This is the first issue," she said looking intensely at the girls.

"Now listen carefully. I will assign each of you to one of the three barracks. That's where your bed and your closet for your belongings will be. I will call up your name and you will stand up and identify yourself. After that, do sit down again and wait for further instructions."

Rosa looked at Frieda, realizing that they may be in different living quarters. Her heart started to pound again. *Dear God, let us be in the same house*, she prayed silently.

Frieda's name was called up early, as the first letter of her last name appeared in the first half of the alphabet.

"Barrack 3" was all the group leader said. Frieda sat down, looking at Rosa. It did not have to be commented on. Now it was a matter of waiting until Rosa was called up. Despite her trepidation she tried to keep her anxiety down. Then, finally, it was over in a few seconds. Rosa rose from her chair as if she was going to receive a verdict.

"Barrack 3."

Rosa then dropped back into her chair.

"Now we have to get a bed next to each other," Frieda whispered between clenched teeth.

After a few more announcements everybody had been assigned their living quarters and the noise level in the room rose somewhat to a subdued humming.

"Silence," the group leader shouted. "Each of you will now go back outside into the yard and get your luggage. With it you walk to the barrack you have been assigned to. They are right next to each other as you can see. There are two entrance doors at either end with the number of the house above each door. Go in and select a bed for yourself. I expect this to happen without any hiccups, fights, or arguing. Then you put your belongings neatly into your assigned closet. At 1800 hours you will come back here to the dining hall for your first evening meal. That will be all for the moment. Good luck."

"Come on, quickly," Frieda said to Rosa, pulling her on her sleeve. Without questioning the urgency Rosa jumped up and followed her new friend. Out in the yard there was a lot of luggage spread out on the ground.

"Grab yours, Rosa, hurry. We want to be at our place first to select the best beds and next to each other." Understanding flickered in Rosa's eyes. This city girl knew how to deal with crowds. They arrived at Barrack 3 with Frieda panting heavily and Rosa watching her with interest.

Frieda did not stop to catch her breath, however. She pushed open the screeching door and stepped inside, followed by Rosa. They stood still now, after all.

"This is where we are supposed to sleep each night?" Rosa asked with panic in her voice.

She saw the bunk beds and feared immediately her privacy was threatened. In fact, the whole room with about 20 such beds in it seemed to be too crowded. It smelled from soap scent, clean and fresh. It was no wonder – even the floors had been scrubbed that one could eat off of it. At least it was a clean place all over, and this made Rosa feel somewhat more comfortable, despite the noise of footsteps from the girls coming after them into the barrack. The building was entirely constructed of wood. Only the foundation consisted of brick.

After a while of taking it all in, Frieda answered.

"I guess it will have to be. Do you want top or bottom?" she asked Rosa without looking at her. But Rosa's mind was spinning. *Neither, I don't want to be here. I want to go home*, she thought desperately. *In the bottom bed so many more people can see me. I want top for sure.*

"Top," Rosa answered.

"You do? I want bottom. Up there I am too close to the ceiling," Frieda said with a questioning tone.

Each of the two young women quickly threw a piece of luggage onto her future bed to mark it as hers. It was settled then. They stayed together for mutual comfort and reassurance. Perhaps it was a good start.

Shortly before meal time Rosa and Frieda left the barracks together with all the other girls, only to meet more out on the path to the dining barrack. At the door they were greeted by another woman in a green uniform. She told them to take a tray and walk by the food counters in an orderly fashion. The evening meal was placed on their trays by the kitchen helpers. They were allowed to sit as they pleased but not to leave when finished. The group leader would join shortly and give them further instructions for the next day. Only then could they leave.

At the table Frieda looked at her food with disgust. She could not eat this, she said. Rosa, however, had no such reservations. It was a typical evening meal for her.

"I like it," she said and ate her thick vegetable soup. The jam-filled pancake also was tasty to her. Sure, it did not have extra sugar on top. Still she would have liked another one. But it was out of the question that she would ask for a second helping.

"Eat it," Rosa commanded Frieda. "You won't get anything else." Frieda eventually followed Rosa's example, especially after another blonde girl sitting next to Rosa said in an accusing manner that no-one would be treated special in here.

Finally, the group leader came into the room and clapped her hands. Everybody went silent. She had the full attention of everybody.

"Listen to me," she demanded. "I hope you enjoyed your first meal with us. I wish you a good night's sleep. You are going to need the rest. When you hear a whistle tomorrow morning it will be six o'clock. We expect you to be here in this room for breakfast at six thirty, washed and dressed properly. After breakfast, at seven o'clock I will collect you and take you to Barrack 4 to get you fitted with your uniform and work clothes."

I will get a uniform? And what work clothes? What work am I going to do? Rosa thought, alarmed. But she liked the idea of being given that brown-colored uniform. *We will all look the same*, she considered. That was not bad at all. She would blend in.

"And now we are all going to stand up and sing one of our precious folk songs that you all know, or should know," the woman in the uniform added. Frieda sang, so Rosa thought, enthusiastically. She really seemed to enjoy it. Rosa, however, since she knew from the first grade, could not hold a tune, so she tried her best to keep her voice low.

Nonetheless, the first time since her arrival a good feeling came over her. Had she been asked about it, she could not have named it. She just felt calmer now than practically all day before, like being a part of it, being included, no questions asked. Was it not always said that people who sing one should stay with as bad people don't have any songs? That was exactly it! For Rosa it looked like it was going to be good company.

These emotions rose to an even higher level of intensity the next morning. Again the whole group of newcomers assembled for breakfast. It consisted of fresh bread, various jams and coffee. Frieda again pulled a face after smelling it.

"What coffee is this, Rosa?" she whispered. "Are you sure it is coffee? How come you drink this brew so readily?"

"It is the coffee we always have at home. What did you drink?"

"We drank coffee, c-o-f-f-e-e. What is this?"

"Be quiet, Frieda. Don't get yourself into trouble. This is ersatz coffee. It is made from chicory root. Drink it or you will have none," Rosa implored her friend, getting a bit worried about her attitude.

"Oh boy," Frieda said and took a sip. Rosa put her head over her plate and tried to hide her smile.

After breakfast was finished and the dishes cleared away the group leader clapped her hands, waiting for the humming to cease.

"Please walk in file, two and two, and follow me to Barrack 4 to get your uniforms."

The girls did as they were told, and followed the group leader to the barrack. When they got there they found other group leaders behind a counter, stocked with piles of folded uniforms and caps. Rosa and Frieda waited a while until they were handed a uniform and were directed to the big change room.

"You are not so tall. Try this one on," the young woman behind the counter said to Rosa, handing her folded clothes and a small cap. It took two more tries until the outfit matched Rosa's figure close enough. There was no mirror in the room where everybody had to change. But after an almost dust-raising, chaotic hour, most girls stood there in their brand new uniforms. A new chatter rose accompanying the appraisal the girls gave to each other. In this way Rosa received some compliments about her looks. As she was not used to such appraisal she blushed in embarrassment. But only Frieda had the comment that Rosa liked to hear: *it makes us look like somebody important. And we look all the same*, Rosa thought. She liked the effect of the brown uniform the most. Nobody was different and everybody was equal.

However, on the third day after her arrival, Rosa's relative comfort was severely disturbed by a sky-high anxiety level. After breakfast, each one of the new recruits was assigned her work place for the next year to come. Their group leader called up each woman by name and asked her to come to the front. There, in front of everybody, Rosa would have to stand and get her assignment sheet and her slip to obtain the appropriate clothing for the job. Rosa waited for her turn with a pounding heart and sweat in her palms. She did not like to be exposed like that. Finally she had to walk to the front, feeling dizzy as she approached her group leader. *Dear God, please let me work on a farm with animals*, Rosa prayed silently.

"You are assigned to the Thaler family farm. There your first responsibility is to tend to their three children. You also must assist with other chores if the mother of the children requires you to do so."

The group leader's piercing eyes looked into Rosa's face, which made Rosa feel tense and frightened. Only when Rosa walked out the door to collect her work clothes did she fully comprehend that she would indeed work on a farm, although not with animals. There was no time to converse with Frieda, who grew pale when she received her assignment to a dairy farm. But that night they would catch up on everything. They all were given boots to be laced up, which was just as well, as it was raining outside. For now they had to leave for their work places right away.

"We expect you to behave flawlessly at all times and execute your duties properly. Always remember that you are serving your country and the war effort. You are the pride of this country. Behave accordingly. Dinner will be at 1900 hours on weekdays from now on, as you are working until 1800 hours. We will assemble here then. Good luck."

***

Rosa remembered those words of her group leader as she was trudging through the rain to the Thaler farm. Her anxiety was unabated. She only ever had to watch and look after Hans. After all, she had been the baby in her own family. Would this mother show her with kindness what she had to do? Matter of fact, what if she did not like her? Rosa contemplated all possible things that could go wrong.

Gradually Rosa became terrified of her new job. When she finally stood facing a woman taller than herself but of quite a full figure, her future boss, she no longer felt any pride but was reduced to a shy, trembling girl.

"Here you are," the woman said. "Finally, I need you desperately. Go upstairs into the last room to your left. There you can change into dry clothes. And put on those house shoes when you are in the house on rainy and snowy days. We don't want any water puddles in here. Then you come down into the kitchen."

Rosa calmed down a little. The woman had not been unkind. Her eyes had a hint of sadness in them and her face seemed tired somehow. In no time Rosa was back in the kitchen.

"Sit there, Rosa," the woman said. She herself already sat at the table with a cup of chamomile tea in front of her and a toddler in her lap. One cup was waiting for Rosa at the place she was to sit down. Rosa was grateful for the warm liquid.

"I need you mostly to watch my kids, this one and the twins. They are just four months old and asleep right now. I will be working outdoors and in the cow stable mostly. We have only my elderly father and me to get the work done. I will cook our lunch, but you will then need to clear it away and tidy up the kitchen and the house. You have time for that when the kids sleep in the afternoon. If there is anything you don't know, ask me. And I do expect honesty from you at all times as I will be honest to you. Now I have a few more minutes, so tell me a little about yourself. Where do you come from?"

Rosa felt alarmed. She did not like to be questioned about her background at all, but she felt she had to answer. So she told her about her village and her family's dairy farm she had worked on until recently and loved it. She also described her uncle's blacksmith workshop. Rosa thought it would be enough to stop her from asking more questions.

"So what is your last name? Is it the same as the name of the farm?"

Rosa had been afraid of this all along. Even though she expected it she was still unprepared. She felt the blood rise into her face and a slight dizziness made her vision dance.

"Yes, it is. Our name is Mitter."

"Do you still have a man on your farm or is it all women now?"

"My uncle and my mother are there." At this point Rosa felt very tense but still was ready for the inevitable question.

"And has your father been drafted?"

"Yes, of course; he is fighting in Russia." It was out! She made it, and it didn't even feel like a lie because he probably was somewhere out there, like everybody else… and Alois.

When Rosa and Frieda met in their bedroom that evening they started talking at the same time. Each was full of the day's experiences and wanted to tell the other everything about them. Through the excited chatter it became apparent that they both felt they had hit it right. Frieda was to work in the kitchen, cook the meals and keep the place clean.

"This is great for me, Rosa," she stated. "I have learned some cooking from my parents and our cooks." *Oh, she is a rich girl*, Rosa concluded.

"Our cooks?" she asked back.

"Yes, my parents own two restaurants. I learned to cook in our kitchens, sort of," she added with a grin.

"You are going to have to learn Bavarian cooking, Frieda," Rosa cautioned her.

"Sure, I can do that," Frieda said almost cheerfully. "As long as I don't have to milk the cows, I can learn anything!"

"Come on now, we need to hurry to the dining hall," Rosa pulled Frieda out the door. They could hear the buzz already outside the dining hall. Everybody had stories to tell that night.

However, after the evening song the group leader advised everybody to retire, as tomorrow they all would have to rise early again and then be fit for a full day's worth of work.

"But nobody is to go to bed without drying and cleaning your shoes. Do not leave here tomorrow morning with the dirt from yesterday on your boots!"

"They will be dirty before we arrive tomorrow," Frieda whispered to Rosa. But Rosa just grabbed her sleeve and pulled her along. Like everybody else they stood outside in the yard and brushed and creamed their shoes and polished them with rags as best as the damp would allow.

Exhausted, they slumped down on their beds. It did not take long and everything was quiet. Rosa, however, thought about the past day's events. *This lie was not a sin*, she reassured herself again. *It was not even a lie*. Finally she fell asleep.

***

The first week of Social Service was done. It was Sunday, which allowed another hour of sleep. Rosa woke up shortly after five, like she was expected at home. Still sleepy she sat up in her bunk bed and looked around. It was so quiet! It took her only a few seconds to remember where she was and that it was Sunday, sleep-in time. She let herself drop back onto her feather-stuffed pillow. *They will wake me with their whistle*, she thought. *I will wear my uniform to church* was her last thought before slumber engulfed her again. A little while later, Rosa woke, remembering immediately that she had to get ready for church – wherever it was at the camp. While she was dressing, Frieda looked puzzled.

"What are you putting your uniform on for, Rosa?" Frieda asked her.

"Well, what else should I put on? We are not going to work. It is Sunday and after breakfast we are going to church."

"What? Church? I did not hear that being said! We are to wear our sports pants and have to go for exercises before breakfast. Don't you remember from yesterday?" Frieda looked with astonishment at her friend. Rosa stared back at her. Indeed, she had completely forgotten about that! She changed silently. Walking with Frieda to the center yard she asked:

"Are we going to church after breakfast then?"

"I don't know. We were not told. Do you want to go?"

"Want? You have to go. Are you not coming along?"

"Not really," Frieda admitted.

"But it is a sin not to go to mass on Sunday," Rosa explained.

"It is? I am Protestant-raised. Rosa, they don't care if we attend church or not," Frieda said in a low voice. "You are better off to stay here."

Rosa looked at her friend as if she was making no sense. But her comment and the tone of her voice had scared and warned Rosa to stick to the rules, even the unspoken ones. She did not want to be different, that much she knew for sure. This was to be her first Sunday without mass as long as she could think, minus the days she was sick. It felt utterly wrong and right at the same time. But the cheerful, easy-going, positive Frieda pulled Rosa along through the day.

There was not much time to think and sort out her conflict. She did have fun with the exercises, enjoyed breakfast, and went along to do what Frieda and the other girls thought up. After breakfast their rooms and their clothes for the coming week had to be tidied up, and their shoes to be shined. In the afternoon Rosa was part of a ball game that she enjoyed a lot. She was quick and strong and belonged to the winning team. It was very uplifting – belonging and winning! Finally, the twilight hour before dinner was still filled with a pleasant sunset. Rosa sat on one of the benches outside her barrack, leaning against the wooden wall. It was not particularly warm anymore as the cool fog started to come in. But the wall still warmed her back and she stretched her face into the last rays of red sunlight.

Somebody joined her. Rosa opened her eyes and she saw Frieda looking at her with a smile.

"I found you. Mind if I catch some rays as well?"

"No, glad you came," Rosa invited her.

There was comforting silence between them. But Frieda was a livewire personality and did not keep quiet for long.

"You joined that train where we met at that small train station out in the country side between Munich and here. Forgot the name of it. You live close to that station I assume?"

"Yeah," Rosa said neutrally and wearily.

"What did you do there, Rosa?" The inquiry made Rosa's heartbeat quicken. Quickly she decided to tell Frieda a little about her background. That much was fair.

"My family owns a farm close by," she started to explain. "We raise dairy livestock, grow four kinds of grains, and we grow what we need ourselves. We have a little patch of forest, too. And my uncle runs the blacksmith workshop."

"Oh boy," it escaped Frieda's mouth in a genuine way. She was a city girl after all. But she was in control of her wits anytime.

"That must be wonderful for you to live in such an idyllic environment," she added quickly. Rosa was an equally good match to Frieda.

She burst out laughing, "I know that would not be for you."

"So what do you do there?" Frieda asked on.

"I am learning to run a farm," Rosa was aware that she felt pride rather than bashful and embarrassed about her lack of an academic background.

"Well, I suppose it is the same effort as my having to learn how to run a restaurant business. Don't exactly like it, but I figure that I am going to get married anyway and that will be my rescue from the kitchen and the dining hall. My father actually said that to me."

Rosa flinched when she heard "father". She braced herself for the inevitable.

"What does your father say about your future?" Frieda asked curiously.

"Don't know, he did not say," Rosa answered, feeling the blushing spreading all over her face. Frieda looked at her silently for a few blinks.

Touching Rosa's arm, she asked gently, "What's the matter, Rosa? Did your father get killed in the war already?"

Rosa heard the compassion in Frieda's voice and something snapped in her. It was mixed with anger and defiance.

"I lied to you, Frieda. I don't know my father. I was born out of wedlock." Rosa looked at her friend apologetically. Again Frieda stared at Rosa, causing her to feel resigned to the end of a friendship. She then put her arm around the hunched-over Rosa.

"Don't worry, Rosa, I won't tell anybody and I don't care in the first place. This is not your fault." Rosa trusted her friend and cried tears of bitterness and relief simultaneously.

"Time to go for dinner," Frieda said. Rosa wiped her face with her sleeves and walked next to Frieda, feeling a strange triumph.

***

Over the weeks Rosa had settled into a routine that she quite liked. She did not mind getting up early. It was not even as early as on her farm. She got along well with Mrs Thaler, although she found the care and the constant watching of the three kids tiring. What Rosa liked the most were the evenings and the Sundays in the midst of all these girls her age. It was such a lively bunch, cheerful and playful. They played ball games together or sang the folklore songs everybody knew. They took walks together into the town and might even see a movie. On rainy Sundays there were card games and knitting, embroidering, or sewing. They compared their works and had advice for each other, or joked a lot about items that might have turned out not quite as intended. It was enjoyable company any which way one might look at it. And they all were not too nosy either. Of course, Rosa's friendship with Frieda was the crown on top of it all.

Life was good, despite the war still raging on. That latter subject was always present, for the group leader made sure of that. When there was good news about the fronts she would read to them from the local newspaper during dinner. The German troops were successful and on the winning side. Hearing this news made Rosa feel confident that Alois was fine and safe. She hoped and prayed that he would be home for Christmas. But she had kept those thoughts a secret so far. She did not even tell Frieda about Alois.

Because winter was knocking on the door the girls were allowed a home visit over an extended weekend. Of course, they could not go all at once. But they had three weeks within which that visit had to be completed. Frieda already had told Rosa that she was too far away from her home to go there and be back in time. Trains were unreliable those days. But Rosa could make it over an extended weekend; it was four days after all. Yet, she did not have the funds for a train ride.

However, an unexpected opportunity arose. One day in early November a letter was handed to Rosa on Sunday morning, the time for handing out mail by the group leader. Rosa had received a letter before from Liz, but this address was written in a different style. To her surprise the sender was Thekla. A warm feeling flooded over Rosa. *She has always liked me*, Rosa remembered. She tore open the brown envelope and read with increasing astonishment:

Dear Rosa!

Hope you are all settled in Straubing.

This should be the time when you girls get time off for a home visit. Instead of going home, how about you visit me and little Hans here?

We are closer to you than the farm. I have already spoken to your mother and got her permission. I am not feeling well these days and could really use your help with Hans for a few days so that I can rest. I have enclosed the money for the train ticket. Just send me a quick note when you will arrive. We will be at the station.

Your aunt Thekla

***

Rosa stood at the train station at Straubing and shivered. There was no telling whether she had pulled in her shoulders against the foggy early morning air because she was nervous about her trip to her aunt's, or if the temperature was indeed so low. She was wearing her uniform skirt and jacket. In addition, she wore the coat that the girls had been given just two weeks ago as part of their winter outfit. To be sure, she felt pride in wearing that winter uniform. It gave her a feeling of importance and definition. She was a Social Service girl and very much needed. Rosa was looking forward to present herself to Thekla this way. She must be impressed, not only because of her uniform, but also because she was brave enough to go on this sixty-minute train ride alone. If only Alois could see her! Rosa was quite sure Alois was allowed home for Christmas. The thought of seeing him and being wrapped in his arms was sending a tingling sensation down her back.

Thekla and little Hans waited for her arrival at their train station. With a pounding heart Rosa left the train. Very few passengers departed, so Thekla saw her at once and shouted her name. Rosa ran towards her, forgetting the dignity expected of her in uniform. She was warmly greeted. Hans acted a little shy. But Rosa just lifted him up and swung him around, which made him laugh.

"Where is Uncle Ferdinand?" Rosa asked her aunt upon entering her ground floor flat. Thekla briefly turned to her six-year-old son and answered:

"He is in hospital for a check-up. Nothing to worry about: just some pains and feeling weak. He will be back before you leave on Monday. But let's look at you," she said, turning Rosa into the light from the window. "You look fine and healthy. You like it at Social Service?"

With a hand and a soul-warming cup of tea, aunt and niece exchanged what had happened to them since they last saw each other. Hans sat on Rosa's lap and seemed content.

"It is great that you came, Rosa." Thekla said. "If you could play with Hans, take him outside and keep him busy I would be grateful.

That's all you need to do. I am feeling nauseated often these days and need to rest more." Rosa looked at her aunt with alarm in her eyes.

"Hansi, go play in the living room. Set up your train to show Rosa. She is joining you soon." Hans went off to do as requested, obviously liking the idea of presenting Rosa his toy train system.

After he had left, Thekla bent forward to Rosa and, with an almost whispering voice, she explained that she had just suffered a miscarriage. She had lost a lot of blood as there was no doctor available and therefore still tired easily. Rosa blushed at the unexpected news. Things like that were usually hushed up, but not with Thekla and Ferdinand. But Rosa understood that she was needed here to afford her aunt more rest.

On Sunday Rosa was greeted by Ferdinand when she came into the kitchen for breakfast. He seemed very happy to see her, thanked her for coming, and made her feel welcome. Rosa drew in her breath when she saw how pale he was. Yet, so he reassured her, he was going back to his assigned place at an ammunition depot about a three-hour train ride north. On Monday morning all three of them took her to the train station and stayed until the locomotive pulled out with a black smoke cloud over their heads. Rosa did not have a good feeling about her aunt and uncle as she waved until they vanished from her view.

***

In early December 1942 the first snow blanketed Lower Bavaria. It was then followed by frost. Rosa and her companions in Social Service had to wear heavy winter boots to get to their assigned families and farms. It seemed like a peaceful time. The first signs of Christmas appeared in the form of advent wreaths, candles in windows and visits from St. Nikolaus. A general atmosphere of subdued excitement hung in the air. The girls were looking forward to go home to their own families for Christmas.

However, when the group leader announced that everybody had to knit warm gloves or socks for the soldiers in Russia within the shortest time possible, it was a blow to all the good Christmas and home visit feelings. They whispered to each other knowing that there was something serious happening. Some of the girls could be heard crying at night in bed. They had already lost a family member or a friend in the raging battles of the war. Anxiety so carefully suppressed and ignored had surfaced again. The pride that was supposed to be felt about having sacrificed for the country had made room for the pain of loss.

Rosa watched in horror her peers who walked with red-rimmed eyes. *What about Uncle Kon and Uncle Anselm? What about Georg, Bert, Thomas, Josef, Hans, Ludwig? And Alois?!* She felt guilty of having thought about them so little since she had come here. Now she was told about the extreme cold in the steppes of Russia, about soldiers having gone mad in the constant darkness close to the Arctic Circle, about those who had limbs either frozen off or shot off. She could no longer fall asleep easily. During the day she watched whoever was whispering around her or rushed out of the room after receiving a letter from home.

Knitting was the only relief from the gloomy feeling that had settled over the inhabitants of the barracks and from her own anxiety. She did that furiously and in every spare minute she had. Forget about knitting artful scarves as Christmas presents. She had people to support who might otherwise freeze to death and never come home again.

On the day of departure for the Christmas holidays, the same wagon and horse was waiting for the girls outside in the courtyard that had brought them roughly four months earlier. Frieda and Rosa again sat next to each other. Only this time they hardly talked. They could take the same train until Rosa needed to get off at her station. They hugged each other tightly. Each was afraid of the situation they might find at home.

"Come back safely in January," they said to each other, and Rosa left the train.

Jakob was waiting for Rosa with a bicycle to load her bag onto. There was no more car or horse in the village as they all had to be turned in for the war effort. Slowly they both started to walk through the snow. In a little over an hour they walked the eight kilometers to their village.

Silently they trudged along. Jakob had said no more other than that he and Liz were healthy and were managing the farm alright. Sometimes their elderly neighbor would lend them a hand, as did Jakob in return when necessary. Rosa's heart thumped. Why did he not say anything about the others? Finally, she could not stand the heavy silence anymore.

"Are Kon and Anselm coming?" she burst out. Jakob took a while to answer. He spit into the snow.

"No."

"No?" Rosa shouted. "Why not?"

"Guess they did not get permission. Must be needed on the front." Rosa's eyes filled with tears of disappointment and worry.

"Where are they?" she asked.

"Both in Russia, the last we heard. Kon was still with the horses and Anselm somewhere in the steppes there."

"Is anybody coming home for Christmas that you know of?" Rosa asked neutrally, hoping to get the news she was craving more than anything. She did not want to ask directly about Alois.

"Can't you wait until we are home? We are almost there."

Why? What is wrong with asking now? Rosa thought, getting a bad feeling. *There is something he doesn't want to tell me.* Rosa's anxiety skyrocketed while raising her impatience and urgency.

"Come on!" she almost shouted at Jakob. "What is the matter with telling me now? You know something! Tell me!"

Realizing his niece's anxiety level, Jakob did not have the heart to keep her in suspense. He knew that the news would not be any less of a blow to her hearing it from her mother. He collected his courage, stopped walking and looked at her.

"I know better who is not coming," he told her. Rosa pulled in her breath audibly.

"Georg and Thomas are not coming home, not for Christmas and not later either."

Rosa stared at Jakob. The thoughts in her head were racing until they settled at the awful truth. But still she asked in hope:

"What do you mean with 'not later either'?"

"Their families each received a letter that they have been killed. Georg in Russia and Thomas in France."

"No, no, how can you be sure?"

Jakob cupped Rosa's face with his rough blacksmith hands and said, "Be strong, Rosa. There are more and there will be more. It is a horrible war!"

"Georg, Alois brother? And Thomas?" Finally she could accept the devastating news. She could not prevent her tears from running down her face. She sat down in the snow and kept on yelling, "No, not them!"

Then she shot up from her cold seat and yelled, "And Alois?"

"Don't know. When we are home, go to his house and find out. He is probably alright. But come on now. It is getting later and colder. We should be in our warm Stube in thirty minutes or so."

At the light of dusk Jakob and Rosa arrived on their farm. The Stube was cozily warm and Liz had hot soup on the wood burning stove.

"Thank God you made it before dark. Take your wet shoes off and put them on the rack so that they can slowly dry until tomorrow." Liz put her warm hands to her daughter's cold cheeks as a welcome.

"Bet that uniform is warm, Rosa?" she asked. She was not the kind of person to dish out compliments. Rosa did not answer but instead just mumbled confirmatively.

"What's the matter? Well, you must be tired. Sit down and eat, both of you, and you will feel better." Liz said, while looking questioningly at her brother. He nodded at her.

"Liz, is Alois going to come home for Christmas?" Rosa blurted out.

"Don't know, Rosa. Leave it alone today. Tomorrow you can go to ask his sister. She is back from Social Service."

Rosa almost trembled with anxious anticipation. The wait till the next afternoon seemed endless. She was also exhausted from the trip and the walk from the train station. She had her evening meal of soup, potatoes and homemade yoghurt together with a slice of freshly baked bread. Then she went into her unheated bedroom. It was actually Kon's bedroom, which her mother had prepared for her. A hot water bottle warmed her bed and she fell asleep quickly.

The next morning Rosa got up at five, awakened by her mother's voice. It was understood that she would help with the milking and feeding of the cows the same as before she had left. Every hand was needed in those days, but she welcomed the work. It kept her grief and anxiety in check for a while. Breakfast was taken together and consisted of chicory coffee and the wonderfully tasty bread her mother always baked. Each slice was topped with jam made from their own plums. There were also dried pears in sweet liquid which Rosa loved.

"We don't have butter at the moment," her mother explained apologetically. Rosa had not asked for it. She knew that most fat needed to be turned in and they could only keep a small portion for themselves. She did not mind as she knew that it would go to the soldiers. Perhaps Kon and Anselm would get some too.

"Rosa, can you bake Christmas cookies for us? I have a new recipe. It does not ask for any fat."

Rosa agreed, even though she did not enjoy any work that kept her in the kitchen. But she realized that she could use those cookies as small Christmas gifts. She had knitted socks and gloves for her mother, for Jakob, Kon and Anselm … and Alois. She had used double yarn to make them warm. And with a different color yarn she had knitted a Norwegian snow star pattern on all of them. Those warm things would have to be sent to the Russian Front. Some packages did arrive. Everybody knew that from the Feldpost letters that came through to some families.

The morning was very busy. But by the time the three of them sat down for lunch Rosa could hardly contain her nervous tension. As soon as it would be socially proper she went across the street to Alois' farm. Berta and her sister sat at the table in their Stube knitting.

"Rosa," they both exclaimed holding their knitting needles quiet. "You are back," Berta stated the obvious. Excited chatter followed between them, exchanging experiences they had made at Social Service. All the while Rosa did not forget for a second that the death of Georg had not been mentioned. But finally, the excitement of their reunion decreased and Berta started crying without prompting.

"Georg is dead," she howled. Rosa did not know how to answer. Instead she cried with the sisters.

"Where is Alois?" she finally asked with huge anxious eyes focusing on Berta.

"We don't know," Berta said.

"What?"

"We have not heard from him and we don't know where he is. The last Feldpost we got he said he was close to a place called Stalingrad. But that was so long ago. We don't know where he is now."

Rosa felt dizzy and her face had turned ashen.

"Is he coming home for Christmas?"

"Rosa, we don't know for Christ's sake!" Berta yelled with a cracking voice.

Berta's sharp desperate voice brought Rosa to her senses. Gradually she began to understand that Alois was missing.

"Oh my God, no, Berta, no, I am sure he will write soon." Her mind could not accept the terrible news. The winters in Russia were incredibly cold. She knew that, because her mother had asked her to help sew rabbit fur on top of the gloves she had knitted for Kon and Anselm.

Rosa jumped up and bolted for the door. She ran straight home and crossed her farmyard to find her log behind the barn. But it was winter, and her sanctuary was covered in snow. She went to bed instead and stayed there until Liz came and asked her to get up again. She needed help with the evening milking.

"Work is the best medicine," she said to her daughter in a consoling way. "And tomorrow you will go into the forest with Jakob and cut down a Christmas tree."

"Yes, of course, we need a Christmas tree," Rosa said desperately and without joy in her voice.

***

The Christmas holidays turned out quite different than Rosa had expected and hoped for.

She could sense the tension that Liz and Jakob tried to keep bottled up inside. But watching them both made her uptight as well. All day she felt her anxiety and the worry about all the loved ones that she knew to be in harm's way. Still they took part in all the customs of a rural Bavarian Christmas. After the evening meal on

Christmas Eve, Rosa took slices of salted bread to the cows, one slice for each. She was allowed to take over that tradition from her mother. But the pleasure that this activity had raised in her last year did not come up now.

There was no Christmas play at the local pub. Midnight mass was held by a different and much older priest, for their own priest was also called into the army and was somewhere with the troops out in foreign land. Even the candles seemed to flicker differently. When the congregation sang "Silent Night, Holy Night" the male voices heard were just a few. A number of women cried silently and did not join the chorus at all.

Rosa had to return to her Social Service unit immediately after the second Christmas holiday. She was in a confused state of mind. Being at home with Liz and Jakob, with the animals that she loved, her village, hearing the church bells ring, it all gave her a feeling of comfort and safety. But it had been most upsetting to hear about the death of a number of people whom she had known. And worse, they were buried far away in a foreign land. She missed a grave to visit. She felt grief for the families. Only Mal seemed to have escaped such a hardship for now. But worst of all was the terrible fear of Alois being missing. Especially at night she felt restless and imagined the worst.

***

Rosa had arrived back at the Social Service camp, but did not find Frieda at the place she usually was at this time. Not knowing the reason for this irregularity Rosa waited in her barrack for Frieda to arrive. When she finally showed up Rosa dashed to her friend.

"Are you alright? Is everybody alright at home?" she burst out. Frieda hugged her and answered, "My family is safe. But two of my classmates are dead and another two are missing. And you?"

"Two dead and … and … Frieda, Alois is missing!"

"Oh, my God," Frieda said, but not recalling who Alois was. Then she took charge.

"Let's get our stuff put away and make our beds. Dinner is in half an hour."

They walked to the dining hall together, meeting other girls on the way. Even before they entered they could hear the sounds of excited voices, laughter and little squeals of delight. Once they had reached their places at the dining table and looked around, they could see those who were in mourning as well. Their faces seemed mask-like and pale. Some sat silently on their chairs. Others had handkerchiefs in their hands. Having seen the mourning families in her church at home Rosa had developed an eye for those who had been touched by tragedy. *Tomorrow we will be at work. That will make us feel better*, Rosa thought. She was right.

Eventually youth demanded its need for cheerfulness. The girls went about their assigned work, played games, and worked on their crafts projects on Sundays. Rosa gradually enjoyed being in the midst of peers, the laughter and excitement as an almost constant background noise. She was even admired for her extraordinary knitting and sewing skills, which made her proud. One could almost say that she was happy, had it not been for the constant worry about her uncles and, of course, Alois.

For the next few months life seemed to go on in a rhythm of routine set by the jobs that had to be done. But under the smooth social surface Rosa felt uneasy. This feeling was also nourished by bits of news that were whispered between all. When some girls brought back the news that there had been bombs dropped "up north in the big cities", an additional fear settled over the young women. Once more Frieda helped to calm the level of worries by calling for snowball fight matches and other activities on Sundays. But her success was short-lived. The whispered news kept being brought back from those girls who worked with families who had radios.

Until one day in February, rumor had it that something terrible had happened. It said that the German army that was fighting in Stalingrad had surrendered to the Russian army. The German soldiers had been taken captive. Nobody knew where they were taken.

Rosa grew pale once she heard the news. Her green eyes flickered back and forth, and she began to feel sick in her stomach. In her head frightening images were playing like a movie. Where was Stalingrad? Was that not where Alois had been seen last? Did not

Berta say that? And Anselm, he was around there as well. *Oh my God, no. Where are they now?*

Rosa held on till bedtime. She tried to reason her terrible feelings away. *But they said that our soldiers don't ever surrender, or death – no, they did surrender, so they are alive.* However, her mental efforts did not work very well.

Once she was in her bunk bed a flood of tears opened up; fear overwhelmed her. Frieda heard her and climbed up Rosa's bed, trying to console her by putting her hand on her head, petting her helplessly.

"They will search for them and find them, Rosa. Have faith in our troops. They will come back. Please calm down." There was no answer from her friend but her crying had diminished. She waited until Rosa was asleep and then went back to her own bed. *Dear God, let me be right, and bring my brother back too*, Frieda prayed silently.

For the remaining months of Social Service Rosa executed her duties conscientiously. Mrs Thaler and the children had come to like her. It was tiresome work there, but Mrs Thaler gave her some extras for lunch, like a bit of butter on Rosa's bread. That was very nice of her, as Rosa knew that most of the fat and oil had to be given to the army. Mrs Thaler, however, did other things as well. She listened to news that came from forbidden radio stations. Thus, one time, when she saw Rosa cry during bathing the little one, she whispered to her, "Don't fret so much, Rosa. The war won't last much longer."

Rosa stared at her with frightened eyes, saying nothing. That rumor went through the barracks as well. But Frieda always hissed at her, "Don't listen. Stay away and keep your mouth shut."

With her friend's command, Rosa had no problem at all. She was used to keeping her thoughts and opinions to herself for a long time.

When the whispers of bombings of the cities in the north, the ports and the industrial pot of Westphalia kept circulating, Rosa was upset. But then, that was far away from Bavaria. In August she was going to be released from her Social Service duties and could go home. She would be fine there. What could be worth being bombed in rural Bavaria? But Frieda, she had to travel north to her home.

One day in the last week of August 1943 Rosa and Frieda stood in a long line of excitedly chattering girls to turn in their uniforms, suits, caps, shoes, winter coats and all. The evening before their group leader had organized a celebration in the courtyard. A huge fire was blazing in the night sky. The girls stood around it wearing their uniforms for the last time. Some had to recite patriotic poetry. The group leader thanked the young women for their services to the fatherland. For closure the national anthem was sung by all.

Rosa felt quite sad to leave this place. It was a place where she had been appreciated and treated like all others and where she had found genuine friendship. On the other hand she was internally trembling with anticipation to go home to her family and farm and close to Alois' farm. Perhaps when she returned they would have received a Feldpost from him. She was sure of that as so much time had passed since he went missing. He surely had turned up by now and informed his family. After all, Frieda also had not received a note from her family in Westphalia for a while now. She was very concerned what she might find there after her return. The news about the bombing raids just had never stopped. Actually it seemed to have increased and the bombings had spread further south.

For the last week the two friends had been together every minute they had to spare. It felt good to talk out their fears. They also exchanged addresses and promised to stay connected and, perhaps after the war, to visit each other. Side by side they went one more time onto that horse-drawn wagon to get to the train station. But this time they could not go on the same train, as they ran different routes and at different times now.

Rosa and Frieda hugged briefly but intensely, with tears running down their cheeks unhindered. Rosa did not like a public commotion but their hands separated only shortly before the doors of Rosa's train were slammed shut.

"Good luck, good luck!" they yelled at each other. The steam engine whistle blew off piercingly, and drowned out a third wish. Black smoke rose up into the sky and the train started moving. Rosa hung her arm out of the window and Frieda ran along until the train was too fast for her feet.

Rosa's year of Social Service, which had helped her to feel so much better and more confident in herself, was over. Sitting in a local train she cried tears of separation pain, despite her desire to go home for good. *They liked me*, she thought. *Hopefully Frieda will find her home and her family to be okay.*

Coming of Age

It was an uneventful homecoming, although a sigh of relief accompanied Rosa's return to her family. She could feel how Liz and Jakob relaxed. Part of the work was now returned to Rosa, the young and strong one. Rosa was acutely aware how much her presence was appreciated. The rest of her ambivalent feelings she kept to herself. The struggle of turning loose of her uncomplicated connections to her peers at Social Service and the pleasure of having completed her year of duty on the one hand, and the soothing comfort from her loved ones at home on the other, was a tough one for her to solve. Nevertheless she fought it internally and on her own. Quietly she picked up her chores and quietly she adjusted to her old life. Nothing had changed at home, or so it seemed on the surface.

But Rosa was not quite the same person who had left a year ago. With her peers in Straubing she had learned that her fatherless condition was not necessarily important. Moreover, she now had spent time out there in the world, away from the familiarity and relative safety of her home. She had done a good job of it too, both socially and in her work. Now Rosa understood even less why her mother would not let her leave home to acquire an occupation. Was that it then? Was she back home for good now? And would the circumstance of her birth rear its humiliating and painful head again? Rosa had no answers but felt plenty of confusion. However, she was intuitively aware that she had changed. She no longer would put her head down should anybody bring up her father issue.

The first Sunday afternoon after her homecoming she went to see Berta. Entering Alois' house, she immediately was aware of the subdued atmosphere. Resi, the youngest sister, was now serving her year of Social Service. The usually cheerful and talkative Berta looked sick, pale, and thinner than before.

"Are you sick?" Rosa asked.

"No, why?"

"Don't really know. You look pale."

"Well, wouldn't you?" Berta snapped. Rosa regretted having asked about her health as she knew already the cause of Berta's problems.

"I am sorry, Berta. I know," Rosa apologized.

"Georg is not being brought home for burial. We won't even have a grave to visit! And we still have no news about Alois. I prayed a lot, but some good it did." Berta's face was flushed now. Her oldest sister, the only other sibling at home now, entered the room. With one look at Berta she said:

"Calm down, Berta. And you, Rosa, don't upset her like that."

Rosa felt guilty and swallowed the questions she still had about Alois. They switched to talk about Berta's knitting work. Rosa genuinely admired her work and the difficult pattern she had selected.

"Where did you get the three different colors of yarn from?" Rosa asked, knowing that it was hard to get any yarn these days. Quietly, holding her head over her work, Berta said:

"I undid an old sweater of Georg's. He would not mind." Rosa gasped at the finality of that statement. It made Georg's death so damn real.

Soon Rosa left. She wanted to be alone with her grief and feelings of terror about Alois' fate. Was he still alive? Was he a prisoner in Russia? She had heard already that this could mean being sent to the lead mines in Siberia. Or was he safe further west? Why was nobody looking for him? Why did he not write? Rosa had to fight to keep those horrible thoughts from overwhelming her.

***

Over time Rosa realized that she had not come back to the life she had known before being called to serve her Social Service year. Sure, the work on the farm had not changed a lot. Actually, she enjoyed the closeness and caretaking of all the farm animals immediately again. No estrangement was there, but rather a peace of sorts settled within her troubled mind everyday when she fed, milked, or cleaned her four-legged charges. For that time with them the ever-present worries about her loved ones out there went away. And that was a most welcome, regenerating break. But those feelings returned to its baseline mood after she had cleaned up herself and turned to other jobs, went for a meal, or settled for the evening. Her fluctuating moods had become a constant in her life.

By now almost every family was mourning the death of one or more family members in foreign lands. Those who had somebody on the list of missing soldiers desperately hung on to a thread of hope. The signs of such suffering and mourning were ever present in day-to-day life. Rosa was very compassionate when watching the signs of hardship around her. Good thing she had her animals.

However, there was another source in her life that could lift her mood. When on Sundays Rosa met with Mal, Lisa, and Berta, they would talk a lot. Berta and Lisa had also completed their social year already and they loved to tell stories about it. That made for a lot of laughter amongst them. Youth demanded a tribute, regardless. But to Rosa it had a different sound to it, not like before. Sometimes she felt guilty for having been cheerful with her small, all-female group of peers.

But times were difficult and the young ladies needed new clothing as twenty year olds do. So out of necessity some Sundays the four women also met for sessions to create new dresses. Where would they get material from? They followed the principle of those less fortunate: from the old make the new. One of Rosa's strong points had always been a creative mind. She took the lead.

"Each of you, go home and see what you can find on older clothes. Ask your mothers what she will let you have from her dresses. We will cut them apart then and make something for us out of those materials."

There were no protests. Rosa was a natural seamstress. They knew that from their crafts lessons for girls way back when in school. In a sort of joint venture they pooled together what was available at home. Under Rosa's guidance they created an haute couture that was a delight. Vanity had found some satisfaction. Those hours of tailoring were fit to make one forget angst and sorrow. If one could not take those new outfits to dances or other occasions for admiration one simply wore them to church, or for the next Sunday afternoon get-together. Those hours of merciful forgetfulness were surely sent from heaven.

But each evening, when all the day-to-day chores were done, Rosa was brought back to reality by Jakob. He had a way to collect news and whisper it during supper. Rosa's anxiety skyrocketed each time he told about the terrible combats abroad that they could not see. The dead soldiers and the casualties from bombs dropped in the cities could no longer be counted. But the worst for her was the news that came out of an occasional Feldpost that somebody still received.

They told about soldiers dug into the earth with only the head protruding and others drove with farm equipment over them. She heard about hunger and typhoid, soldiers shot in the abdomen with their intestines dropping out, rape, the mysterious disappearance of people, children separated from their parents. It was sheer horror. Rosa developed nightmares. Where was Alois, her uncles, friends, school mates? *Good God, let this end!*

Rosa alternated between the natural cheerfulness of her youth and the efforts to absorb terrible reports from the raging war. But the ugly face of war was creeping closer to her farmland community, disturbing the relative protection that it had provided so far.

One cool, hazy afternoon in early November 1943, Rosa had just come back into the warmth of the Stube when a knock on the window made her jump. Liz stood up to see who was there. Rosa stood right behind her. A woman stood outside holding a small boy on her hand. She was dressed in a shabby-looking grey coat and a black head scarf. The boy, perhaps two-years-old, wore a little coat that did not look any better. At least he had warmer boots than his mother. His red woolen cap protested the dreary colors both wore. The woman looked tired. Her skin showed deep mimic lines and she appeared overly slim even in her winter coat. With wide, anxious looking eyes she stared at Liz. Her free hand held up an electric iron.

"This is a good iron," she said. "I would like to exchange it for one of your chickens."

Rosa felt puzzled. Why would anybody want to give away a good piece of household equipment? But Liz responded calmly.

"I don't have any young chickens. They had to be turned in. You must know that," she answered. Silence followed. The woman was still holding up her iron.

"Do you have something else then? Please," she pleaded with intensity. "I have another daughter and my mother to feed. My husband and my father are both dead."

"Oh, no," Rosa exclaimed. Liz turned around to look at her daughter.

"Liz, we could give them eggs instead," she implored her mother with harsh intensity. Liz raised her eyebrows in astonishment. "What is it to you?" she said to Rosa.

"They don't have a father!" Rosa began to shout. Liz understood instantly.

"Wait a moment," she said to the woman outside. "Come with me," she demanded from her daughter. Both went to the naturally cold pantry and wrapped a number of eggs into newspaper. The woman held out a small bag for the eggs.

"Keep the iron," Liz said to her.

"God bless you," the woman said and left.

Such visits from hungry and desperate city dwellers increased dramatically during the following months. Rosa was eager to trade tit for tat. However, Liz kept a watchful eye over the food items as well as the quantity that her daughter was handing through the window or the front door. Food had been rationed and Liz was concerned to feed her small family enough. She reminded Rosa not to forget the care packages that they sent to their own city dwellers Thekla and little Hans, especially since his father was somehow feeling weak so much of the time. Liz's reminder made Rosa anxious every time and she held back with the food she gave away. It was not the time to be sick. It frightened her.

And so they all struggled on into the next year and on through another harvest: calves being born, grain being brought to the mill with a wagon drawn by two oxen, fertilizing the fields by hand, harvesting all the potatoes and cabbages from the fields and more. The village inhabitants helped each other when called upon. Everybody needed help occasionally as all male, able farmhands were absent.

New relationships developed out of necessity and unexpectedly. One of those helpers who came to Rosa's farm when needed was Alois' youngest brother, Johann. Rosa had always regarded him as a kid since he was five years younger than Alois. Now Johann turned out to be a very strong teenager who could lift things or apply force if necessary. He had no problem lifting heavy sacks of grain onto the wagon for Rosa's mill trip. She, in turn, realized that this kid was no longer a kid, although he was not a full grown man yet. *Dear God, let him be spared from being drafted*, Rosa prayed often. For herself, though, Rosa was not nearly as concerned. But she was going to learn differently soon.

***

One day, in the height of summer 1944 the old, slightly bent-over mailman handed in a postcard from Thekla. It was addressed to her sister Liz.

Dear sister,

I hope this reaches you soon enough.

The time seems near where I have to go to hospital. Since Ferdinand is not feeling well at all he is not fit to take care of Hansi while I am giving birth. And afterwards I will have a newborn to take care of. I am asking you kindly to send Rosa to take Hansi for at most two weeks. That way we can keep him out of the mess here. Almost every day there is a bomb alarm now.

If Rosa takes the 8.30 train she should arrive here around noon. Ferdinand will be at the station to pick her up. She then can return with Hansi the next day.

Thanks for the last package. We ate the cucumbers in a few days.

Your sister Thekla

The three of them ate their supper of freshly boiled potatoes, homemade yoghurt and bread, and white radishes that Rosa just pulled out of their vegetable garden. They ate in silence until Liz dropped the news from the postcard.

"Thekla wants Rosa to fetch Hans immediately. The card was already taking a week to get here. It is urgent."

"Let her go, but she needs to come back at the latest the next day. Work is too much for just the two of us. I have work in the blacksmith workshop, too," Jakob said.

"But the trains don't run properly now. And what if they bomb something?" Rosa clearly was frightened.

"They don't here, Rosa. That's up north," Liz calmed her. "You have to get Hans. What should she do with him while she is in the hospital and Ferdinand is in and out of the clinic all the time? Don't you think it would be nice to have your little cousin here for a while?"

Rosa could see her mother's point, and yes, she liked Hans a lot.

"Ok. But I can only travel during the daytime hours," she said with finality.

The next day at noon Rosa arrived safely in Passau. She was startled how pale Ferdinand looked. Yet he greeted her with a broad smile and a tight hug.

"Hello, young lady," he said to her. *Young lady*, Rosa repeated in her mind. She liked the sound of that. Chatting away they walked to the family residence. There Rosa received another warm embrace from her aunt. Eight-year-old Hans flew right into Rosa's arms and nearly knocked her over. Rosa noticed the huge protruding belly that made her aunt walk slightly bent backwards. Nonetheless, she had managed to prepare a lunch that was pleasant and satisfied her hunger. In the afternoon both Hans' parents needed to rest while Rosa went outdoors with Hans. He knew the city quite well and took her through the old, narrow lanes to the Danube. He showed her how to throw flat stones into the water so that they bounced several times. They dipped their feet into the mighty river, and they watched the ships floating by.

"Come," Hans pulled on Rosa's arm to get her up. "Let's go to the inn river now. The water is faster there," he explained. "But we have to stay back from it," he cautioned. "Papa said that one can easily be taken away by the current of that river. And the water is so cold."

They spent a playful afternoon together. It made Rosa forget all about the war. As the sun began to set Hans got uneasy and wanted to go back home. Not knowing why, Rosa had similar feelings.

"Clean up, the both of you," Thekla exclaimed when she saw them. "We are having supper soon." And so it was. First they had some vegetable soup. It was followed by sourdough bread and white radishes that Rosa had brought with her. They would have eggs the next day for breakfast. *What a feast*, Rosa thought. She had not seen eggs in the grocery store for probably a week.

"After washing up we can perhaps have a cup of tea, Rosa. But then we should go to bed to catch some sleep in case the alarm goes off. Usually they come at ten pm. Put your clothes somewhere, and spread them out so that you can dress in the dark if we have a bomb alarm. You need to do it quickly. It is not far to the bomb shelter. Don't worry, we are safe there," Thekla tried to calm her niece.

But Rosa went pale. Her heart was racing and she felt herself breaking out in sweat. She had to share Hans' room. To her amazement he was already asleep when she came to settle down. At one point she dreamt of church bells ringing. But she jumped up when Hans yelled at her.

"Get up, Rosa, quick!" Instantly she realized that the church bells in her dream had been the sirens. Rosa flew into her clothes. Thekla was already waiting at the door.

"Where is Papa?" Hans asked in alarm.

"Quiet, darling, Papa wants to stay in bed. He is not as worried."

They joined the other people on the streets running to the shelter. Thekla could no longer run. Many passed them by, but they also got to the shelter before the gates were closed. They sat there in silence while listening to the noises of airplanes. Soon they heard a humming tone that got louder and louder. The earth was vibrating when the bombs dropped. Rosa and Hans were both in Thekla's arms, which were pressed against her body. Finally the noise stopped and everything went silent again. Then the sirens blared again and Rosa's hands trembled anew. Her eyes were wide open and looked questioningly at her aunt.

"No, no," Thekla calmed her. "This is the signal that it is over for tonight." The gates opened and they all streamed out onto the street, going home to claim some more sleep. Rosa took a while to calm down. Eventually she fell into a deep sleep. *Thank God we live on a farm and not in a city*, she thought.

Rosa enjoyed Hans' two-week stay on the farm. He followed her most of the day and at his age he already was some help with light chores. Since it was the height of summer and the days were long, they used the little spare time they had for fun activities. They both enjoyed evening bike rides on small dirt paths through meadows and forests. Often they saw rabbits, or deer grazing in the distance. Occasionally, after a hot day, they went to that pond behind the western forest. The water was pleasantly warm and yet refreshing. That was great fun because Rosa's female friends also came along.

And some of them, like Lisa, could actually swim. That was reassuring since neither Rosa nor Hans had been taught that sport.

But Rosa was also experiencing a storm of memories of the times she had come here with Alois. A burning, painful longing for him and his reassuring hands was raging in her mind. Her imagination let her see him in terrible situations in Russia so bad that she shook her head to stop her thoughts. *Dear God, where is he? What happened to him? How long is this still going on?* Tears ran down her face.

"Rosa, why are you crying?" Hans asked, noticing Rosa's distress one day.

"Silly! I am not crying. You are splashing around so much."

"Yes, come on, splash back," Hans yelled and hit the water with his flat hand.

The sun was already setting and the air had chilled a little when Lisa walked up to Rosa. Without a word she wiped the tears from her friend's face and said gently:

"Come on, Rosa. It's time to go."

***

At the end of those two weeks Hans had changed into a cheerful kid. One Sunday Rosa took her cousin back to his parents. She regretted that he had to go back home to a city that had scared her so much. This time she was determined to take the evening train back home. And so she did – after she was allowed to hold Hans' new baby sister.

Liz, Jakob and Rosa missed Hans more than they wanted to admit. With him gone the last cheerfulness seemed to have vanished. Gloom had re-entered their days. Nonetheless, life settled into a routine again, but some routine it was! Sure, each of them completed the work that was theirs to do. They discussed procedures and priorities for each day during their meals together. But they avoided touching on the most burning questions: Where were they, their loved ones and friends and neighbors? Nothing had changed in that respect. Rosa had heard many horrific stories of soldier's fates. Nightmares had become a common occurrence for her. But whenever she met her girlfriends and school mates on Sundays they could talk it out; and that helped a little for a while. Somehow they came to agree that it was best to avoid thinking thoughts along those horror lines. Mal was a firm believer in that. She seemed to be less troubled by it all. Rosa eventually also learned to suppress thoughts about the unthinkable. It worked for her to some extent.

With this tug of war in Rosa's head she struggled on in between calm and terror. A new fall came into the land and winter knocked on the door. All along Rosa had been hoping to receive a letter or a postcard from Frieda. Finally, she sent a card to her, but she had yet to receive an answer. Frieda's silence annoyed Rosa, as it felt like Frieda had not lived up to her promise. But when Rosa heard about the bombings of some cities in the north another awful suspicion entered her mind. Rosa was glad about the load of sometimes back-breaking work she shared with her mother as it did not allow for a lot of dwelling on all the worries. Work is the best medicine – it was said by everybody. But soon she was going to get more help in keeping her inner balance by distraction. It came from an unexpected corner of wartime life.

***

January 1945 turned out to be as cold as they come with temperatures below zero degrees. Every morning the bedroom windows had beautiful ice flowers on them as there was no heating for the upstairs rooms. It had always been this way, and nobody complained about it. Personal hygiene was done with almost cold water and with lightning speed. Those who needed it a bit warmer went downstairs to a pot of leftover warm water in the Stube. Liz habitually was the first person up. It was her job to make a fire in the wood burning stove and boil water for coffee made from roasted barley. Liz had some cream set aside for that heart- and soul-warming beverage. Rosa knew that only a very small amount of cream could be kept back for their use. Thus it was really a precious treat. Home-baked bread and homemade jam completed breakfast.

At the end of the last summer one farmer who always came to the blacksmith workshop had brought a small ball of wool from his sheep. Rosa had washed and dried it with pleasure. Now she had started to spin it into yarn. It would be of a natural color, of course, and somewhat scratchy on the skin, but it would keep the wearer warm. Thanks to her grandmother's instructions Rosa had mastered the craft of spinning wool to perfection. Her yarn was admired by her peers, as she could make a very evenly thick or thin thread. This was a skill that not many had.

It was on one of those bitterly cold afternoons when Rosa was working on her wheel spinning fine, even yarn and Liz was knitting next to her. It was silent between mother and daughter; each concentrated on her task. Nonetheless they both jumped when they heard a rather strong knock on the window. A woman's head was straining to see into the room. Her cheeks were almost bright red from the cold. Liz stood up and opened the window. She then saw that the lady was holding the hand of a little boy. She guessed him to be about four years old.

"Yes?" Liz inquired.

"Greetings," the woman said, holding up a piece of paper for Liz to read. "We have been bombed out and been assigned to your farm for accommodations for my son and me. May we come in?"

"You have what?" Liz asked.

"We are to live with you until we can get our own flat again. They said it won't be long. My husband is in uniform."

"I have never heard of something like that," Liz said more to herself than to the woman. She was puzzled and did not know what to do.

"Well, come in out of the cold for the moment," she said and went to open the front door.

The woman carried in one tattered suitcase. Liz held open the door to the Stube.

"Rosa, get them a cup of tea," she ordered her daughter and disappeared back out. Liz was looking for her brother in the blacksmith workshop. She quickly explained the situation to him.

"What should we do? She has papers. Do we have to take them in?"

"Yes, we definitely have to. Sepp told me the other day that one farmer in Niederberg also has such a family living with them. For the moment they can use Anselm's room. And the woman needs to do her share of work while she is here. That way she can earn her keep."

"Dear holy Mary," Liz said and went back into the Stube. She was not looking forward to the next day what with strangers in their home.

"I am Liz. What is your name?"

"Ina, and this is Denis," the lady said pointing at her son. With that the formalities were taken care of. The paper with the swastika on it eliminated the need for any other considerations. Only one more thing had to be clarified.

"Are you Catholic or Protestant?"

"Protestant," Ina answered. It sounded a bit aggressive.

Holy Mary, Liz thought.

In a couple of days it turned out that Ina and her shy boy were not as much a nuisance as the three inhabitants had feared. Ina assisted in the kitchen and her son stayed close to his mother all the time. He had not spoken at all yet. If asked he either nodded or shook his head as an answer. He appeared really frightened. Rosa made every effort to entertain little Denis and gradually he began to respond. It was not long until he took Rosa's hand and let her show him the little kittens and calves. By now Ina had taken over the cooking almost entirely. Liz was freed up to help her daughter with the farm work.

Contrary to expectation, things had worked out well amongst the natives and the strangers. In spite of all the more or less suppressed feelings of terror, the agony of not knowing about their loved ones, and the atmosphere of sadness in the village, Ina and Denis provided occasionally for a bit of laughter and cheerfulness. Nobody could have guessed then that Ina and Denis were going to stay for more than a year.

As the familiarity grew amongst this patchwork family Rosa found the courage to ask Ina where Denis' father was.

"We don't know, Rosa," Ina said softly. "Where is yours?"

Rosa's heart skipped a beat. For once, she had not anticipated this question. Possible answers raced through her brain. She could say he was dead and buried somewhere in Russia. Or perhaps he was missing in action. Or perhaps he could be in a field hospital, wounded. Perhaps it was most plausible that they had not heard from him?

"We don't know either," Rosa said firmly. This answer was the best. It was not a lie. Rosa had become skillful in navigating her responses to such an inquiry. She could afford to forget this incident quickly.

There was more need for adjustment skills coming Rosa's way. This time, however, Rosa jumped with joy, although the reason that provided the opportunity was rather terrible. In the second half of this bitter cold January Thekla with her five-month-old infant and nine-year-old Hans had come home to stay. Ferdinand had died. Thekla was devastated and Hans along with her. However, there was not a lot of time for mourning. An extra bed needed to be found for Hans. The occupancy of the available bedrooms needed to be sorted out and arranged immediately. Jakob put his bed out into the upstairs hallway to make room. Rosa, Thekla, the baby and Hans were all going to sleep in the biggest bedroom. Since this room was directly above the Stube it was also a bit warmer from below. Liz moved back into the northern bedroom where she had given birth to Rosa. All had found a place to sleep in relative comfort. It would have to do for now.

However, the next day the slight overtone of occasional cheerfulness had already given way to a gloomy mood, worse than it had been already. Thekla seemed to have lost her smile and her speech. Instead, tears kept rolling down her face again and again throughout each day. She kept her head down, or stood by the window staring into space. Her face was drained of all color and her son often stood with a worried expression next to her. Her voice sounded hoarse when she talked to her infant daughter or to him. Rosa also felt inexplicably sad. All her happy anticipation for her aunt and Hans' arrival had vanished. Not even the baby could change her mood.

She tried her best to get her cousin to come with her to feed the animals, which he always had liked. And in a couple of days she began to be marginally successful. Hans would come along and even help feed the cows. He seemed to enjoy the activity. But his laughter returned fully when he played with the recently acquired puppy dog, Lux. They all became best friends with Lux, who followed Hans around everywhere he went. Rosa observed that development with relief. Yet it did not significantly improve her own emotional disposition. Thekla in her black clothes and her sad facial expression was a daily reminder that death could be looming over her family's head any time.

Rosa had a hard time watching her aunt in her grief. She often started crying with her. But what was worse for her was little Hans crying in unison with his mother. Rosa could not find her inner equilibrium. Her heart went out to Hans and his mother in their enormous sadness about losing their husband and father respectively. *But then, I don't have a father and my mother did not have a husband. I wish they would stop crying.* Such were Rosa's conflicting thoughts. In despair and in a case of emotional overload she asked Liz:

"Is Aunt Thekla ever going to stop crying?"

"Rosa, watch your mouth! And besides, it has just happened."

But Thekla had overheard the exchange and she found the strength to confront her sister and Rosa.

"It is easy for you here in your warm nest. You have no idea what is happening out there! Do you want to hear?" She did not wait for an answer and continued to set the record straight.

"Just barely two weeks ago I lost Ferdinand, and Hans and Susi lost their father. I took Susi to a neighbor to take care of her while I went with my son on an almost six-hour train ride to put my husband into his grave. Did you know that the trains ran only at night because during the day they are shot at from planes? And did you know that this train was unheated and some windows were broken out. In January! And when we arrived there was no room available in the whole place to stay for two nights until the funeral. I had to ask the mayor for help. If he had not called that inn and ordered them to take us in, I don't know what we would have done.

"Did you know that Ferdinand's friend from Passau, Heinz, his friend from his university days, came to the funeral? I was not completely alone. God only knows how he managed to get there, what with the hundreds of maimed soldiers in the trains. Did you know he had brought his own medal from their fraternity when they were students and put it on his friend's coffin? Do you know how that felt to me?

"And then we had to come back in the same cold train again during the night. So we waited for hours in the train station, again, unheated that is, not knowing when that damned train would take off again. It is a wonder that we both did not get sick. And when we returned home there was no milk anywhere for the baby and no gas to warm it up should there be a drop. I came back here because I could not feed my kids in the city. What would you have done and how do you think you would have felt?"

Thekla's chest was heaving. She seemed spent. Liz was the first one to find her speech again.

"Well, calm down, Thekla. We took you in and you can stay as long as you must. Just calm down. You are not alone. This is our home, for all of us siblings."

Rosa's mouth had dropped open during Thekla's account of her horrendous experience. She had not known any of this. Now she could almost personally feel Thekla's and Hans' grief.

One day Rosa ran behind the barn, wiped the snow off the wooden planks and sat down on them. *Good grief, I hate this, she thought. When is everybody coming home? Where are they? Why don't they write? Alois, Alois, my Alois, where are you?* "I miss you so much, I need you," she howled. And finally Rosa could cry as if she could never stop. After a while she heard her mother call her name and she knew she was needed and had to go.

She stood up and brushed the snow off her back. And then another piercingly painful thought was revisiting her: *Hans and little Susi don't have a father anymore! Oh my God, what is this with us? Aunt Thekla was married and did not sin! But at least they had had a father, and were not out-of-wedlock kids. They were luckier than me!*

As the winter dragged on these eight people learned to live together in relative peace. Food had to be carefully rationed, which caused some friction. Often there was not enough hot water left for everybody's personal hygiene in the evenings. When the two boys played too noisily on the Stube floor, Jakob scolded them. He wanted to listen to any news he could get. Rosa, though, was glad that there were more people in the household. Sure, it made everything feel a little crowded and tight, but there was also more distraction from the worries. Moreover, together everything was a little easier to bear.

Of course, those little breathers from the unthinkable and the moments of pretence that life could be enjoyable were losing its effects fast. Not a day went by without a shocking reminder of a war going on close by; that bombs were dropping on the big cities was known. But at least it was happening further away. What was worse was there was no cheer left in the village, that every family wore the black colors of mourning, that it was known some men might return with one leg or one arm, or not ever. The daily stream of barterers and beggars coming by put the family through hard trials, as the family could not give away so much food anymore. Rosa alternated between generous help and hard denial when she felt there might not be enough for them. Sometimes guilt bothered her. She was acutely aware of her position of power to be able to hand out some food. *How good we live on a farm,* she thought. But soon the terrors of war would be experienced more closely still, even being on a farm and away from big cities.

***

One day in mid-March 1945 Ina came storming into the Stube and yelled, "There are bombers coming towards us!"

Leaving the door open she ran back out to collect her son playing with Hans in the last patches of snow. Rosa ran after her outside.

They saw and heard bombs dropping from the sky but could not see from the farmyard where they hit.

"They're bombing our little provincial town," Jakob remarked in disbelief, with a calm exterior on his pale skin. Nobody had contemplated this possibility as they thought there was nothing worse than destroying that town down in the valley.

It was a spring day with a little sun between white clouds. Rosa and Hans grabbed two of the bikes and pedaled hard to get to the hill by the forest, from which one could overlook the whole valley and observe the bombings. When they got there other villagers were already present and had dropped their bikes where they stood. Rosa told Hans to let his bike fall on hers and to stay close to her. Hans started counting the planes.

"I think there are twelve," he said.

Big clouds of dust and smoke rose from the little town.

"They are bombing the train station," somebody remarked.

Some planes turned and came closer to their observation point at the edge of the forest on that hill. Suddenly Jakob appeared with an old rusty bike. He was gasping for air.

"Are you guys crazy?" he yelled. "You are standing here in full view of the pilots. And your bloody bikes are sparkling in the sun. Grab your bikes and hide amongst the trees and stay there until they have left!"

Rosa grew pale and knew instantly what a big mistake she had made. But Hans wanted to watch the show. Rosa grabbed him by the arm and jerked him amongst the pine trees. Then she ran back out into the open and pulled in both bikes. Everybody else did likewise. *Uncle Jakob saved our lives*, Rosa realized.

Rosa could not tell how long she, Hans, Jakob and all the other people from the village had stayed hiding in the forest. After the sirens had signaled the end of the bombardment it took Jakob once again to get her and Hans to go home. She still trembled when he approached.

When they came back Liz, Thekla and Ina stood by the front door and shouted at them simultaneously, their fear, frustration, and anger running freely off their mouths. They had been beside themselves with worry. Little Susi screamed along. Only Jakob found the words:

"There must be hundreds of casualties. They bombed the train station and the canal bridges and the whole town. Something dropped on our side of the valley. I don't know why Anselm and Kon don't come home, goddammit!" He needed support, too.

Nobody could go into the city or out of it just like that. But anybody who could walk or had any vehicle with wheels, such as a bike or a little hand-pulled wagon, left for another place that seemed safer. Thus the people from the bombed town started coming to the village by mid-morning the next day. Rosa wondered how they crossed the canal. They must have walked to another bridge from a wide detour. They wore what they could rescue, in tatters or not, as long as it was warm. They swarmed out across the village to every farm house that looked like it could have food. They were offering items to trade.

"Liz, how many eggs can I give her for this shovel?" Rosa asked her mother.

"There's nothing left today. Ask her to come in for a bowl of soup."

"This one has a baby and needs milk."

"Well, fill her bottle."

Rosa worked tirelessly. Ina and Thekla tended the bread and soup in the house. Water puddles formed in the Stube from snow stuck on shoes.

Eventually the stream of desperate and hungry people lessened. Rosa and Liz had to tend to the dairy cows. New milk was collected and a new day could be faced. Rosa fed her cats with the still warm milk. That much had to be.

"Come, my little ones," she would talk to them. "We will always have milk." After all the work was done for the day, at least one of those five cats would settle in Rosa's lap and purr while she knitted. It always gave her a peaceful feeling. Hans and Denis also each held a cat before they had to go to bed.

One evening, a few days after the bombing, and after the milking and the cleaning of the stables had been completed, Berta knocked on the Stube door and entered without waiting for the customary call "come in". With a cracking voice she asked for help because one little calf had trouble being born.

"Is Johann not there?" Jakob asked.

"No," Berta said and started crying. Rosa put her knitting down and looked up alarmed.

"Where is he?" Rosa's voice was almost shrill.

"He has been drafted. He was picked up yesterday morning." Berta looked straight at the adults in the room with her eyes swimming in tears.

"No, no, I don't believe it!" Rosa had jumped up.

"What? Now?" Uncle Jakob said in disbelief. "Now?" he repeated. "But the war is lost, it is over!"

"Be quiet, Jakob," Ina shot at him, bending forward.

"Where is Alois?" Rosa shouted.

Without another word, Jakob took his jacket from the hook and walked out. Berta followed him. Rosa ran after them without dressing warmer. She was devastated and felt she wanted to be close to Berta and on Alois' farm.

This blow also was absorbed by Rosa and her extended patchwork family. For the next day all living creatures needed to be fed: the cows, the cats, the chickens, Anselm's doves, and the people. There was no timeout from that. Like many times before, Rosa said to herself, "*Work is the best medicine.*" She was glad for the chores that had to be done. It provided a feeling of routine and the illusion of stability in the midst of chaos. The former had to make the latter bearable. Thus, and almost spitefully, the Easter holidays were marked by providing a colored egg for each of the kids and Rosa. Thekla had hidden them while carrying little Susi in her arms. Hans and Denis screeched with delight when they found their egg. The Easter bunny had not forgotten them.

Time to Get Married

8 May 1945 was not a typical day of this glorified month of warm air, sunshine, and trees saturated with blossoms. Instead it was a day of cold temperatures, wind and enough snow that still would collect on the ground before it melted again. Thus, the American tanks that rolled around the schoolhouse into the village made enormous tracks on the dirt road.

Rosa was in the shed to collect firewood for the evening meal and a few lumps of dried peat when she heard a strange rattling sound. She stepped into the yard to see what made that noise. When she saw the giant tanks she turned white like a sheet and felt her knees go weak as if they wanted to buckle. Then she saw Jakob in the door frame to his shop. His jaw had dropped open. Rosa wanted to bolt for the house but stopped dead when someone shouted something she did not understand. But it was not necessary to run inside for Liz, Ina, Thekla and Hans appeared. The little ones were napping.

To the horror of the observers one tank came rattling into their farmyard. Two more stopped out in the square where normally the farmers parked their horses and wagons when they needed work done in the blacksmith workshop. But there was no more space for another one of those monstrous war machines. Some still came only to keep moving on and through the village without stopping. The soldiers that climbed out of the tanks swarmed out into the neighboring houses. One of them stayed and told the three women in a harsh and no nonsense tone to step aside as he was going to go in and look for weapons and other forbidden material. Thanks to Ina's ability to speak and understand English this operation happened peacefully.

A second soldier stayed next to his tank with a gun pointing into the air. No-one had spoken a word except the first soldier and Ina. Speechless out of shock, Rosa stood motionless where she was. After a considerable while the army man reappeared in the doorframe. He held and bundled up little Susi in his arms.

Thekla let out a bloodcurdling scream. That caused the soldier to turn and walk straight to Thekla. Quietly he talked to her. She did not understand a word and did not care. Her arms went for her baby. But the soldier apparently wanted her to understand what he was saying. His voice was calm. Then he turned to Ina and told her.

"Thekla," Ina said, "he says that he will come again when she is one-thousand weeks old." Thekla's terror came down slowly after she comprehended that he was not kidnapping her daughter. Finally her face twisted into a weak grin and she stretched out her arms for her baby again. Gently the man put Susi into her arms and she pressed her quite tightly to her chest that the baby started a furious cry. Everybody breathed a sigh of relief. But the soldiers were to stay on in the village.

***

Somehow the occupiers and the townspeople lived with each other. Life had to go on. The cool May of 1945 had yielded to the warmer summer month of June. By now the farmers and all the other people in the village, natives and refugees, had found a fragile co-existence with those foreign soldiers. Under the latter's watchful eyes they pursued the tasks of everyday life. Farmers fed and milked their cows and harvested hay. Even the church bells rang again for Sunday mass.

But there was no jubilation about the end of the war. Every house and every family was anxiously waiting for their men who were assumed to be alive to return. That, however, was not readily forthcoming. Hope, however, received a boost when Alois' younger brother Johann, the teenager, walked into the village. He was briefly stopped on the square in front of Rosa's farm by an American soldier. But since Johann did not wear a uniform nor carry a weapon of any kind, the soldier let him go, watching him step through the gate into his farmyard. When Rosa was told about Johann's safe return she dropped her bucket of water and ran to the same gate and through it. She did not even see the soldier grin.

"Johann," she yelled, storming into the kitchen. But Johann was preoccupied with his two sisters and his father asking too many questions to answer. When he finally turned around to Rosa she stared into his pale face as if she had to reacquaint herself.

"Are you okay?" she asked quietly. All inner uproar seemed to have left her. Instead, concern flooded her. But Johann was tight-lipped.

"Yep," he said. She looked at him a little longer, studying his pale face and his eyes that had changed so much. It seemed to Rosa that they were scanning as if he felt hunted. It unsettled her. Then she shot out the most burning question in her heart.

"Have you seen Alois?"

"No," Johann answered. And Rosa realized once more that something was different about Johann. Feeling helpless she turned without another word and left.

"You okay?" the olive green-dressed soldier in the square asked. Rosa automatically shook her head as if she had understood the question, walking on to her place behind the barn.

***

Already the village was filled with refugees from far away and from places closer, from foreign lands and homelands, from all the bombed cities. Most, however, moved on, but enough stayed for a lack of place to go to. Many wore a wardrobe in tatters; all of them seemed to be starving; children cried, and some were obviously sick. Some came with their belongings on their backs; some had an animal to pull a wagon; and some wagons were pulled by their owners.

They slept in barns and stables, some in their wagons, some preferred the open meadows. It was chaotic. All the while the foreign soldiers tried to keep order with some success. The already tight food supply had to be rationed some more. On Rosa's farm a whole clan of Hungarian musicians had taken refuge in the barn. They mostly kept to themselves and were no trouble. Food was shared with them which they accepted with gratitude. Rosa watched them with interest and she liked it a lot when they sang songs in their language in the evenings. Even the soldiers came to listen. One could almost forget that these people were enemies meeting in peace for a short time.

It was a short stay for the Hungarian musicians. After a few days they moved on to wherever they could. Rosa regretted their departure. For a few hours each evening they had brought lightness to their gloom. Their music brought back memories of a life that now seemed hardly possible amidst all the trauma of loss and confusion. *When was the last ballroom dance?* Rosa considered.

Rosa also was aware of the handsome young soldiers amongst the congregated crowd. One of them in the olive-green uniforms kept on looking at Rosa. It was the one who inquired about her wellbeing after she had seen Johann with a heavy heart. At first she was uncomfortable, almost frightened about his attention to her. But then she began to look forward to the evenings and those pair of grey eyes on her. With the Hungarians' departure, however, those mind-saving evenings also had come to an end, and the grey pair of eyes looked at her only when her path crossed that of the olive green-uniformed soldier.

***

The barley had ripened and it was time to harvest. It was followed by the other grain varieties. Rosa knew it would be another summer of back-breaking work, what with the cutting and bundling fields of grain by hand. Jakob helped when he was free from the blacksmith workshop. Thekla had taken over the cooking so that Liz could work in the field with her daughter. Ina was watching the small children. Still it was hard work for the women.

Every day low-flying planes were blasting through the sky. It scared man and animal alike. Rosa and Hans would run to lie in the ditch until the sky had cleared and they could continue their work. In the evenings, after all the chores had been completed, there was some fun to look forward to.

Rosa met with Mal, Lisa and Berta to walk to the pond by the forest. The July nights had been warm enough to jump into the water and cool down from the heat of the day. Usually Hans was allowed to come along. Since both Rosa and Hans could not swim they stayed close to the shore in shallower water. That was the time when Rosa remembered how Alois had used to float her to the reeds out into the pond. How sweet it was and how much she missed it. Where was he? The war was over and he must come back soon! Had not the elderly father of those five children that lived at the edge of the forest come back? And Hans, the man from the small house down the western meadow, had returned. Of course, he had been close by in a hospital for many months as he had lost one leg.

Berta said that they still had no word from Alois. That was one moment when Rosa felt extreme anxiety. Her tears were hard to hold back as she feared the worst. The best was not to allow those ruminating thoughts to get a hold of her.

Yet a few weeks into July Rosa's dwindling hope for the return of her loved ones received a tremendous boost. Even though it was still early morning the air was humid and warm. Rosa was sweating. She had just finished milking her last cow and was pouring the content of her milk bucket into the filter when she saw a man walking slowly and with an unsteady gait towards her. She screamed, dropped her bucket and ran towards her uncle Kon. When she raised her arms to hug Kon he quickly stepped back and said:

"Don't do that. I am dirty."

Rosa stared at him. With a pounding heart she began to take in his picture. Indeed, he was very dirty. His uniform was hardly recognizable as such. It lacked any signs of stripes and it was torn front and back. His face was sprouting a beard that was unclean and uncombed. With a shock Rosa noticed the grey in her uncle's hair, which was growing off around the cap. Silently she followed him walking towards the front door. She noticed his tired, insecure steps. Her euphoria began to give way to anxiety.

Liz, Jakob, Thekla with Susi in her arms, and Ina all had gathered at the front door staring at this man who barely could set one foot in front of the other. Yet he did muster a grin. His brother Jakob slapped him on his back, whereas his two sisters tried not to show any tears.

"Kon, this is your newest niece," Thekla said, showing him her baby. Kon let his tears flow freely now. He was at the end of his strength.

"I better not touch her," he said apologetically. "I have lice."

"Let's all have breakfast," Liz said and walked ahead into the house. Kon sat down at his place at the table. He looked into the faces of the people around him as if he needed to believe that he was indeed home. Ina's and Denis' presence did not seem to surprise him at all.

Liz and Rosa served roasted grain coffee, which contained the rich milk from their own cows. Liz had baked some bread. There was plum jam to be spread on the slices. But after one slice Kon did not feel too well. It became apparent how exhausted he was. It had taken him all night from the train station to get home – eight kilometers, he explained. Because of the curfew he could only walk from one ditch to the next as the U.S. army was driving with search lights over the roads to check for curfew violators. Each time Kon heard a jeep coming he would dive into a ditch and keep still. That way he got very cold.

"Lay down on the sofa and sleep," Jakob demanded.

"Yes, but I need to change into different clothes first." Kon said weakly. "These ones need to be burned."

Kon slept, but briefly. He was awake before lunch was served. Now he was almost ferociously hungry. But again, he ate only half the food on his plate. Rosa looked questioningly at the adults. Kon had always eaten his plate empty, so she remembered.

After lunch Kon attempted to help in the field to bring in part of the grain harvest. But soon he felt nauseated and faint. Rosa went to Thekla and told her about this.

"Do you think he is sick, Aunt Thekla?"

"Well, he is just still very weak from what he has just been through. The last few months he was a prisoner with the American army." Thekla tried to calm Rosa while her own concern was rising. After all, she had a nine year old and her baby to protect.

The next morning Kon's eyeballs had turned yellow and he still felt worse. Thekla was alarmed and immediately went to the U.S. military authorities in the small bombed city, and told them that her recently returned brother had jaundice and needed to get to the next functioning hospital. Within the hour Kon was picked up by a U.S. Army ambulance and taken to hospital.

The consensus in the family, including Ina, was relief about Kon's luck to get into a hospital as they were very crowded at that time. But after nearly a week of no news they grew worried, Rosa the most. One day during lunch she asked for permission to bike to that hospital in the next town of Altötting, where Kon had been taken to.

"Out of the question," Liz and Thekla said.

"Why?" Rosa yelled.

"It's just too dangerous with all the soldiers and jeeps and creeps on the loose," Liz shot back. It suited Rosa fine as she had just realized that her mother had a point and fear had entered her mind. But she used Liz's arguments to her advantage.

"If it is too dangerous for me alone, why can't Ina come with me? She even speaks English!" Ina liked the idea. She had been on this farm for too long without leave for anywhere.

"Thekla, if you can manage my son for a few hours together with your children I will accompany Rosa."

"I guess I can for an afternoon. But what if something happens to you? It is dangerous out there." Rosa's heart skipped a beat. She was increasingly scared to leave the house. But she needed to see Kon and reassure herself that he was recovering and coming home soon. Everything was about coming home now, wasn't it?

"What should happen?" Ina asked. "We need to go to the military representative and get a permit to travel. I can do this after lunch and tomorrow we can go." And so it was agreed.

"Do we have two bikes?" Ina asked.

"I'll get the second one ready before tomorrow afternoon," Jakob promised.

"And which bridge can we use?" Rosa asked.

"I'll ask that when I get the travel permission," Ina offered. "Everything will work out, Rosa. Tomorrow afternoon we will go."

Rosa did not sleep well that night. She could not stop thinking about all the possible scenarios that could go wrong. They might be stopped and arrested; they might be shot at; the airplanes might come back and drop bombs; or they might never find that lone bridge across the canal. But having worked all day her body needed a rest, so she fell asleep at last.

***

Ina and Rosa felt hot and thirsty when they reached the hospital. The sixteen-kilometer bike ride had actually been quite uneventful, although they both had been stopped and checked by soldiers several times. Ina showed them their travel permit and they were waved on. Rosa held her breath each time they came to a checkpoint.

Now, at the hospital, she jumped off her bike with great relief. But a new wave of anxiety gripped her when they entered the hospital. The entrance hall was overcrowded with patients, all male. Some of them smoked a cigarette. *Where did they get those from?* Rosa wondered. Most had dressings of various extents and at different body parts. Some dressings even had blood oozing through. Rosa stared at the scene and become aware that seemingly all eyes rested on her and Ina.

"Come on, Rosa," Ina called her, "we have to find Kon."

After asking around repeatedly, one nurse finally knew which room he was in on the second floor. They had to walk a long corridor almost to the end. Rosa had to be called to move on again. Horrified, she looked at those men walking or limping up and down the hallway. Some were on crutches as they had only one leg, and some were in wheelchairs as they had no legs. Some walked along with one or both arms missing. Others had their heads, or one eye, or the whole head with only the eyes visible, wrapped in white bandages. Rosa began to feel nauseated. She had not seen that side of the war till now. She thought about Alois and Anselm. Were they maimed like that as well?

They found the room number the nurse had given them, which was somewhat isolated at the end of the long corridor. Ina went in first and Rosa followed with a pounding heart. There were six white beds in rows of three at the two opposing walls. Rosa felt intimidated when six heads turned to look at the visitors. Yet she scanned every face frantically looking for Kon.

"I am here," a familiar but soft voice said.

Slowly Rosa walked to his bed. Her heart rate went up a notch when she saw Kon's yellow skin color and the white of his eyes being awfully yellow as well. He looked very sick. She just stood at his bed and looked down at him, feeling at a loss of words. But despite his years of absence Kon still knew his niece.

"I am better, Rosa, than when I came in. I can eat a little and my color will change back," he tried to reassure her. Rosa found her voice.

"When are you coming home?"

"Don't know yet, but I hope soon." He started to feel tired. Turning to Ina he said:

"You should be heading back. You must be home before dark."

"Yes, I know," Ina said. "Don't worry. We will be home by then."

Without a handshake or a hug they left. Rosa felt elated. Kon was there and getting better. He had said so. But he did not talk a lot at all. *Oh well, he will when he is home,* Rosa thought. They had to leave the same way they had come in. Rosa kept her head down as she could not bear to look at those terribly injured men again. The sight made her sick.

After nearly three weeks in hospital Kon was permitted to return home. His skin still looked a bit tinted yellow, but he had a slight grin on his face and walked better. Rosa and her mother had refreshed and tidied up Kon's bedroom. He was home! Rosa and her family were happy.

But Kon's safe return was also a reminder of those who were still away. They knew that Anselm was a prisoner of war in France, nothing more. At least he was alive. But Alois, what happened to him? As so often on Sunday afternoons, Rosa went to visit Alois' family. This time she dared to ask again about news.

"We have an official notice that he is missing in action. He went missing in Russia." Berta looked straight at Rosa.

Rosa finally burst out after a length of silence. "What does that mean?"

"It means we have no idea whether he is alive or dead, whether he will come home or not," Berta almost yelled.

"That can't be," Rosa yelled back. "They have to look for him!"

"Who, Rosa, who is going to search for him in Russia?"

"Oh my God," Rosa whispered now. She stayed on with Berta and Resi. She felt better in their presence, and she felt closer to Alois in his home. Of course, it was a more crowded home now. The U.S. administration for the region had assigned a mother, daughter and grandmother to their farm house. They were refugees from the east. Nearly every home that had a room empty had to take in assigned refugees from the eastern territories. Everybody was crowded now. The village was packed with strangers.

"He will come, Berta," Rosa said before she left to do her evening chores with Liz.

Rosa's mind refused to believe that her love was dead or that he had simply vanished. But her heart had started to doubt her thoughts. Horror scenarios came into her mind and made her feel terrible. What if he had lost his legs or his eyes? Could he be kept prisoner and tortured, kept hungry, or kept working sunrise to sunset in a quarry? What if he had been taken to Siberia into the lead mines? Overwhelmed with pain, Rosa did what she always had done to get on top of her feelings.

She started to run for her place behind the barn. But midway she changed her mind, turned sharply in the middle of the barnyard, and ran upstairs to her bed. She tore open the drawer of her bedside table and pulled out Alois' card. "'Wait for me, Rosa',' she read and reread again. Tears started streaming down her face. She cried until her pillow was soaked where her face lay. Rosa yelled into the room,

"You have to come back, you said so, you can't be dead, I am waiting for you. Please, Alois, please!"

This was not the last time that Rosa would cry for her lost love.

***

In the face of disaster, destruction, death, endless pain and mourning, life in this village raised its head again like a new plant growing out of a wall that once was hit by a bomb. They even said that school would be reopened come September and a very young teacher would be sent there. He was still missing one exam for licensure, but nobody cared. There was nobody else for the job.

Mothers chatted excitedly in the grocery store about getting their children back to school. There had not been any at all the previous months. Now they would have a free hand for a few hours each day getting their housework done, or go and do odd jobs for the farmers or even in the city in exchange for food to take home to their fatherless children.

The villagers had arranged themselves with the people in olive-green uniforms. It was not least because the soldiers had withdrawn to the cities and came only in irregular, unpredictable intervals to see if things were going their way. Most soldiers had been exchanged for new ones. Some were standoffish and rude, and others were reaching out to the population they controlled. Some spoke a few words of German. The village girls, like Rosa and her school mates, were now, since the scare had diminished a little, more aware of the young men inside the uniforms. The latter had become a familiar sight.

On Sundays, when the young ladies took walks to the very edge of the forest from where the bombing of their city in the river valley was once watched, a few of those young soldiers showed up. They would sit with them in the grass trying to talk to them. Rosa felt uncomfortable about this. But then it was nice too. They offered chocolates and candies, and that stuff that you could chew forever. Mal once even got a pair of very thin see-through stockings. They looked great! And then there were these stinking but also chic cigarettes that they offered to the girls.

One time, to Rosa's surprise, that soldier with the grey eyes came along. *He's still here!* He sat down by her side. Mal looked at her with a wide grin on her face. Rosa blushed furiously. She remembered how these eyes had followed her in the early days of the occupation of their village. *His eyes look good and kind*, Rosa thought. Silently he offered her a cigarette. Rosa shook her head.

"Well, maybe you want to try?" he said. Rosa understood the gesture and shook her head again.

"Try that then," he said with a calm voice.

Rosa reached for the chocolate. He unwrapped it for her and put it into her mouth. It tasted heavenly. How long had she not had any?

After that Rosa began to look forward to Sunday afternoons. It felt so nice to be treated so kindly and to be looked at with those grey eyes. Of course, they could only meet when the weather was dry and warm. Rosa always felt rather timid in his presence, as there was no conversation taking place. But then, she liked being with him as well. It was so nice when he took her hand and put a little chocolate into her palm, or when he smiled at her, or when he just looked at her. She felt ambivalent and confused. Something was not right about this. And it would come to an end when the cold season came in. Summers don't last forever. At the latest it would be over then. That lessened Rosa's concerns considerably.

At night before falling asleep she would reread Alois' words on his card. *Wait for me, Rosa*. Something was not right about this with Jim. *I like him a lot but not more,* Rosa reasoned. B*ut he had chocolate and other sweet things to eat and stockings and such. And he was nice, kind, calm, and he looked at me with those grey eyes.* Mal even got silky fabric from one guy. It was from an old parachute, he had confessed to her with a grin. She had made a nice dress from it.

Inevitably, by October the temperatures had dropped low enough to forbid sitting on the ground at the edge of any forest. The sun was still warm, however. But her friends did not like to come with her to that vista by the forest anymore. Jim was able to set times when he still could come to meet her, and Rosa went to meet him. She told her mother that she was running over to Berta and Resi. Rosa was aware that it was a sin to lie.

She could not help it as Liz was too strict with her. She never did find out how her mother learned about her dates with the American soldier. But the result was a furious scolding from Liz.

"Are you crazy to meet an American soldier? Have you lost your mind? You are never going to meet him again! What are you doing together out in the cold anyway?" Liz carried on. Liz was really scared for her daughter. But she kept her fear to herself. *What if she got pregnant? Unthinkable!*

From then on Rosa was watched fiercely by her mother. But Rosa had one ally. Ina had also been meeting a nice soldier. She spoke his language after all.

One day in early November 1945 she waved Rosa to her.

"Rosa, I thought you might want to know that the troops have been exchanged. The ones that have been here till now have been sent home and others have replaced them."

"All of them?" Rosa whispered.

"Yes, all of them. Yours and mine, both are gone."

Rosa's eyes filled with tears. Ina hugged her tightly.

"All men leave, always," Rosa howled. "Even Alois did not come back. With Jim here I did not have to think about him that much. But now my thoughts about Alois' fate will come back terribly. And Jim, he did not even say goodbye. He just dropped me! Men always just disappear, Ina! I can't stand this anymore!"

"Yes, we can, Rosa. We must. There is nothing else we can do. Look at Thekla. She has lost her husband." Ina reached out to dry Rosa's tears. But she could not take the pain away from her. It would take time. It surely would.

Rosa's pain was pushed aside soon by another worry about physical pain. It was going to turn out to be a problem she had not even heard about in her young life. It felt weird and, thus, instinctively she kept quiet about it, just to be on the safe side.

Rosa had not met Jim the previous week. She had gone to their meeting place on Sunday and was puzzled when he did not appear. Disappointed, she went back home. What had kept him away? Was it the cooler weather or, more likely, had he tired of her? Perhaps he was with another girl? But now, after Ina had brought her the bad news of his departure she understood. She was distressed. Sunday afternoons were going to be boring and there would be no more chocolate, cigarettes, or silk stockings. And the ruminating thoughts about Alois were going to come back with a vengeance for sure. She was afraid of those.

***

The week following Jim's transfer Rosa noticed a burning sensation every time she had to go to the toilet. *I have a bladder infection*, she diagnosed her problem. *I should not have been sitting on that cold floor. That blanket did not help one bit. We should not have met there in the forest anymore. Although, what would we have done then?* Rosa tried to reason.

But her burning sensation got worse. Each night she took a hot water bottle to bed with her, hoping that it would cure her bladder infection. Liz recommended some awful tea to be drunk several times a day. Yet, that did not help either. Actually, something new had come up. She noticed a sort of pus-like discharge in her panties. But then it did not really look like pus. Rosa's anxiety level skyrocketed. What was going on? She knew that she had to talk to somebody, but to whom? Her own mother was a definitive no-no. Ina? No, too embarrassing. But Thekla, she might not tell anybody, and she had been able to get Kon to a doctor, hadn't she? She slept together with her aunt in the same bedroom, so it was easy to talk to her without anybody else listening.

When Rosa described to her aunt her symptoms and the pain she had to endure, and how she was afraid to go urinate, Thekla's eyebrows rose slowly.

"Rosa, did you do something with your soldier when you met on Sundays?"

Rosa turned crimson red, which Thekla could not see. Rosa was deep in her feather bed covered to the chin. But the silence was telling.

"Rosa, that is important to know. You have to tell me because it could mean that you have caught a disease from this man."

"What disease?" Rosa shouted at her aunt from her bed. "He was not sick!"

"Well, this is not a disease one can see from the outside, Rosa." Rosa had started to sob.

"You are scaring me, Aunt Thekla!"

"Don't be frightened, Rosa. It is not so bad that it cannot be healed. Tomorrow I will find a doctor and then we will both go see him."

"Don't tell anybody, Aunt Thekla – not my mother and nobody." Rosa pleaded with her aunt.

"No, I won't tell. But I'll have to shape the truth a little, Rosa. They are going to want some explanation for your doctor's visit without you being visibly ill. So brace yourself. And I hope you are learning your lesson, my dear niece."

Thekla could not stop herself from adding that last sentence. *Why did you do that, you stupid girl? You were taught differently and you know about that sin. You are lucky that I won't tell your mother. I would not want to listen to that drama!*

"What? Why would she want to see a doctor? Does she look sick to you, sister?" Liz was angry. Not only do doctors cost money, but she would also have to do her own work plus Rosa's on the farm that day.

"Well, she has a bad urinary tract infection, I think. You know that – you have given her stinging nettle tea after all."

"Yeah, but this does not call for a doctor's visit, does it?" Liz looked at her sister with a question in her eyes. Thekla began to feel hot. *She must not know more*, she thought.

"No, Liz, she has to go. That thing can get worse otherwise." Thekla hoped that this threat of losing her helper would do. Liz started to waver.

"So go, the two of you, then," she said. "But come back as soon as you can, at least before milking time."

"We will. But don't forget that we have to take a detour to get over a bridge."

Liz signed a cross on Rosa's forehead and left without another word.

Later Thekla and Rosa leaned their bikes against the wall outside the doctor's practice rooms. There were already a number of bikes before theirs. Thekla gasped when they entered their family physician's waiting room. He was a kind, grey-haired man who had treated Grandmother. He was way beyond retirement age but could not close his practice, as there were no young doctors around who wanted to take over. Rosa felt comfortable with the old man. She had known him all her life. But now, he was busier than ever. Every rickety, uncomfortable chair in his waiting room was taken. Rosa counted the patients waiting.

"Thirty-two," she announced. There was no place for her and Thekla to sit down. So they stood until a patient was called in and vacated a chair. After a while they were called in. Rosa's anxiety was sky-high.

"How long have you had that, Rosa?" the doctor asked.

"Don't know, not long, maybe a week. But it burns so bad." Rosa was deep red in her face and could not say more. She started crying. The doctor turned to Thekla:

"Could you please wait outside?" Thekla left without a word and settled in the waiting room. Thankfully, there were a few empty chairs. After a while, which seemed very long to Thekla, the door opened and the doctor waved her back into his room. Immediately Thekla saw Rosa sitting there with a hanging head and crying.

"Doctor, what…"

"Calm, calm," the doctor interrupted her. "She does not have a urinary tract infection like we thought. I mean she does, but it is not the same."

"What do you mean?" Thekla asked, but she thought she knew the answer.

"Well, she has caught some really bad bacteria that will get worse if we don't treat it immediately. She has to go to hospital for that. It has to be closely watched." He did not mention the American forces wanted to know about venereal disease. He had known Rosa since she was a little girl with two thick, beautiful auburn braids. He knew that regardless of her shyness she could be very stubborn too. But he was not going to violate the rules during these days of foreign occupancy.

"Oh Jesus, Mary, and Joseph," Thekla exclaimed. "Then we need to go on our bikes and go down to the hospital now?" *This is where Uncle Kon was*, Rosa thought. She was very frightened.

"No, I have another patient that I am going to take there after I have seen my last patient here. I'll take Rosa with me," he said.

Rosa went berserk. She jumped up and shouted at Thekla:

"But we promised Liz that I will be back for the evening work. What is she going to think? That we broke a promise?"

"I'll take care of that, Rosa. Don't worry. I can handle my sister. And the doctor will take care of you. Don't worry."

"You are going to be in a room with other women your age, Rosa. It won't be long, perhaps a week," the doctor tried to comfort her and to ward off fierce resistance.

"But my people at home will be upset. I am not sick either," Rosa shot back. Thekla put her arms around Rosa and held her close.

"I said I'll take care of them, Rosa. Don't you worry. And now I'll wait with you until you leave for the hospital. We have to cure this problem of yours, dear. You understand that, don't you?"

Rosa nodded weakly.

When the friendly old physician finally came out of his treatment room into the waiting room he looked tired. He had exchanged his white coat for a grey jacket. With an encouraging smile on his face he turned to his two patients, Rosa and another boy, perhaps an early teen, and said joyfully:

"Let's go and get you two cured!"

Rosa jumped up and addressed her aunt hopefully, "But I am not sick, Aunt Thekla. I want to go home with you." Thekla took a deep breath and took her niece by the arm.

"Rosa, be a big girl now. You have to get rid of this problem. It will only get worse. They would ask more questions if you were hanging around at home with pain written all over your face. When in hospital, and it's only for a week, they can't ask so much." Rosa had not considered this yet. Without a further word she turned and walked after the doctor and the other kid.

With relief Thekla looked after the three climbing into the doctor's old, rickety car. She, however, went to her bike, leaving Rosa's at the doctor's place, and started the uphill ride back to the farm. She was not looking forward to the questioning from Liz, Jakob, and Ina.

However, she was determined to further explain the seriousness and painful matter of that urinary tract infection that Rosa somehow had caught. She executed her task with conviction and diplomatically. Jakob was the first to walk away to his blacksmith workshop. Next, Ina left with an "Oh my word!" Kon and Liz, however, stayed wanting to get a detailed account as to the proceedings in the doctor's office. But soon Kon had heard enough as well. He kept silent. When Liz heard that the doctor had taken her daughter to the hospital himself, she finally slowly turned to go outside while shaking her head.

And indeed, precisely after a week, the doctor had to make a house visit in town. He dropped by and asked to speak to Liz. Jakob greeted him first outside and spoke to him briefly, standing very close and whispering.

"I understand, don't worry," the doctor called back while taking the three steps into the house.

"There you are," he greeted Liz in the kitchen. "Your daughter is doing very well. She can come home."

"Thank God," Liz exclaimed. "What actually was so bad that she needed to stay in hospital, doctor?"

"Well," the doctor said calmly, "you know after what we have going on around here these days, there are lots of germs around. And Rosa just had caught a very aggressive and painful one. The medicine that can cure that is only administered in hospitals. But don't worry about what caused it. Let's be happy that she is back to full health and be grateful to God for that." *Yes, I am grateful*, Liz thought.

"Thank you very much, doctor," Liz said.

***

During the winter season the weather was not as cold as the previous two years. Yet, people's warm winter clothes had been worn for almost three seasons now. They all needed new, warmer ones. That was a challenge as new material was scarce. The women in Rosa's family needed woolen fabric, especially new wool yarn. Thekla and Ina bravely went to the farmers, who had always been customers of

Jakob's, in the hope that they would get some raw wool from their sheep. They actually did. It was not enough for them all but they would take older, worn-out sweaters and undo them. If the yarn was torn it would be knotted together. Then this old yarn would be joined with the new one. However, the raw wool from the farmers needed to be washed, dried, and then spun on their old spinning-wheel.

"Watch, Rosa, the thread needs to be evenly thick. Don't feed too much too fast into the wheel." Liz was teaching her daughter the skills that she herself had learned from her own mother. She ignored that Rosa was already quite proficient in that task. There was urgency to their business. Kon, for example, was in dire need of a warm sweater, gloves, socks and more.

Thus, the sound of the spinning wheel or the clicking of knitting needles made for cozy winter evenings. One could even listen to that old radio without fear. And there was even music. But that upset Kon a lot.

"Rosa, turn that off," he would yell almost instantly.

"Turn it off, Rosa," Jakob would tell her calmly as if his brother needed his backup. She did not dare to ask for the reason for this, but she saw that Kon looked relaxed when the music stopped. What ever was the matter with him?

On one of those winter evenings Kon said to his brother into the quiet:

"Did you know that Sepp Reichert was brought back home in a Jeep today?"

"What? Why in a Jeep?" Jakob asked.

"Guess they needed the place in the hospital. His stump is healed."

"What do you mean, 'his stump'?"

"Well, one of his legs took a full hit in Russia and it would not heal up. So they shipped him home. If it had not been for that he would not be home now. He was lucky that he made it home. So he has one leg less, big deal." Kon spoke with a raised voice. Everybody listened up as he had talked monotonously ever since he had come home. Rosa stopped spinning her wheel.

"Did anybody else come home?"

"Yes, Sepp's father came back. He just walked through the village towards his house. Don't know where he came from." Kon had visited one of the village pubs where he had heard the news.

"Do you think there will be more coming back now?" Rosa looked with raised eyebrows at her uncles.

"Nobody knows," Jakob said. Kon turned his head to face his niece.

"A few perhaps," he mumbled. Liz, Thekla, and Ina kept their heads bent over their needlework. They understood the base of Rosa's inquiry well, for each of them felt the same anxiety. Who is going to come back from that devastation? Which family has received a note from the Red Cross about the whereabouts of their men? Everybody missing a loved one was filled with trepidation and expectation. Will it be a death notice, or a note about being prisoner of war, or a note, perhaps the worst one of all, that says "missing in action"? Rosa knew about all possible answers.

Rosa's most dreadful times were experienced in the evenings in bed. Her mind would play out the stories she had heard from Mal and Renate, from Ina, and from the mothers and wives who stood in groups after church on Sundays. In her mind she saw her uncle Anselm hungry and freezing in a makeshift cottage where he had to sleep on the floor without any cover. She saw her school mates living and working in a lead mine in Siberia hungry, with frozen fingers and toes. One of the most horrifying scenarios that played in her mind was a story somebody had heard where soldiers had been put into the earth up to their neck. Then farm equipment was driven over them. *Alois! No!*

Once this caused her to break out in sweat and jump out of bed. She just stood there then next to her bed and shook her head, violently yelling:

"Aunt Thekla, I can't sleep!"

Rosa still slept in one bedroom with her aunt, Hans and little Susi. Only the baby slept through those anxiety attacks. But Hans had developed a subtle sense of dangerous noises during the bombing nights in Passau. He woke up easily when Rosa had trouble.

Sitting in bed he would watch silently how his mother got Rosa back to her bed and tugged her in tightly talking gently to her all the while. Finally, Rosa would fall asleep, which allowed him and his mother to huddle down in their feather beds and drift off into sleep as well. But before that Hans enjoyed his mother tucking him in as well. Hans missed his father and his childhood in Passau, his school and his friends terribly. He was in dire need of comforting himself.

Rosa's night terrors continued. But it was not particularly noticed by the rest of her family. Everybody had painful issues to deal with. There was the worry about Anselm, from whom no note had been sent for a long time. Was he even still alive? Was he being tortured? Was he hungry or sick? When will the French let him go? Kon also concerned his family as he was so different from before the war. He was jumpy, did not like loud noises, had trouble sleeping, and he ate either a lot or had no appetite. He looked thin still. Ina had let her host family know that she had no idea what would happen to her now. She wanted to move back to the city with her son but did not know how. But Thekla looked the worst of all. Her cheeks looked like hollow dents in her face and her eyes were dull. She had little appetite and cried a lot.

Rosa felt terrible for all of them despite her own anxieties. She liked to go to mass on Sundays as it was nice to meet her female friends after service. Together they felt better. Yet she still dreaded seeing all the women dressed in black and in tears. She had not gotten used to this sight. Few men had returned from the war as yet. Hope and anticipation would start to return to the townspeople, but would devastate them again when the Red Cross delivered notice mostly about the deaths or their imprisonment in foreign land of their men

Rosa did not dare to ask Berta or Resi about Alois that often anymore as they had started to snap at her.

"We don't know either, Rosa, stop asking all the time!" Berta would reprimand her, with tears in her eyes.

"Don't you think about Georg at all? He has been dead for over three years. We don't even have a grave for him," Resi would add.

So Rosa retreated and started to hope and wait, so that Alois might walk into the village one of these days, just like his brother Johann did right after the war ended. But that was not to be.

As time went on Rosa finally began to lose hope that Alois would return soon. She had closely watched all the refugees living with various farmers in the village. Every one of them was also waiting and hoping that one of their men, and sometimes even women, would show up. None of them did.

During the summer of 1946, Kon started to improve. He had put on some weight and had a healthier appearance. Rosa loved to work alongside him better than with her mother. The close relationship that she had shared with her most favorite uncle seemed to return. Little by little he taught her the business that a dairy farm had to do. He did not snap at her like Liz and he was not as critical of her. This is not to say that Rosa was not aware of the different person that he now was. He hardly laughed anymore. She saw him jump with the slightest noise and he smoked a cigarette every time he got a chance.

The village store had more and more items for sale now. *He must buy them there*, Rosa thought. *Perhaps Jakob gets them for Kon when he buys his own cigarettes.* That actually was not so bad. Rosa collected the cigarette buds from both and smoked them secretly on the outdoors toilet where nobody would catch her for sure. Nobody was thinking anything of the cigarette smoke around because Ina smoked as well. Ina knew about Rosa's little secret and kept it to herself.

One day in August, shortly after lunch, Ina received a letter from the Red Cross. Jakob stood next to her when she opened it with trembling hands. He also saw the tears dropping on the paper in her hands.

"What is it, Ina?" Jakob asked impatiently. Ina could hardly talk. Between sobs she said:

"My husband has been found alive in the hospital where Kon and Rosa were before. Apparently he has been there for months as he was wounded with grenade splinters all over his body. He is to be released shortly."

Ina was as surprised and happy as everybody else in the family. During supper it was decided that Ina would go to the hospital immediately and bring her husband here. It was assumed that he would be in better care than in that overcrowded hospital. So Ina obtained a discharge permission. In those chaotic days permission to let a patient go was taken a bit liberally. There were so many more patients to treat. How she managed to get the U.S. army to send a jeep to bring him home, nobody knew. But he recuperated nicely, and eventually had recovered enough to be hired by a bakery in another small city to work.

In September Ina, her husband and Denis left to begin a new life. Rosa felt very sad about it. Ina and Denis had lived with them now for all these terrible times. She had been not only a help in a tight household; no, for Rosa she had often been a calming influence when she had fights with her mother. More than that, Rosa had felt understood and accepted by her not to speak of the times when she had acted as her ally. Ina was almost a friend. The house would be emptier without her. But now by way of saying goodbye Ina had left her with an idea that nobody had presented to her before.

"Rosa, you are a good girl and a pretty one, too. And you are smart. Make something of your life. It is getting time for you to get married. But be careful whom you select as your husband. Won't be easy now!"

***

Rosa was twenty-three years old now, an age commonly perceived as the time to look for a candidate as a husband. Never had she given it some thought. But ever since Ina had pointed out the idea of marriage to her, she had a hard time sorting out her conflicting, troublesome feelings about it. This was also the time now where she realized that no-one in her family had ever brought up the subject, not even Liz. Was it not an issue to them all? Or could it be that they did not want her to marry because they would certainly lose her as a worker here on the farm? Marriage surely was not a sin? She had never looked at her male peers in that regard. Alois? Well, maybe him. No, Alois was her love, and that was different. Suddenly she remembered that plea of his in his last card: *Wait for me!* Could it be that he had had marriage in mind upon his return? The thought made Rosa feel shivers running down her spine. *I think I am blushing. Alois!*

Rosa could not conceive any other man as her husband. But he was missing. Nobody whom she had asked knew about his fate. Rosa felt again the deep pain that she had endured so often in the last years in silence most of the time. Now there was an additional twist to her determination to wait for Alois and belief in his return: resignation.

Over time Rosa had learned to bring down her inner turmoil by working hard. That way she did not even think about all these questions that were bothering her now. Kon, as a matter of fact, had already expressed his admiration for her part in running the dairy work of the farm. And that was a very nice thing to hear for Rosa. She felt valued and needed, not to say respected. *They love me*, she thought over again, the all-important issue for Rosa. *And Alois! But he has not come back. He never might.*

***

Rosa had put the thought of marriage out of her mind again. She had no urge for matrimony. Work with Kon at home was fun and much easier than before. She particularly loved to learn how to assist an animal, a cow or a pig, during and after the birthing process. Of course, the mama pig could only be watched. The little piglets hardly needed her assistance. Cows, however, oftentimes needed help with delivery. But the nicest thing out of everything was the little calf after it was licked clean by its mama cow. It had this wildly wiggling tail when it nursed that was so funny to Rosa. It also loved to run and jump around in the winter months in the stable. It was as if it tried to challenge Rosa. Usually Rosa developed a bond to every newborn calf and loved it to the point of kissing it on its nose.

There was life on that farm that needed to be taken care of and that could be loved. It was a good balance to the anxieties, and pains, and shocks that surfaced time and again in Rosa's life. And even though the notion of marriage was far from Rosa's mind, the issue, try as she might, still surfaced occasionally. Others made sure of that.

***

One part of social life had already re-established itself firmly in village life when the Catholic church took up regular Sunday services again. The people seemed to embrace it. Sunday was the day to attend mass regularly again, as a young priest had returned to the parish. The old priest who had kept two churches going more or less during the war years turned over this one to the young man.

The weekly meeting of friends and neighbors after church was something nice to have back. Rosa was looking forward to meet Mal, Lisa, Renate, Berta, Resi, and all the others from the farms located further away. It felt so good to talk to peers. It provided for sharing pain about lost brothers and fathers, and fears and expectations for the future. They could give each other comfort in waiting for those who had not returned yet, or those whose fate was not known.

Moreover, the young women seemed to get their youthful spirits back. They exchanged ideas how to get a decent wardrobe again and how to get material to make new dresses for themselves. The latter was really exciting as Lisa had heard that this year they were planning to hold a Kathrein Dance again. Now that was news! It looked like they had to undo older dresses and re-model them. Regardless, one thing was sure: they had to attend that ball at the end of November. They hardly could wait for that evening to come around.

When the local inn finally opened the doors to the dance floor for the Kathrein Dance, Mal, Lisa and Rosa walked into the dance hall in unison. Each of them wore a new ballroom dress made out of several undone dresses and some of Mal's parachute silk. Heads held high, they were a catching sight. They sat down and ordered their lemonade while scanning the people already sitting at the various tables. But instead of chatting nervously like they used to do before the dancing stopped during the war, they became more and more silent. It looked so different. They knew the people but they were either the older generation or the very young who attended such a ball the first or at the most the second time.

"Nobody from our classes, our friends, are here," Lisa remarked.

"Where are they?" Rosa asked and knew the answer at the same time. Stunned, she looked at Lisa and Mal. There was silence between them.

"Oh my God, how could we not think of that?" Mal asked guiltily.

"Thomas and Georg have fallen, remember? The others are simply not back yet." Lisa added.

Rosa realized with equal guilt that she had done a good job blocking thoughts of Alois. Now she was suddenly devastated, realizing that he won't be here to ask her for one of those wonderful dances with him. Her heart sank. Her eyes were searching for Kon. She stood up and walked over to him.

"What's up, Rosa?" Kon asked.

"I want to go home," she said.

"What? How come? You just came. Dancing has not even started yet."

"Yeah, but it is not nice. Nobody is here!" Rosa complained.

Kon understood without asking more.

"Rosa, look, there are guys here that are a bit younger than you. They may not be what you have expected, but they are good dancers as well and you can enjoy a dance. You have not had this for years now. Stay and enjoy the ball and dance. I am sure you are going to have fun."

With that support from her uncle, Rosa returned to her friends and sat down.

"Where is Bert?" Rosa asked.

"Bert is also not back yet." Mal said. And being less troubled about the dance room situation than Rosa, she also suggested to stay. Mal finally wanted to dance again. There were enough guys, some a few years younger and some much older, but good dancers just the same. Rosa was annoying with her concerns and worries. This night was a night to do one step towards normalcy, to be cheerful. Tomorrow the worries and anxieties would return. *Then we would keep on waiting and hoping for the return of those still missing tonight.* Mal's thoughts matched those of the others present. Everybody was desperate to return to the familiar village life that had been suspended for so many hard years.

Rosa did accept the requests from those males present to dance with them. She had always been known as a fantastic dancer before the war. Evidently, her reputation was still known in the village. Still, she was astounded how many older men asked her for dances. It did not take long and she was absorbed into turning the rhythms of the music into the movement that the dance required. Yet she was aware that fewer from the younger generation asked her. Johann did not change that when he repeatedly asked her for a dance. Despite the elation from dancing that she felt, it never did feel the same as before when Bert, Thomas, and most of all, Alois, led her around the dance floor.

During a break Rosa and her friends rested at their table and sipped their lemonades. Lisa pointed into the corner by the window.

"They are Paul, Hugo, Karl, and I don't know the other guy's name. Have you seen them dancing yet?"

"No," Mal and Rosa answered in unison.

"Why are they not asking any girl for a dance?" Lisa asked.

"Don't know," Mal said. "Perhaps they are shy. I mean they are not from here after all; they are from the refuge families from the Bohemian Forest."

"So what," Lisa exclaimed. "They have been here now for more than a year, at least some of them. They come to church and they work at the farms where they live."

"Well, would you accept, if one asked you?"

"If it is that one there, you know, I mean him, Karl, yes."

"Yeah, you like his looks? But he has only one hand – how is he going to lead?" Mal wondered.

Rosa followed the dispute between Mal and Lisa in silence. She was not aware of the blue eyes from that table that had hung on her all the while. But when the music started again, the man with those eyes stood up and walked towards her. With a slight bow he stretched his hand out to Rosa.

"Rosa, would you dance with me?" he asked politely.

Rosa's heart missed a beat. She had not expected that. Just barely did she catch her "no" before it slipped out. People were going to whisper, maybe even laugh at her to dance with Paul. But it was very rude to refuse and that she did not want to do either. Paul was a very nice guy, had a kind and gentle personality, and certainly always helpful if need be. But he had a damaged face. One of his cheeks was normal, but the other one was drawn inside, like it had been pulled together with a string. Rosa had not gotten used to his face.

It looked so odd. However, she also knew that it was not his fault. He had been shot in the face during the war. Often she felt sorry for him.

"Yes, of course, Paul," she answered as she stood up and took his hand.

Paul was a very good dancer and led really well. He suited Rosa. She had to admit that it was a great pleasure to dance with him. But he was so odd-looking and damaged. She felt guilty for her feelings about this nice young man for he had been screwed over twice. He had not found his family since he was taken away from them and brought to Germany to work here and he had been so badly disfigured. *I'll dance with him any time, though. Poor guy he is*, Rosa thought and felt better for it.

***

Another winter had arrived. This one was not quite as dreary as those before. Some people found work in the city to which they could walk or bike as the winter situation allowed. Work on the farms was not as back-breaking anymore, thanks to so many refugees that shouldered a great part of the chores in exchange for room and board. Nicest of all were the regular meetings of Rosa and her girlfriends on Sunday afternoons. It was so nice to talk about their issues again: clothes, their cursed days, lipsticks, and the last and the next ball. However, the ghosts of the absent guys were always with them, overshadowing their natural inclination to be cheerful. But it felt good to contemplate their whereabouts together, their fates, and exploring all the possibilities of their return. Sometimes these talks gave Rosa hope again. Also, they remembered the dancing lessons at Lisa's place and Bert, Alois, Georg, Thomas and all of the others from their peer group. Once Mal, in her pragmatic and direct way, dropped a question into the middle of them:

"Whom are we going to marry now?" It was answered by silence. Until Lisa found her tongue again and offered a solution.

"Just wait, they will be back. You just have to pray more." That was also followed by silence.

Nobody could quite say how it happened, but eventually during the winter Paul and Karl were accepted into Rosa's circle of friends. It was always great fun with the two of them. The girls taught them the traditional Bavarian card games. They caught on quickly. It was so cozy on those Sunday afternoons. They could even drink the coffee-like brew from roasted grain. It was a treasure. What was strange, though, was that neither Paul nor Karl wanted to talk about their stories or anything from their homes in the Bohemian Forest. After a few attempts they were no longer asked. In turn, Paul sometimes said ever so little about the winters in his childhood world. Rosa's heart went out to him. He had lost it all and she could feel his pain.

***

Dancing in Bavaria was a firm and treasured tradition. The Maitanz was one of these traditions, which was always a holiday. Before any Maitanz, however, a Maibaum needed to be erected. Two wreaths had to be made with pine tree twigs and ribbons of all colors. Then the men fastened them to the top of tree, which had been shaved and painted white and blue. Also sausages, or satchels of candy, and gingerbread hearts were tied way up the Maibaum. Then the Maibaum was raised with sheer manpower and dug into the earth deep and tight enough that no wind could topple it. It was the idea and the challenge for the young men to climb up the smoothly shaved tree to get a treat for their girls.

The Maitanz of 1947 brought out the villagers from almost every house. It had been so long since the last Maibaum had been raised. Even the people still dressed in black came to watch. Of course, in this year there were not so many men who attempted to climb up that slippery pole to catch a sausage or a gingerbread heart for a girl. They were much younger than usual and the elders had to instruct them in the technique of climbing and warning them to hang on tight. In the end there were two young guys remaining who had not attempted to ascend: Paul and Karl. There were still some small items hanging up there. But Sepp, the father of those five children, who had walked through the village more than a year ago to his house, spoke up.

"Do you guys want to try?"

Instead of an answer Paul took off his shoes, went to the pole, spit into his hands, and jumped on the Maibaum, pressing his feet into the trunk. Cheers went up. He went higher and higher inch by inch. After unhooking a gingerbread heart at the top he slid back down, put on his shoes without haste and went to Rosa and gave it to her. Rosa blushed terribly.

"Thank you," she whispered.

"Can you reserve a dance for me tonight?" Paul asked.

"Yes," Rosa said. Neither of the two had heard the cheer going up to encourage Karl's climb.

It was a slow waltz when Paul came to claim his dance with Rosa. Under his lead she hardly touched the floor. Paul's vividly blue eyes looked at her steadily. Eventually he spoke.

"I am going to emigrate to Argentina, Rosa. I would like for you to come with me." Rosa stared at him with increasing intensity and disbelief. Slowly she understood what he had proposed.

He is crazy, was her first thought. Paul was watching her face.

"We can get married before we go, Rosa. Maybe you would come as my wife?" Paul sounded like he was pleading. Rosa's mind was churning, her heart racing wildly. *How am I going to tell him no way?*

"I don't want to get married yet." Rosa stated eventually and hoped that the little edition of "yet" would soften the rejection for Paul. "And I am not allowed to leave home," she added. That she would never go so far away to a foreign country, that she would be scared to death of it, and that she could not get used to Paul's distorted face, she kept to herself. Suddenly she fiercely missed Alois.

"I am sorry, Paul," she whispered and left him standing on the dance floor. Later she could not remember Paul's reaction to her gentle refusal as she rushed back to her table.

"I am going home," she announced to Mal and Lisa by way of putting on her coat. And she was gone. Mal and Lisa stared after her.

"What is wrong with her?" Lisa asked. Mal did not answer.

***

The following Sunday afternoon Rosa met with her girlfriends as they often did. This time they met at Lisa's farm. Rosa was hesitant to go, but was urged by Mal and Berta to come along.

"What is wrong with you? You never had a problem before to come with us." Mal asked, while she and Rosa were on their way to Lisa's.

"I don't know," Rosa replied. "It is not the same as before."

"Well, sometimes I feel like that too. But it still is fun for us girls to be together for these lousy two hours a week, don't you think?" Berta said, looking for confirmation from Rosa. Her friend, however, fell silent for the rest of the way. When they arrived the door to Lisa's place was already wide open.

"There you are, come in," Lisa shouted from inside with an inviting grin.

They settled giggling and talking around the square table in the Stube. Lisa's parents were taking their customary Sunday nap upstairs. Rosa sipped her lemonade but did not participate in the chatter very much. Instead she looked around, remembering the dance lessons they had had here in this room some eight years ago. She was reminiscing. It had been so much fun, especially with Bert, the marvelous dancer, and, yes, Alois.

"Rosa, why are you so quiet? Where is your head?" Lisa asked.

"No, I am here. But you know what? It is sunny and warm today. Could we go outside and sit under the apple tree behind your house?"

"What? In our Sunday dresses?" Mal protested. Lisa agreed with her. But Berta looked thoughtfully at Rosa.

"What is wrong with being in here, Rosa?"

"I don't like it," Rosa said, becoming upset. "It reminds me of our dancing times in here. It was so nice. And now it is empty. Nobody is here! Where are they?" She did not get an immediate answer. But then Berta came to Rosa's aid.

"I also feel uncomfortable in here. I am sorry, Lisa. Perhaps we are better off outside. Maybe we can sit on a blanket that we don't get stuff on our dresses." There was silence. Mal and Lisa looked at each other.

"Let's go outside," Lisa decided with confidence and authority. They left without giggling and chattering. Their mood had sobered up a little. Yet it was better to be together, talk about things and then come back to a cheery, giggly walk back home.

Eventually, Rosa and her classmates had learned to talk about tragic stories they had heard. They shared their fears, their concerns about those male classmates who had not returned from the war or those who were missing. They could talk about their own experiences during the Social Service time.

Of course, there were issues that were kept inside. It would take a lot longer to approach those. Rosa's nightmares had decreased, which was very comfortable. She even went along to the next important balls in the village – the Kathrein Dance in November and the next Maitanz in May 1948.

Nonetheless, she still could not enjoy the ballroom dancing as much as before the war. It just was not the same with all her classmates either dead, or being in prison camps in a far away land, or missing. It felt downright wrong to enjoy a ball, music, and dancing when the men might be suffering somewhere. But then it also seemed wrong to avoid a ball.

One day in the dying days of summer 1948, when the days were already shorter, the incredible and long-hoped-for happened. The day's work had been completed, and the family was gathered in the Stube. Jakob and Kon were smoking while each reading part of the four-page paper. Rosa sat knitting by the radio and Liz was mending torn pants. Thekla had just put little Susi to bed. As she came down the stairs there was a strong knock at the front door. Thekla was instantly frightened.

"Kon," she called her youngest brother. "There is somebody at the door. Can you open it?"

Kon came, unlooked the door swiftly and opened it. First there were a few seconds of silence until Thekla screamed. Jakob and Rosa came running and stared at the pale, disheveled, dirty-looking man standing in the door frame. He looked back at them having a tired grin on his face. He had an equally dirty bag slung over his shoulder and back.

"Let me in," Anselm said. "I am home."

Four pairs of eyes stared at him in utter disbelief.

After the initial shock, which gave way to recognizing now that both of the family's young men had miraculously returned home after six and eight horrible years away, euphoria set in. And guilt followed quickly. So far there was no other family in the village that had such luck.

Thekla took Susi out of bed again and proudly presented her to her brother. At the same time Thekla keenly felt the loss of her husband, paired with the bitterness that he would not ever come back. A few weeks later Jakob, the owner of the farm, reassured her that she could stay as long as needed despite the full house. Wherever should she go with her two children, no job, no strength of her own and destroyed cities where the jobs would be. Thus, there would be no income to raise her children.

Rosa was the happiest of all. Everybody who was back was there when she grew up. She felt comfortable and protected in the middle of her family circle. There also was more farming to do now what with so many more people to feed. Anselm's and Jakob's workload also had started to increase. Some farmers brought their horses that had been brought back from the battlefields. They needed their hooves tended and horseshoes fitted. Farm equipment had to be restored. Life had taken an upswing.

Only one issue caused her pain and sadness periodically. Alois. *Why could he not return? But if Kon and Anselm, Sepp with one leg and the father of those five children came back, perhaps Alois might just appear in the village, too. One day!*

Rosa knew that those who had returned so far had been caught by the Allied forces in France, Italy and Germany. *Perhaps those from Russia just come later,* Rosa reasoned, with a fluctuating level of hope, if truth be told. But generally she had mastered the art of suppressing those thoughts about Alois by now.

So strong was the boost from the miracle of both her uncles being back for good that she blossomed. Quickly she overcame her dreadful feeling about going to the various dances with her friends. Mal and Lisa even wanted to walk to the neighboring village that celebrated the same occasions with dances, but at slightly different times. Even Renate came along. Rosa felt safe because wherever they went to a ball Kon would show up for sure. Usually he sat with other older men somewhere and watched her. It did not escape his watchful eye that Rosa was often asked for a dance by one young man who was not a local.

His name was Gus. He was a refugee living in the neighboring village and worked on a big farm. He was a teenager when he was brought to that farm alone. He had lost his family on the long escape from the east. He did not laugh at all. Perhaps a shy smile would come from him. But he had vivid blue eyes and almost black hair. Rosa found him to be handsome. He could also dance, almost as well as Bert.

Gus became a constant in Rosa's life. He came to the dances during Carnival season. When she went with her friends sledding on Sunday afternoons during the winter he was suddenly there. He came to watch the Christmas play in the inn. He seemed to know where to find Rosa. Her friends started to tease her. Finally, the next first of May of 1949 came around and with it the Maitanz. Of course, she was going with Mal, Lisa, Berta and Renate. It was so much fun. She was looking forward to dances with Gus.

And so it was. They were an outstanding pair on the dance floor. Rosa let go of her problems and just let Gus lead her. She did not even jerk back when Gus kissed her. It was nice, actually. Then somebody clapped his hands next to them. Both Rosa and Gus looked up. Rosa's eyes stared at the man. She looked at him without recognition until he said something very familiar to her:

"May I have this dance, Rosa?" She sucked in her breath deeply with an open mouth.

She turned loose of Gus. Her arms reached out.

"Bert, Bert, Bert!" she shouted at him. "You are back," she shouted, stating the obvious.

Bert nodded at Gus and took Rosa in his arm.

"I am not so good a dancer anymore, Rosa," he warned her. "I have been in hospital for many months. I was transferred back to Germany because of my injuries. My hips were fractured and my left leg was hit. But at the end I was made prisoner of war just this side of the Rhein river. And in November or so, they let a bunch of us go home. So I have been back a few months. But I was sick when I came back and did not leave my place at all, not even to go to church." Rosa had listened silently to Bert. He did dance differently.

The fresh spark was out of his step and he had a slight limp. After just one dance Bert brought her back to her friends.

"That felt good, Rosa. Thanks. Perhaps my legs will improve still."

"I can't believe this." Mal said when Rosa sat down to take a sip of her lemonade.

When the music started up again Gus was immediately there. Rosa took his hand and gave him another dance. She did not see Bert again for the rest of the night.

***

Gradually, hesitant step by hesitant step, old habits got picked up again, as if the Maitanz had opened the door to more daring activities. The American soldiers had retreated to the cities and were seen only occasionally in rural environments. They were perceived less of a danger now. The people had accepted their presence and had gotten used to the status quo.

Thus, swimming in the pond by the forest had again become a regular activity on hot summer days. Of course, neither of them owned a proper swimsuit now. Rosa had to apply her sewing skills to create something suitable to wear for the occasion. Her friends also had to make do with various outfits. Some suits were left over from years back and thus too small. Mal wore one too large for her small frame, surely handed down from somebody. In that way, Rosa did not feel disadvantaged and enjoyed the outing. Everybody was in the same boat.

One day Gus showed up there as well. He stayed close to Rosa, but she did not allow him to attempt a swimming lesson with her. This scenario was forever connected with Alois. She could not shake the memories. They came back strongly just as they approached this idyllic area.

Gus noticed Rosa's slightly different mood. She was keeping him at a distance, emotionally as well as physically. He started to get nervous, as he did not want anything interfere with his plans. *I must act now*, he thought. She was the right one for him: she was good-looking, young and functioned as a security blanket for him. The time had come to be brave.

"Rosa, let's take a stroll. It is cool in the forest," he offered. Rosa thought this was perhaps a way to get him off her back trying to teach her swimming.

"Well, okay, but it is too cold in the shade. Let's walk along the edge where we are still in the sun," Rosa said. Gus put his arm around her and they walked off well in sight of the other bathers and friends. He waited until they came to that huge oak tree with the thick trunk. There was some long grass they could sit down on.

"Rosa," Gus started out, "you surely know that I am very fond of you, don't you? And I think you have feelings for me, yes?"

Rosa turned to look at Gus' face. Her heart had started to pound. She did not like the drift. Frantically she searched for the right answer.

"Well, I sort of like you, yes." Gus did not hear the "sort of".

"This makes me happy, Rosa. You see, I think we fit together. Don't you?"

"What do you mean?" Rosa felt alarmed.

Gus pulled her close, ignoring Rosa's resistance.

"I mean, Rosa, that I would like to marry you."

Rosa jumped up and stared at Gus. This was the last thing she had expected. Gus stood up as well reaching for Rosa's arms.

"What's the matter, Rosa? Why are you so upset? I thought you liked me as well."

"I do, but I don't want to marry you! How did you get that idea? I don't want to marry anybody," she exclaimed, staring at Gus with flashing eyes. But Gus was not somebody to take no for an answer easily.

"But Rosa, think about it! I also grew up on a farm. I know I don't have family but I can't help that I lost them on our escape from Sudetenland. I have asked the Red Cross to look for them, though. But the two of us would be the perfect pair. We could run your farm together and make it better, don't you think?"

"My farm," Rosa hissed. "It is not my farm; it is my uncle's."

"Jakob is your uncle? I thought he was your father."

"He is not!" Rosa was truly upset now. "Go away and leave me alone!" She turned around and ran to her friends at the pond.

Mal knew by one look at Rosa's face that something had happened.

"What happened to you?"

"Nothing!" Rosa snapped.

"Is it because of Gus?" Lisa inquired gently.

"Yeah, he is an idiot," Rosa shot at her friends.

"Oh, I see," Berta said. "Did he want to go into the bushes with you?"

"No," Rosa shouted, "the idiot wanted to marry me!"

"Holy cow! What did you say?" Berta asked.

"What do you think?" Rosa challenged.

"Well, good for you, Rosa. Not that one. He has tried with another one from Bergkirchen before. He just wants a place for himself." Rosa felt she was right to reject Gus in no uncertain terms. But it still felt good to get the blessings of her action from her friends.

Gus never came close to Rosa again, not even for a dance. In time the incident disappeared from her mind. Even the idea of marriage Rosa put out of her mind. It actually was that easy, for there was no man around who interested her. And Alois, Alois was still missing. *The war had ended four years ago*, Rosa sometimes sighed. They said that those who had not returned by now would most likely never come back.

Gus' upsetting offer brought back Rosa's longing for Alois. It made her mourn her lost love again. She again raged at his fate, and alternated between hope for his return in whatever condition and the possibility of his death. She did not talk to anybody about her bothersome, conflicting thoughts in her mind. It only would instigate the answer that she was not yet prepared to hear: *Forget him. If he has not returned by now he is either dead or in a lead mine in Siberia. Alois, there will never be one like him.* That she knew for sure. Perhaps, however, she really should make more effort to forget him. But marriage?

No. To whom, anyway? She was not alone with that problem. Her friends had no prospects for marriage yet either.

Rosa knew that she and her friends were expected to get married as soon as they had passed the age considered best for starting a family. Rosa was twenty-seven years old now. One time she received a shocking confirmation that she and her friends were already considered too old and undesirable by the guys younger than them.

It was one of those so enjoyable Carnival dances that she attended with her group of friends as they had done since before the war. As they sat at their table waiting for the music to start up, they heard it from the neighboring table with the village youth congregated there.

"What are these old cows doing here?"

Berta, Mal, Lisa and Renate looked at each other as if they were checking if the others had heard it as well. Rosa was stunned. But one look at her friends' faces confirmed the ugly statement had really been said. While Mal and Berta turned red Rosa's face was white as a sheet. In another few seconds she grabbed her coat and bolted out the door. She ran home and jumped into bed. Thekla heard her crying under the covers.

Rosa took that "old cow" label to heart. She questioned if it was presumptuous of her to look for a groom now at her age. Such criticism was serious and must be considered lest people would laugh at her, and that Rosa could not handle at all. She was the conformist who did not step out of the prescribed lines or asked for extras. Was it not a case in point when she was not chosen to carry the statue of Holy Mary for the Corpus Christi parade? Her size was matching the other three carriers' perfectly. She was not given a reason for her rejection. But a school mate several years older than Rosa, a rejectee herself and born out of wedlock as well, whispered to her that girls born to unmarried mothers were not entitled to carry the Holy Mary statue. Rosa believed it instantly. Moreover, it reminded her of Xaver, the out-of-wedlock boy living in the village and being raised by his aunt and uncle. He very much wanted to become an altar boy, but strangely enough he was not selected for that job, even though he would have been in line age-wise. So who was she to want a groom now when so few were available anyway?

Despite this line of reasoning, deep down in her soul something felt akin to anger. It was an uncomfortable feeling interfering with her thinking. Something was definitely not right here. Her illegitimate birth was not her fault! How come that this should be a reason to be denied certain things? Of course, she was a sinner because her mother was one. But she had been to confession often and asked for forgiveness. She was not sure if God loved her, but her family did. She knew that for sure. Well, one way to change her plight considerably was being selected by a man for marriage. Come to think of it, a marriage would give her legitimate status! It would give her value in her community.

This fact of gaining a higher status by marriage was going to be demonstrated to Rosa soon, for, unexpectedly, in April Renate announced that she was getting married. At first it shook up her friends considerably as they were unaware that Renate was in love with anybody. Renate was a school mate but not a close friend. She did not go out with her friends often, but kept to herself and her work as a seamstress. How then did she find a groom? But all the same her marriage announcement was displayed on the blackboard right by the entrance to the church.

At first Rosa could hardly believe it when she saw that piece of paper pinned up. She felt immediate envy. How come some always landed on their feet? Much later, Rosa and her friends learned that another friend, Regina, had a groom found for her. Thus, it could not be known whether it was really a love match or not. As for Rosa herself, she was not inclined to marry under such circumstances, if at all.

Holy Matrimony – A Niche for Life

Almost a year had passed since that fateful question about the presence of "the old cows". Rosa carried on with her work. As always, she loved her animals and felt that they loved her. Every calf born in their stable she took care of tirelessly. One time another farmer from the village had given her a newborn lamb, a twin that had been rejected by its mother. Rosa nursed it with a bottle, loving and kissing it on the soft white wool. The little lamb imprinted on Rosa and followed her everywhere throughout its lifetime.

Therefore it appeared that Rosa was content with her life. But that outward social side of her was deceiving.

Renate, however, was happy indeed. First off, she had found an organ player to give her piano lessons. She even was taught to play the organ – well, as much as could be expected within the short time given. Nonetheless, she was allowed to play the church organ in their village as there was nobody else available at that time.

In addition, she had even found a groom! How did that happen? It was said that somebody had acted as a matchmaker. Her groom was from a distant village further north, and that he was a tailor like Renate and a good man. It appeared to be a perfect union. Renate knew that marrying this man was better than waiting for someone she could fall in love with. Her male peer group was lost on the battlefields of that incredible war, just like Rosa's.

Renate's groom had survived because he was badly wounded and had to be shipped home to be treated in hospital. One of his legs had been torn up by a grenade. His foot was blown off completely and he walked with a limp.

Rosa's envy lessened when she heard this. She doubted that she could accept such an invalid man as a groom. What would people say? Good enough for a woman without legitimate birth? This to Renate was not an issue. Nonetheless, she would attend her wedding together with Mal, Lisa, and Berta and whoever else would come.

It was no problem to attend the church ceremony. But there was this second part of a traditional Bavarian rural wedding. It was the wedding ball dancing, which would go on from after church until the wee hours of the night. Rosa felt a bit apprehensive as she had not been dancing since the "old cow" shock. But this was the wedding of a friend, and thus a different reason to join the dancing. Maybe Bert would be there and she would be fine anyway. Since that was decided, it followed naturally that she needed a new dress. She was going to show them how beautiful and desirable she was, more than Mal, Lisa, Berta and any others. For deep down in her soul Rosa's feelings of fairness rebelled.

The following Sunday after mass the young ladies met. They had decided to tackle the wardrobe problem for Renate's wedding together as it would take some creative thinking. The wedding was set for June 1951. That was enough time to create and sew a dress.

"Good thing that that old teacher is playing the organ now. Otherwise Renate would have had to play her own wedding march," Mal said with some malice in her voice.

"Not so sharp, Mal," gentle Lisa reprimanded her. "She will have enough to do once her husband has moved into her house. What, with joining her man in tailoring, the household, and, mind you, there will be babies! And they are going to take on the custodianship of our church as well."

Rosa had kept silent all the while, as it sounded that this was not going to be a bed of roses for Renate. Nonetheless, she was going to be a respected married woman, Rosa thought enviously.

"What are you going to wear for the wedding in June?" Mal brought up her most burning issue.

"Well, a summer dress, a nice one," practical Berta said. "I did get that pink one last summer for Corpus Christi Day. I'll wear that."

"I don't know yet," Lisa said. "I'll probably ask my mother for money to buy material and make myself a new one."

"I have my flower dress and my polka dot dress," Mal mentioned.

"Wear the flower dress," Rosa suggested. "Everybody has a polka dot dress." *It will make you look much heavier*, Rosa thought maliciously.

"And what about you?" Mal asked Rosa.

"Don't know," Rosa answered.

Secretly Rosa had already designed a dress for herself in her head. She had asked Thekla if she could remodel that beautiful dress of hers that she had not worn in years. It was of a wonderful turquoise color and the fabric made a rustling sound with every movement the wearer made. The color would match Rosa's green eyes. She knew that this would be very much to her advantage. She would have to take the dress in to fit her own slim figure, which made for an even wider skirt that would flare out wonderfully when dancing. Thekla had already agreed! But she was not going to tell her friends all that. She would surprise them and hopefully blow them away.

Almost feverishly Rosa and her friends had been waiting for Renate's wedding day, the first wedding for one of their classmates after the long war and when the fun things of life had almost come to a complete halt. When finally that June day had arrived Rosa and her friends stood in a row lining the path Renate and her wedding party had to walk into the church. But first the young ladies reacted with various expressions of awe to Renate's magnificent self-tailored wedding dress.

It was as white as the cherry blossoms in May. The upper part of her dress was tight around her figure, thereby emphasizing her youthful breasts. But most breathtaking was the lace, which was a gift from Liz. The skirt was wide and floor-length, covering even her shoes. To top everything off, with her beautiful blonde hair she had made two thick braids wrap around her head like a crown. There somebody had fastened the four-meter-long train, which was carried by her two five- and six-year-old nieces.

For the church service Rosa was allowed to take her six-year-old cousin Susi along. The little girl watched mostly in silence, but when she saw her two little play- and school mates carrying the train, she shared her thought with Rosa.

"Rosa, when you get married, I want to carry your train," she said to her grown-up cousin.

"Sure," Rosa answered evenly.

After the church wedding ceremony, the bridal party went to the local inn where the ballroom was all decorated and ready for the midday meal and the dancing that was to follow. In the evening, traditionally, the villagers could join for the rest of the day and night. Rosa and her friends had agreed to meet for the evening dancing at Mal's place and walk into the ballroom together.

Rosa was very nervous about entering the dance hall. She walked in behind Mal and Lisa. But once inside she scanned the guests and calmed down. She should have known that there were people of all ages attending except for children. This was a wedding after all, not a Maitanz. Still, Mal wanted to sit at the only table still available right next to the dance floor. But Rosa had spotted another place a bit further back and convinced her friends to sit there. Shortly after they had settled down the music stopped and the dancers left the floor. Rosa looked around. She saw Bert sitting further away and talking to some older farmers. Hopefully he was going to see her. Over by the open window stood Hans, Alois' younger brother, smoking a cigarette. *He looks like a grown man now, not like a boy,* Rosa thought.

The music started again with a big bang but switched immediately to a slow waltz. Franz, an older man from a farm outside the village, was approaching their table. Rosa's heart sank. This was not the kind of guy she wanted to dance with.

"May I have this dance, Rosa?" he asked politely. Rosa knew that it was an insult to refuse. She did not dare to do that and accepted. As she left she saw that Lisa was also asked by an older man for the dance. However, Franz turned out to lead really well. She began to enjoy the slow waltz. After it ended Franz asked to add another dance, this time a fast polka. Franz had no problem with the tempo. Rosa was in her element and enjoyed the dance. The evening looked promising as far as dancing itself was concerned. Rosa relaxed a little more.

When the music started up again Rosa saw with utter pleasure Bert walking towards their table. With expectant, sparkling green eyes she watched him approaching. *His limp has improved*, she thought.

"There comes your favorite dance partner, Rosa. Aren't you lucky?" Berta said.

"Shall we, Rosa?" Bert asked with the grin of familiarity on his face.

Rosa jumped up and took Bert's outstretched hand. Her turquoise dress rustled as she walked with Bert to the dance floor, her head held high. Surrendering to Bert's lead with easy confidence, she was totally happy, just like she did when they were teens. It was wonderful. They stayed on the floor dancing through three different dances until Bert confessed that his leg was hurting.

"I cannot dance anymore for tonight, Rosa. I will sit with those two farmers at my table talking for a while longer and then go home." Almost as an afterthought and as if to comfort her he asked Rosa:

"What is it with you, Rosa? No groom in your life yet?"

"No," she said simply. But Bert knew about Rosa and Alois.

"There is nobody like him, Rosa, huh?"

"No," Rosa said again, as her eyes filled immediately with tears.

"Does anybody know what happened to him?"

"Not really," Rosa said. "Berta said that he went missing somewhere around Stalingrad. The Red Cross is looking for him. But they have not found him yet."

Tears were running across Rosa's cheeks. Bert put his arms around her to help her hide them.

"That is the worst, when we don't know what happened to them," Bert tried to comfort her. "But don't close out the future because of the past, Rosa. I think there is a man in this ballroom who is a few years younger than you, but that does not matter. He has been watching you all evening. Give him a chance when he comes to ask you for a dance. His name is Sepp. His father owns that big inn in Hartdorf."

"Was he in your unit?" Rosa asked Bert. *How come he is back from the war and without a scratch?* Rosa was wondering.

"No. He is a bit younger than you. He was one of those kids drafted at the end like Alois' younger brother. They were sent home by the enemy as soon as they saw them. This is not to say that Sepp was not lucky to come back unharmed."

Dumbfounded, Rosa watched Bert walk back to his table.

"Rosa, what was that all about?" Mal asked.

"What?" Rosa turned to her friends as if she had just remembered that they were here. "Nothing!" Rosa responded without thinking.

Presently Mal, Lisa and Berta were taken away to the dance floor. Rosa sat at the table alone sipping her soft drink. When they returned, the dance floor was cleared for the last dance for Renate and her new husband. After that they were going to leave. But the dancing could continue even without the newlyweds.

"Let's leave after their bridal dance," Lisa suggested. Berta and Rosa readily agreed.

"There are only old men anyway," Mal added.

But as soon as the first notes of music were played after the bridal party had left, a tall man with dark, almost black hair suddenly stood in front of them, looking at Rosa.

"May I have this dance before you go home?" Rosa looked at him in surprise.

"Did Bert not tell you? I am Sepp. I am from Hartdorf." And Rosa remembered.

"Yes, he did," she admitted in a quiet voice. "Okay, one dance only," Rosa said boldly. "I don't like to have to go home alone and my mother would be mad if I came back so late."

"If you like I can take you home. Can you tell your friends that?"

Rosa did signal to Mal that they should not wait for her. With raised eyebrows her friends left.

Rosa realized immediately that Sepp was as good a dancer as Bert. So it became three dances, not just one. He kept on looking at her, which made her a bit nervous. Then Rosa insisted she had to leave. Sepp took her to the front gate of her farm.

"This Sunday there is a summer dance in Niederkirchen. Would you come with me?"

To Rosa's own surprise she agreed.

"I'll pick you up with my motorbike. Take a jacket for the ride." He hugged her quickly and left.

Rosa went to bed with churned-up thoughts in her mind. She knew she had to get up at five am to help milk the cows. The milk had to be in huge, heavy metal containers and placed out on the side of the road where the milk truck would pick them up and leave the exchange containers from yesterday. Thus, Rosa tried to will herself to sleep without much success. The dances with Sepp kept intruding her mind. And it was a pleasant feeling. The dances with him were superb. He led with ease and his hand on her back had felt comforting. It had actually given her one of those goosebump showers that she had experienced a long time ago. Yes, she was looking forward to go dancing with Sepp again next Sunday. Finally she fell asleep.

All the next week Rosa took a little longer to drift off into dream land. In the warmth of her bed she questioned her meeting with Sepp again. He was probably three years younger than her and she did not know him well either. With Alois this had been entirely different, although Rosa pushed this thought aside quickly. This was no more! Truth be told, she had felt comfortable with Sepp at Renate's wedding ball.

He was good-looking as well. Actually, she was looking forward to see him on Sunday night. It was just to get to know him a little better, of course, just to check him out. But she was nervous as well, nervous also to admit to her mother that she was dating a guy without her friends coming along. But then, to her own surprise, Rosa felt a bit angry at the thought of her mother forbidding her to go. *I am an adult. I have been away from home to do my Social Service year. Why should I not go?* It was a rare moment of defiance she felt. It was a recognition that she did not have to hold her head and her wishes down. Others did not either, like her friends. Most significantly, she was no longer the only one without a father. Rosa's moment of contemplation came and went, but it would surely come up again.

Until Sunday Rosa fluctuated between courage and anxiety. However, when she heard that motorcycle approach the front gate of the farm and then stop, she did not hesitate. She grabbed her jacket and put it over her rustling, wide skirt dress and left the Stube without a word. Neither her mother nor Jakob made a comment. Only Thekla shouted after her, "Have fun!"

Rosa, the enthusiastic and skilled dancer, enjoyed the hours on the dance floor with Sepp. Dancing was easy with him. He also was attentive and almost protective of her. When a few of his friends and acquaintances saw him with this beautiful, green-eyed woman they made appreciative gestures. He even agreed to allow two of them a dance with Rosa. *I think he is proud of me*, Rosa thought with surprise. At midnight, when she then asked to be taken back home he agreed readily without making a fuss.

He drove his motorcycle slowly through the summer night to keep the wind down as he did not want Rosa to get sick. He stopped and turned off the motorcycle at Rosa's gate. Both stood facing each other until Sepp reached for her and drew her close, putting his arms around her. He pressed her to his chest and tried to kiss her. Rosa struggled strongly to be released from his arms. Something was wrong. All the courage with which she had started out had suddenly left her. Her heart was pounding wildly. She did not want to be kissed. This seemed wrong to her. She felt embarrassed and sorry for Sepp. But she could not help herself. Her feelings suddenly had gone haywire.

"What's wrong?" Sepp asked her, annoyed. Rosa gave him the first answer that came to her mind.

"I don't know, I can't. Not yet."

She did not want to tell him what she just had realized herself. She had remembered Alois's kisses at the same place. Without agreeing on another date they separated for the night.

For the next three Sundays Rosa listened out for that deep sounding rumble of Sepp's motorcycle to stop in front of her gate after dark. Her emotions were totally unsettled. She liked to go out with Sepp, but she also was fearful of his reappearance. She relived the nightly scene from three weeks ago. Had she been right to refuse to be kissed? Had she insulted him? Was she too complicated? Why could she not take it easy like Mal or Lisa? But she knew that she had to avoid that kiss from Sepp. It suddenly seemed so wrong when she remembered the last kiss from Alois and his written plea to wait for her. What was she to do?

Well, Rosa did nothing but wait for the motorcycle sound in the evenings. Sepp did come by in irregular intervals. He even had become a bit bolder and picked her up after lunch time in broad daylight. This caused Liz to implore Rosa before she left with Sepp to be back at five to help with milking and feeding the cows. Kon's reassurance that he would take over Rosa's part did not change Liz's request.

It was summer and Rosa enjoyed the rides. What with the warm weather they took tours to ponds, lakes and rivers further away. Rosa had declined to go to the pond by the forest where she had been with Alois and her friends. Sepp had tried to kiss her again and she had let him, but did not respond. Sepp looked puzzled but did not approach the issue. Rosa felt confused about herself but remained passive. On rainy days, and they were plenty, Sepp mostly did not show up. She did wonder, however, what he did on those rainy Sundays, but did not ask. She was in a state of indecision. Often she would go to Alois' farm to visit his sisters. She also enjoyed activities with six-year-old Susi, who could ride a bike by now. In winter they had great fun sledding together with Hans and all the other village kids. This was always a lively and lighthearted time with the kids. Moreover, it kept her from thinking about Sepp.

One day in spring of 1952 Thekla wanted to take Susi to her first movie in the county town. The town had recovered from the bombings to a considerable extent and actually had even two movie theaters now. Thekla invited Rosa to come along.

"Oh, I want to come along," she exclaimed. "Are we going to be back in time for the milking?"

"You would be a bit late for that," Thekla guessed.

"Then I need to ask Liz first," Rosa said.

"You do that right now, Rosa, and then tell me that you are coming with us." Rosa went to find Liz.

Everybody owned a bike at that time. Susi had a brand new bike for adults, which had the saddle lowered so far that she could sit and pedal. And she biked with great and careless skill. "Watch, watch, slowly, stay behind me," Thekla shouted at her daughter almost throughout the eight-kilometer ride. Neither Susi nor Rosa had asked what the movie was all about. Who cared! It was exciting just to go to a movie theater first time. It was a documentary film featuring the life of Albert Schweitzer. Susi was partially frightened by some scenes and held on to her mother. Rosa just stared at the screen in wonder. She really enjoyed herself.

***

When the next Maitanz was held in Rosa's village, Sepp came midweek to ask Rosa to let him take her. Rosa was pleased and looked forward to the dancing. She could hardly wait to tell Sepp that she had been at the movies. She guessed he had never been at one such theater. But more importantly, he then will know that she had spent Sundays without him in great fun. He must not think that she would sit at home and wait for him. Rosa had guessed right: Sepp was astounded that Rosa had gone to the movies at all and even without him.

"That is something we both could do, Rosa," he said with muted enthusiasm.

"Oh, yes, of course. We just need to look at the newspaper to see what is playing and when." Rosa looked at Sepp triumphantly. She did know things he did not.

"Okay, I'll do that," Sepp volunteered.

That was the beginning of a love for movies that they both shared. Rosa bought a program for each film they saw. Keeping that habit roughly for the next two decades she collected inadvertently a history of the post-WWII movie scene in Germany.

Sepp and Rosa developed a habit to see films on weekends. Even in winter they went on Sepp's motorcycle heavily bundled up. Movies and dances were mostly the occasions for them to meet. However, there were also sporadic Sunday afternoon outings. Sepp tried time and again to have a more intimate relationship with Rosa. But he did not succeed. Rosa still did not feel any great pleasure to kiss him, as far as he could tell. However, he had fallen in love with her. He had hope because Rosa questioned him about his whereabouts when he did not show up on some Sundays. Rosa was undecided about Sepp, but she liked to see him a lot. She was even confused about her own reactions. This, however, was to change soon.

One Sunday afternoon Berta came over to visit Rosa and whoever else had come to that bench under the walnut tree in front of the gate to Rosa's farm. It was often a social gathering place for the neighbors on Sundays. One time, when all others had left, Berta remained. Sitting next to Rosa, she told her the latest news she knew about Alois.

"We have received a letter from the Red Cross," she said with eyes filling with tears.

Rosa's heart started to beat faster. She stared at Berta.

"They can't find him, neither dead nor alive," Berta continued. "They had found a survivor from his unit – actually, his officer. He had seen Alois last before they approached the area of Stalingrad. He was sick then with badly frozen legs. Apparently a group of Russian soldiers had taken his boots from him when he was thrown on the ground by a stray bullet. The officer thinks that Alois might have died from that, as it was winter in the steppes and brutally cold. And that's where his trail is lost. His unit was driven into a run when grenades and shots came to them. They don't know anything about him beyond that."

There was shocked silence after Berta finished talking.

"We will never know what really happened to him, Rosa," Berta added.

After a period of stunned silence and both women's eyes almost fixated with terror Berta turned to leave.

"It's late. I have to go help with the milking."

"Me too." Rosa whispered as if she was hoarse. But she did not go to the cow stable. She went to her sanctuary behind the barn to let go of her tears. This was not the final blow that Rosa and her unwavering love for Alois received. It followed on Memorial Day in November.

The village, like most villages in Bavaria, had erected a shrine on the graveyard right next to the gate into the church building. It had a long stone plate fastened to the back wall. All the men's names of the village who had been killed in WWI and all who remained missing had been chiseled into the stone plate. Every year on Memorial Day there was a ceremony in honor of them. There were wreaths laid down and a three-shot salute was fired. Then the flags would be lowered and that incredibly emotionally stirring song "Once I had a Comrade" was played. Every year at that point Rosa observed her female family members cry together with many others. It always frightened her to see her mother cry. She did not like that day.

In this year the shrine had been renovated and a new black stone plate, longer than the first one, had been added. When "Once I Had a Comrade" was played and the three salutes had thundered off, and the echo had been thrown back from the forest, there did not seem to be a dry eye amongst them all. Rosa was trying to hide her distress as she remembered Thomas, Georg, and the rest of her friends and school mates.

After lunch she went back up to the graveyard to look closely at the new plate and all the flowers without anyone else present. She read through all the names on the new WWII plate. Each one stood for a man Rosa knew. She howled loudly by herself when she found her male classmates, entirely, on that list. Finally, she saw Alois' full name on the missing soldiers list. She started trembling uncontrollably. Her tears streamed unhindered down her cheeks. This was the time and place when she finally started to accept that the love of her youth was not to return.

Alois was lost forever in the depths of Russia.

This time she did not run to her log behind the barn. She went into the warm Stube where her mother and the rest of her family had gathered on a Sunday afternoon. She made no effort to hide her pain. And no-one asked. Only Jakob spoke up.

"It will get better in time, Rosa. And life will go on. You are young still." Rosa was twenty-nine years old.

It was just as well that Sepp did not call on Rosa for the next two weekends. She had no desire to see him. Her grief to let go of Alois was with her every day. Coming to a closure with her love was something she knew she had to do; but her mind and her heart did not work together on this.

When one early December evening she heard Sepp's motorcycle stop outside the gate, she felt disturbed. Yet she did grab her coat and went outside to see him. He grinned at her apologetically for not having called the past weekends. "I have a free evening, Rosa. Shall we go somewhere?" He asked quietly.

"I don't feel like it tonight, Sepp. I actually don't feel well at all. Can we postpone it?"

Sepp felt a bit surprised. Usually Rosa came along spontaneously. What was this tonight? He had no idea what was the matter with her. *Perhaps it is wrong to stay away for so long each time. I need to pay more attention to this courtship,* he thought.

"Okay," he agreed with Rosa. "It is pre-Christmas time in our Gasthaus and we have several large functions the next weeks until New Year's Eve. My next free day is probably New Year's Day. I would like to see you before then, Rosa. Please say yes."

"Yes," Rosa said automatically.

"I'll see you then," Sepp said, reaching for Rosa's hand. He pulled her closer and kissed her chastely on her cheek. Without any emotional charge she simply let it happen.

For the next few weeks Rosa worked with great intensity alongside Kon. He taught her detailed skills and knowledge about agriculture and dairy business. She liked that. As she was an animal lover in particular, she was enthusiastic about watching the birth of a calf. She petted the mother and the baby alike. Kon had to keep her back from rubbing the baby calf dry.

"That the mother needs to do herself," Kon instructed her. "For if she refuses the calf, we have a problem."

Rosa owned five cats by now. She was the sole caretaker of them. And when the little kittens played wildly with each other Rosa finally laughed out loud.

"Susi, come and look," she would call her young cousin.

A week before Christmas Eve in the local inn the school was having a Christmas play. Susi was to sing a Christmas song solo on stage. Rosa went with Thekla to watch. Mal, Lisa and Liz also showed up. It was great fun. It was a nice pre-Christmas time. Rosa's spirits lifted. But the nicest day and evening were still to come.

Since Thekla had come back home with her two children, Christmas had become even more special as it usually was anyway. Folklore demanded that when it was dark Thekla took little Susi out to walk through the snowy street on Christmas Eve. They had to watch the star-covered sky in hope of seeing the little Christ child fly through the star-sprinkled heavens to visit all the children in the world. It would bring them a Christmas tree and gifts. While Thekla and Susi were outside, Rosa and Hans had to decorate the Christmas tree in a hurry and put the gifts under it. Then the two walkers in the Christmas night came back in from the cold and, voila, the Christmas child had been here! Rosa loved that tradition with Hans and the sparkling eyes from everybody. Everybody had a smile and everybody received one or two gifts. It was the coziest time in her family. On Christmas Day everybody attended church service. Rosa especially loved to hear her community sing "Silent Night, Holy Night" with the church organ playing along and all the many candles burning.

After Christmas she suddenly remembered Sepp. She was anxious. He said he had a day off on New Year's Day. She realized that she actually wanted him to come.

Sepp did more than keep his word. The sound of his motorcycle stopping outside the gate reached her already on New Year's Eve. It was completely quiet in the Stube and everybody had heard it too. Rosa put on her warm jacket and went outside without a word.

"Rosa," Sepp greeted her. "I can't spend this night without you. We have a ball at our inn. I need to work. But I thought you could come with me and just be there. At least we would be in one place together. And I would take care of you anyway. Perhaps we can even get a dance or two in. What do you think? Are you coming?" Without thinking Rosa agreed.

"I need to change and dress warm. I won't be long."

She changed in a hurry. On the way out she stuck her head into the Stube and announced to all that she would be celebrating with Sepp till the New Year came in at midnight. It was but a short ride on the motorcycle. Still, Sepp drove slowly to keep the icy wind down and to make sure he did not slide on the snowy road to his home.

Rosa sat at the bar most of the time. Sepp came by often on his way to the kitchen or to wait at a table. He kissed her quickly and asked what she might want. A few times she was asked for a dance from men she knew remotely. All in all she had a good time that New Year's night. When Sepp stood next to her during the countdown to midnight she was pleased. He kissed her with passion at midnight and wished her Happy New Year, looking into her eyes. She felt good in his embrace. 1953 started out well!

"Would you like to spend the night and I can take you home tomorrow?" Sepp asked, trying to keep a tremble out of his voice. Rosa felt a hot wave going through her.

"Not tonight, I can't," she shot out quickly. "I have to be there to do my chores with the cows early tomorrow morning."

Sepp understood better than she realized. But he also had heard her say "not tonight".

"Tomorrow we are closed. Could we go see a movie later in the afternoon then?"

"Yes," Rosa said.

Sepp helped Rosa to pack her up tightly. With careful and slow driving he took her home through the cold winter night.

The following days Rosa's thoughts kept on returning to Sepp. She almost surprised herself with her mental stocktaking of Sepp. With a bit of disbelief she became aware that she actually liked him a lot. Remembering his kisses and embrace made her still feel warm and protected days after it happened. *He was kind and attentive to me*, she thought. *He made sure I was warm and safe on his motorcycle. He was not pushing me. And, not to forget, he did not ask me about my father!*

Sepp did come on New Year's Day to take her to town for a movie. However, his motorcycle slipped on ice, but neither got hurt. Rosa had torn up her winter boot and felt very distressed about that.

She would have to answer to her mother. After all, she had provided Rosa the funds to buy those boots.

Since that incident, Sepp came every Sunday afternoon to go places with Rosa until she had to be back home for the milking and he had to help his parents with the evening guests at the inn. When winter temperatures went below freezing, Sepp finally asked Rosa again to come home with him. It was just too cold on a motorcycle. In his room it was warm and cozy. Rosa agreed while her heart beat faster. She knew she would be committing a sin. But she did not care too much anymore. There was confession available to clear her sins. She only worried about her mother and the village people. They would be down and unforgiving on her for being a loose woman. Even though she was very cautious that nobody found out about the loss of innocence between her and Sepp, she knew that in this village nothing stayed a secret forever.

However, she was unaware that at least her family was on her side. Her uncles did not ask anything. Jakob and Thekla had implored Liz to refrain from her attempts to keep her daughter restricted with curfews, and moral and religious threats. *She is all grown up and she should get married now if she did not want to wind up as a spinster*, or so their reasoning went. Rosa had fallen in love again. That not only was her right, but it also was about time.

Rosa and Sepp spent a wonderful summer together enjoying their feelings for each other. They went to the movies, went to summer dances farther away, and they made love out in the meadows. Only when Sepp wanted to go swimming in little lakes and quiet rivers did Rosa feel uneasy. She came along but did not like it when he wanted to float her along in the water. Rosa had little time for her friends. She saw Mal and Lisa only when their paths crossed by way of their village lives or on Sundays in church. Renate was a new mother and had no time for her friends anymore.

There was only one pain during that summer that Rosa felt deeply. Her nephew Hans had to move back to Passau to attend an advanced education school. She had watched him during his babyhood, and she had watched him when his mother was pregnant with his sister. Later he had followed her around during the hard times of war and after war times. He had become a playmate to her when he got older. She was very attached to her nephew and he loved her. Rosa felt very sad about his departure and considered it a loss. Nobody could tell what the future would bring and when he would return. The only consolation was that his vacations would be spent at the farm. That had to do for now, as the day of his departure had not come yet. There was still time to prepare for that day.

Sepp did not quite understand Rosa's sadness when she told him. But he did try to kiss her tears away and she was grateful for that. Their relationship had become closer over the summer. She felt very comfortable with him and loved him for what he was and how he treated her with kindness and respect. She did not get upset when he wanted to know about her father. She told him that her mother had given her only the most minimal information about him. He lived in another village further away, but she did not know where and he was not an issue in her life at all. There had never been any contact and there never would be any.

When in late summer the weather turned moist and cooler and the days grew a bit shorter, Sepp and Rosa had to find warmer places, such as cafes and bars and, of course, Sepp's room at his parents' place. One still warm and sunny autumn Sunday they sat in the grass at the edge of the forest overlooking the valley. The Alps were clearly visible. It was a melancholic day. Sepp put his arm around Rosa's shoulders and turned her to face him.

"Rosa, we should think about getting married," he said to her. Rosa's eyes widened in surprise, even though she had had that thought herself. Playfully, though, it had been. But this was serious now.

"You think so?" Rosa managed to stutter.

"Yes, I do," Sepp responded. "Don't you?"

"I think I would like that," Rosa mumbled, looking down.

"Rosa, look at me," Sepp demanded, putting his index finger under her chin to make her look at him. "Rosa, I think you just said yes."

"I think I did, yes," Rosa smiled at him. Sepp threw his arms around her and held her tightly to his chest. They both started laughing. They would get married!

"Okay," Sepp finally said. "Give me a bit of time to bring this to my parents."

Rosa had already decided that she would not reveal the news to her family until Sepp had his parents' agreement. For the next few weeks they would carry on as usual. Rosa, however, went around like living in a dream. She would get married after all. She would even be the next one to follow Renate. No matter that he was a few years younger than her. He was good-looking, comfortable to be with, and they got along well. It was nice and comfortable between the two. And imagine, not only by marriage but also by becoming the lady of that inn she would get the status and recognition she always wanted. *Just like Renate*, she remembered.

The following Sunday Sepp did not show up. Rosa was not particularly worried. After all, it was still harvest time and work was plenty. Instead, her mind was mostly preoccupied with an upcoming separation.

The day of Hans' departure had arrived. Her cousin Hans, the very one whom she did babysit the first time in Munich when he was barely walking, was preparing to leave home. Over the years they had become very close. Sharing a bedroom with him and his family often made for nice chatting before falling asleep. But now this was all coming to an end. Rosa experienced this painful loss acutely. She hugged him goodbye and bravely tried not to cry.

The weekend after Hans' departure Rosa did start to feel concern about Sepp's no-show. It was Saturday and she considered riding her bike to his house Sunday afternoon. This had been their usual date time anyway. Before she could make a decision on Saturday evening well after dark, she heard the familiar tune of Sepp's motorcycle stopping outside the gate. Without hesitation Rosa took her sweater and went outside. Thekla, Susi and Liz had already retired to their bedrooms, and her uncles were at the local inn for a beer. She greeted him with a kiss. He kissed her back fleetingly, and sensitive Rosa felt the difference immediately. She leaned back and looked questioningly into his eyes. Sepp did not hold her gaze. He looked down.

"You look nice, Rosa. How have you been?"

"Fine," Rosa answered and told him briefly about Hans leaving home. "But what about you? It is quite a long time you stayed away. Everything alright?"

"Actually not, Rosa," Sepp said, still looking down. Rosa's eyes widened.

"What is it? Come on, talk!"

"Well, let me hold your hand." Rosa complied but felt also alarmed.

"I had told my parents that I want to marry you. And they said they do not agree with this. I was surprised and started to argue. It turned into a violent shouting match. So I have to tell you that we cannot get married, Rosa."

Now he looked at her and squeezed her hand hard. Rosa jerked her hand back. Without a sound she had started crying. Her heart thumped furiously. *No, this is not true*, she thought, *he is teasing me.* She kept on staring at him. Finally, she shouted out at him:

"Why?"

"My parents like you, Rosa, but they said they have another bride for me, one who will bring a very large dowry into the family and our inn. They figure that you would not." Rosa was speechless. She had not figured the dowry matter at all.

"But surely, Uncle Jakob and my mother Liz would provide me with some sort of dowry," she tried to argue desperately, not knowing if she actually could expect any.

"Well, that was not their only point," Sepp informed Rosa further. "They said that one also does not know who your father is." Sepp could not see how Rosa turned pale and stopped breathing and crying for a moment.

"They threatened to disown me if I marry you against their will."

Sepp was quiet and just looked at Rosa. She stared at him with her eyes swimming in tears.

"You see, Rosa, I cannot marry you. I feel terrible about this but I came to tell you that we cannot go on. It is over."

Rosa stood motionless a few seconds. Then she started to step back, turned abruptly and rushed through the gate and into the house. She did not look back or hear the motorcycle drive away.

Rosa went straight upstairs to her bedroom. But she did not go to bed. Instead she turned on the big ceiling light. Thekla was awake instantly. Rosa's face was red and awash with tears. She started talking immediately, telling her aunt what just had happened. Susi was sitting in bed by now looking at her utterly distressed cousin. Rosa did not care having woken her up. Eventually Thekla would soothe Rosa enough to go to bed and tell her to "sleep over it". Rosa followed her aunt's advice. However, she knew that the next day would be no different. The pain and shock were too great. The second time in her life she had fallen for a man and into a disastrous end. Tomorrow she would start another kind of life without Sepp. She was grimly determined to fight the humiliation she felt and to keep her pride and dignity.

After a night of crying spells and fitful sleep Rosa still got up early to do her work in the cattle stall as was expected. Her face appeared mask-like. She kept her head down, avoided eye contact with everybody, and spoke only when addressed.

"Rosa, don't fret over it so much. You will get over him. Things always look up again," Kon tried to console her. She did not react at all. In fact, she was afraid of reliving the whole memory. It was just too painful. She was determined to hide her feelings and what she considered her shame. But she also felt an unfamiliar sensation rising.

For Rosa, it was not humility anymore but pride and fury. *He did not love me as much as he had said. That son of a bitch had an issue with my father! After all these years!* For the time being Rosa dealt with her tumultuous feelings alone and entirely inside. *Work is the best medicine, they say. Well then.* She tried to keep her sadness hidden away while holding her head high.

Work that fall was plenty. There was the harvesting for the potatoes, the cabbage, the nuts, and the fruits from the trees in the garden around the house. Two days were spent to thresh all the wheat, barley, rye, and oats. Those days were always quite cheerful times as a few more people were hired to help. It left not much room to rehash how Sepp had ended their relationship and the ramifications for Rosa. As every year in fall the cows were driven out into the meadows to graze. Rosa still knitted pure wool socks and gloves for everybody in the family. However, she did not like the quiet, tranquil environment any more.

Sometimes Lisa, watching her farm's cows on the other side of the valley, and Rosa met midway. That helped to direct Rosa's thoughts away from her grief. But the best distraction for Rosa was Susi, who was now nine years old. Often she stayed with Rosa out on the meadow. She also liked to knit. Rosa helped her and taught her the craft. She also, occasionally, told her stories about her childhood, her youth and the war. Susi was an attentive audience. Rosa liked her around.

"It was a nice time," Rosa told Susi at the end of one of her tales.

Movies also gave Rosa peace of mind for a few hours. Every weekend she read the advertisement for each movie theater in the two small towns reachable by bike. Mostly she found what she would like to see. Often, Rosa would take Susi to an age-appropriate film. Susi was a skilled bike rider. After the movie and before they rode home they would go into a café for coffee and cake. These rides to the cinema on Sunday afternoons enabled Rosa to ban her sorrows from her mind.

One time in late November of that year Rosa again went alone to see a film. She was a bit early but nonetheless went into the theater as it was already cold outdoors. As always she bought a program describing the film and the actors. She was reading it when a man came and took the seat next to her, even though plenty of other seats were still unoccupied. With a bit of concern she turned her head to look at the person. Her heartbeat leaped forward dramatically and on the spot. *Sepp!* She was speechless and just stared at him.

"No," she yelled sharply.

"Rosa, please," Sepp pleaded, "let's watch this together." Ignoring his words, Rosa jumped up. Sepp did not turn to let her pass.

"Let me out," Rosa shouted. She was aware of other visitors watching the scene, but she did not care.

"Let me pass by," she yelled again. Slowly Sepp stood up to let her go.

Rosa almost ran out of the theater and on to her bike. She pedaled furiously once she had cleared the town limits.

"You are already back?" Liz remarked with raised eyebrows when her daughter came home.

"Yep," Rosa answered and went upstairs to change her clothes.

Thekla was in their still common bedroom, writing a letter to Hans, when her niece stormed in. With astonishment she saw almost instantly that Rosa was not sad but furious. That was unusual with her, almost new.

"Rosa, was the movie bad?"

"Sepp was there," Rosa hissed. Nothing more was said, and Thekla knew better than to keep probing further at this moment. She understood enough. Her niece had developed pride. She was not going to be a mistress ever. Rosa never mentioned Sepp again until Susi was almost an adult.

Pride and Dignity

One year had passed since that fateful evening when Rosa and Sepp's marriage plans had come to an unexpected and abrupt end. For all close observers like her family and her female friends, her pain of rejection was visible on her face. She was subject to quite rare mood swings. Often she did not participate in family discussions and stared into space. When she suddenly joined in conversations, she did it in a new snappy mode that surprised everybody. Of course she was reprimanded for it, especially from her uncle Kon, which made her feel bad. But her angry explosions happened again and again. This was not the Rosa that one knew from before. In time, however, she did find a bit more equilibrium. But her snappy, sharp verbal ways remained.

Rosa put on a brave face all along. She rejoined village life like nothing had happened, such as joining church services on Sundays and holidays. She also participated in church celebrations. Of course, she did not attend any of the Kathrein or May dances. Although, neither did her friends attend anymore on the grounds that they were no longer considered young. On the surface Rosa seemed to be healing from her emotional wound. Only Thekla knew differently. Frequently she heard her crying in her bed. Thekla only had told that to Liz but kept it completely to herself otherwise.

Rosa had also taken solace in her cats. Especially the young kittens, for they could cause her to forget her pain for a while. When they played with each other out in the cow stable, charging through straw and hay, one could hear Rosa laugh.

In late fall, after Sepp had ended their relationship, a farmer asked Rosa if she would accept a little lamb to be raised by hand. The mother sheep had bore twins and rejected this one. Rosa agreed without hesitation. It was a gift that gave her great pleasure. She raised it with a bottle and loved it dearly. The lamb for the rest of its existence followed Rosa everywhere. Rosa could sublimate and shower her rejected love over her animals.

During that time of her slow return from the pain of rejection, a man, Blasius, a few years younger than Rosa, came one Sunday afternoon to speak to her. Since he was from the same village as Sepp had been, he was not unknown to Rosa. He also had been drafted towards the end of the war. It left him with hand grenade splinters in his face. The scars were on both sides of his mouth. He showed Rosa pictures of his time in hospital where he underwent several operations. Still, scars remained and his mouth was a bit twisted when he talked. He said he had watched her in church and, in general, knew about her. After all, the two villages had always been close. He said he would like to marry her, if she would take him with his scars. Rosa was surprised. But quickly she knew her answer.

"I like you as a person and could imagine a friendship. But I don't intend to get married ever." Rosa felt a mixture of empathy and defiance when she told the man her decision. Blasius sighed.

"Yeah, I was afraid of that," he responded. "I know that women don't want me what with all my scars and my crooked mouth." That statement presented so sadly made Rosa feel even worse for rejecting him. After all, she understood rejection well. But she did not change her mind. She could not even imagine another partner after Sepp. *No, I cannot, never again.*

Rosa did not give this proposal a second thought. Yet that event had shaken her a bit, pointing out the raw spots in her heart. Obviously, that unhealed place in her needed to be protected and buried deep inside. And she knew ways to accomplish that.

It became a habit for Rosa to take Susi along with her. That way nobody could accuse her of being out on the loose, looking for a man. There was the annual State Fair, or the Carnival parades in late winter. They both biked to the river on warm summer evenings just to watch the bathing scene from the bridge. Rosa was not willing to undress in public and never learned to swim. If she was seen by a person from the village she would explain that Susi wanted to come.

However, Rosa's relationship with her young cousin was not always comfortable for her. When she was in one of her defiant, negative moods she would turn on Susi. One time when Jakob had a visitor in the Stube, Susi was reprimanded from her adult cousin for making too much noise and acting too fresh forward.

"Keep quiet, Susi," Rosa whispered in her ear. "Who do you think you are? You are not that important here." Susi looked dumbfounded at Rosa, then put her head down and kept quiet for a while. She felt degraded and hurt. Eventually she left the room.

Such puzzling occasions came up repeatedly. When in spring of 1954 there was a traditional street market in one of the small towns in the county, Rosa and Susi meandered up and down the main street with all the stands. One day Blasius suddenly stood in front of Rosa, greeting her with a smile. He started a conversation with her, to which Rosa politely responded. Susi stood by happily licking her ice cream. When she was almost finished with it Rosa turned to her abruptly and asked:

"What? You have to go to a bathroom?" Susi looked surprised and replied with the innocence of a child:

"No. Why? I did not say anything." Rosa flashed her eyes at Susi and made her understand that she just had made a blunder. With that Susi realized that Rosa wanted to get away from that man.

"Oh yes, actually, I do need to go," Susi complied.

In early summer of 1954 another event took place that caused Rosa to come out of her lethargy. It helped her find a completely new and, for women of that time, unusual interest. It was the second

World Soccer Championship after the war that was taking place in Switzerland. Germany had qualified and was participating in it as well. That fact raised Rosa's attention to a sport she had never considered an issue. People were excited and she caught the hype. Game after game the German team played she followed via radio. It was understood that work did not stop because of a soccer game, championship or not. It was summer after all, a busy time for these farmers. But radios were blaring out open windows everywhere. When Germany won the final game and became world champion, Rosa was euphoric.

"We won, we won," she chanted, jumping up and down out in the field where she just happened to work with Kon. Tears of joy followed. Her mother, her uncles and Thekla looked puzzled. Soccer championships or any other sport events did not mean a whole lot to them. It was nothing they grew up with. But since she, and everybody else for that matter, remembered the championship-preceding debate if Germany should be allowed to enter the competition at all that victory had taken on an additional meaning.

"We did it, we made it," Rosa stated repeatedly. She talked as if she had been instrumental in bringing about that victory. Civilization had triumphed over madness. A wounded and beaten soul saw light at the end of a dark tunnel. Hope was regained!

From that day on Rosa was a soccer fan. She was interested in all national and all international games. Every Sunday evening she watched the sport report no matter what. Mal, Berta, and Lisa shook their heads at Rosa's fanatic soccer interest. Of course they teased her. But this time Rosa did not care. Soccer was not only her hobby but also an uplifting support for her inner peace. It had come to stay.

In September of that year Rosa, by way of looking through the Saturday newspaper, found the announcement of Sepp's wedding. It was to happen in his village. After church there would be the wedding meal and dancing in his parents' inn. Rosa was pale and unusually quiet on his wedding day. Almost the whole day she felt her elevated heartbeat while her mood fluctuated between sadness and fury. She did her various tasks with vigor adhering to the motto, *Work is the best medicine*. But once, when she had a break, she went behind the barn to sit on her log again. There she could listen to her inner rage and feeling of betrayal and rejection. Yet the day passed eventually. Pride rose in her mind about her strength of having gone through it without anybody seeing her cry. *Not because of you*, she thought defiantly.

It was fall again, and, as every year, the cows were let out every afternoon to graze on the meadow. It was still Rosa's job to stay out there and watch them. She did not mind. She had, as in the years before, her knitting with her. Moreover, Lisa also was still on the other side of the valley on the hill with her cows. And as before, they met in the middle to talk and gossip. Only this time Lisa had some news for Rosa that took her by surprise: Lisa had been connected to a somewhat older man and he had found her to be the bride he was looking for.

"I'm getting married next May," Lisa announced with a smile on her face. The news took Rosa's breath away. She had taken Lisa's single status for granted.

"What? Who is the man?" Rosa exclaimed. Lisa explained how her parents had known this man for a long time, especially since her father had often played cards with him in the pub. Lisa had found him to match her needs and wants and she agreed to be his wife. She knew better than to wait for the miracle to find a partner her age, as it was obvious that war had taken them all one way or another. With this man, after all, she would be the lady of the house of another farm in Moosding. Yes, he was twelve years older than her, but he was still good-looking.

"Why are you marrying him?" Rosa asked incredulously.

"Why not?" Lisa returned the question. "There are not too many around for us, Rosa. He is a good man; he has only a hidden scar left from the war and he has a farm in Moosding." Lisa tactfully refrained from asking Rosa about her potential wedding plans.

Rosa accepted Lisa's engagement with trepidation. To her it meant losing support as a single woman. But then there were still Mal and Berta and her sister. She was not going to be the only one "left over" whom no men wanted.

On Lisa's wedding day in the first week of May 1955 a warm spring sun rose on the horizon. It lit up the baroque church in Moosding beautifully as if it were a good omen. Mal had talked

Rosa into at least joining church services to see their friend getting married there. They went to the first row of pews on the balcony right below the church organ and the choir. Mendelssohn's famous piece of music thundered through the church when bride and groom slowly walked to the altar. Lisa was dressed in a white, floor-length wedding gown with a train just down her back. The groom was in Bavarian traditional finery suited for a wedding.

"This groom," Mal whispered into Rosa's ear, "is much older than she is."

"Yeah, I wouldn't marry him." Rosa whispered back. "But she said that he was a good man with a farm and that we can't hope for young men our age."

"Yep, that much she is right. How did she find him, though?" Mal was wondering.

"Don't know. Her parents connected them." Rosa replied.

The ceremony had started and they both went silent. Rosa's mind was churning. *No, I would not want him*, she thought. She was not envious. But she did have to swallow her tears throughout the wedding service, remembering what could have been for her. She also suddenly thought of Renate's wedding and Susi's wish to carry her train. She never will, Rosa knew. How lucky she was that Mal and Berta also had no wedding plans, as far as she knew.

After the church ceremony Mal and Rosa joined all the other guests outside the portal lining the path the newlywed couple had to walk through. This was a chance for many to offer congratulations and best wishes to the couple. Lisa took each of her friend's hands with a happy smile on her face.

"Thanks for coming," she said to Rosa and Mal. "At the latest we will see each other again in mid-September when Bert has his wedding." With that she turned and shook other guest's hands.

"Mal, did you catch what Lisa just said?" Rosa asked her friend with big, round eyes, expressing confusion and surprise.

"I heard her say that Bert is getting married after harvest time in late September this year."

"No, I don't believe that. How would she know?" She challenged Mal in disbelief.

"Well, Rosa, he is distantly related to her, which is why he is a guest at her wedding."

Mal pointed further back towards the church gates. "Look, there he is," she exclaimed. Rosa's head whirled around. Indeed! There was Bert, who approached them with his slight limp. He smiled at them both.

"I hope you also come to my wedding in a few months," he said. But he only looked at Rosa with almost pleading eyes. Mal's eyes darted back and forth between Bert and Rosa.

"Look at that," Mal uttered in surprise. Bert had moved on.

"Mal, another one of us is getting married! I won't be going!"

"Oh yes, we will," practical Mal said with determination.

***

It did not take Mal a whole lot of effort to talk Rosa into attending Bert's wedding.
However, she did not know that Bert had caught up with Rosa one Sunday after church to invite her personally to his wedding.

"You have to come, Rosa, please." Bert pleaded. "Not only to church but also later to the dance. It would mean a lot to me. We have to dance together again. At least one waltz with you on my wedding day, Rosa. Can I count on you? I'll be waiting for you!"

Rosa succumbed to Bert's intense look in his eyes staring into hers, and just nodded. But something puzzled her. On that same day Rosa asked her mother for some money to purchase material for a new dress. She found green rustling material that matched her beautiful green eyes almost perfectly. She made herself a ballroom dress with a daring cut as she saw it and tight long sleeves. September was not a hot month anymore. The skirt was wide and would swing nicely during a waltz.

Yet, she was in a nervous state of mind. After all, she had not been at a dance in a long time. But this one she could attend as it was Bert's invitation, which legitimized and negated the "old cow" issue. Moreover, Mal, and even Berta, would be with her attending the evening wedding ball.

Bert, after the wedding, would just move from his home farm to another a bit further away. He still would belong to this village. So Rosa did not have the intense feeling of loss as she did during Lisa's wedding.

Finally it was evening and time to go to Bert's wedding ball. Rosa knew Bert's wife and felt comfortable about her, as she was a very quiet woman. Together with Mal and Berta, Rosa was able to enter the ballroom, albeit with the loud heartbeat of anxiety.

There were many people already. But they did find a place to sit together with another unknown couple at the same table. Bert and his wife sat at their wedding table, which was decorated with many fall flowers. Rosa gradually lost her nervousness as she was asked for dances by various men from the village. She began to enjoy the dance movements almost like during her youth before the war. Her face flushed from exertion. She looked radiant and beautiful. She saw Bert dancing with his wife and a few more times with other women. Rosa was aware that he often sat down. *It must be his leg*, she thought.

The evening had already progressed late into the night when Bert came to her table just like in the times before the war. He stretched out his hand for her.

"Rosa," was all he said. She took his hand and walked to the dance floor with him. It was crowded and Bert pulled her close to him. Silently they danced the promised waltz. When it ended Bert kept holding Rosa's hand.

"One more slow waltz, Rosa," Bert pleaded.

Rosa had felt heavenly in Bert's arms and his lead. He had looked at her almost constantly. Rosa had completely forgotten about Bert's leg injury from the war. Apparently he had done the same. The music started again. Bert put his arm around Rosa's waist and held her other hand in his ever so gently but firmly. He pulled her close again.

"It could have been us, Rosa," Bert said, looking intensely into her eyes. She searched in his to read out of them the meaning of what he could not have possibly said.

"What do you mean, Bert?"

"You still have no idea?"

"No," Rosa said, puzzled.

"I mean, Rosa, that you could have been my bride today," Bert whispered. Rosa slowly began to comprehend Bert's words and the loving expression on his face. Her eyes grew large looking at him. Her face flushed, her heart started to beat stronger. After a time of stunned silence and Bert waiting for a response Rosa said:

"You never did or said anything that would tell me what you thought about me, the fatherless woman! Or did I miss it all the time? Why did you not tell me anything?"

"You know why, Rosa. I was afraid and actually certain that you would turn me down. You had only eyes for Alois."

"You knew?" Rosa asked naively.

"Of course I knew. I watched the two of you all the time. I had no chance with you, Rosa. Yes, I was a coward as well."

"Oh my God," Rosa exclaimed. "But why then did you connect me with Sepp?"

"I knew you were grieving for Alois and I thought Sepp would not have a chance either. I firmly believed that. Unfortunately I was wrong. Word went around that it was a very serious relationship with him. I mean, you were much courted, Rosa. Why would you want me then? I figured I was your favorite dance partner but nothing else. And then I had this limp. I was damaged goods. I was not sure of myself at all."

"Oh my God," Rosa said again. "I think I would have said yes to you, Bert."

"Please don't tell me this now, Rosa!" Pain and surprise was written on Bert's face.

"But one thing I want to impress upon you and us for that matter. I'll always look for a dance with you, Rosa, forever. I hope you do come to at least some like the Maitanz or somebody else's wedding dance. And if you need me you know where to find me. We will see each other. We live in the same village district. There is something else I would like to tell you. It burns inside of me. Maybe some day I still will do that. But today is not the right day for that."

He kept her hand in his and walked her, like the gentleman that he was, back to her table. Before Rosa could sit down he had turned and walked back to his new wife, leaving a devastated Rosa behind.

***

Rosa, Berta, her sister Theresa and Mal met fairly regularly since Lisa had left their group. During the summer months on Sundays they liked to meet casually in front of Rosa's farm gate. There was a bench under a walnut tree just made for such gatherings. Sometimes they walked to the forest where they had met with the American soldiers, retelling stories of that time. Often other people from the village would come by to sit or stand around that bench under the walnut tree and chat. It usually was a nice social time on a Sunday afternoon. In the colder months of the year they gathered indoors either just for social time or to help each other with crafts projects. But only Rosa went to see movies, if need be also alone and with her bike. Movies had always had a healing effect when Rosa had problems. This time, after Bert's surprising revelation to Rosa, it helped but marginally.

***

Rosa had always enjoyed the traditional female crafts of knitting and sewing. With the complicated pattern she used, it also could take her mind off her turbulent emotional life and gave her some inner peace. Thus she had taken over the production of sweaters not only for herself but also for her three uncles. That was no small task, for her uncles were tall men. Every day throughout fall and winter she sat evenings at her table in the warm Stube. The radio also was placed on that table. Rosa operated it to her liking until Jakob demanded to turn to the evening news. One of her cats usually slept on her lap, covered by the knitting.

She turned out to be very ambitious in terms of producing sweaters with complicated patterns and first class woolen yarn for her three uncles. Her skills improved, and gradually she became known for her knitting craft in the village. Often she was asked for advice by other women, and this made her very proud and happy. In addition, each summer she cut and sewed herself at least one new dress. She had good taste. When she wore one of those creations to the state fair even Susi remarked that so many men and women were looking at her. Of course, Rosa enjoyed the looks and walked holding her head high. Nobody knew that she also was vigilant not to run into Sepp and his wife.

In this way Rosa lived a quiet life. The church had enough holidays to make life not so boring. Rosa took Susi along almost everywhere she went. Susi loved Rosa for that and happily went along. The bond between these two cousins developed as strongly as the one between her brother and Rosa. Susi and Rosa were absolute movie fans and went to many, which Susi was barely old enough to be allowed in. But the highlights in terms of entertainment were the annual visiting circus and the district fair. On warm summer evenings they both still went with their bikes to the bridge over the river, looking down at all the swimmers in the river. Still, Rosa never suggested to enter the river herself. She still could not swim and had no desire to learn it. Only Alois would teach her. Without him, why would she want to go swimming at all?

Hans came to the farm during holidays and his annual vacation time. That always was a fun time for the three of them. Rosa was fair game for her cousin's activities. One time she even tried to ski. Hans got a new pair of skiers from St. Nikolaus. He went the next day to try them out down a rather flat slope to the west of the farm. Rosa took Hans' old skiers that had old, fixed bindings with a spiral around the heel of a ski boot. She did not think twice to go on those skiers with rubber boots. She used broom handles for ski poles. Hans laughed and laughed until he caught his breath and shouted after Rosa:

"No, no, Rosa, you'll get hurt! Are you crazy?" Rosa let herself fall into the snow when she picked up too much speed and stayed in one uninjured piece, laughing.

Rosa was supportive of her cousins. This sometimes required her to go to the Gasthaus, where she had had her great time as a dancer and where she also had heard the question what those "old cows" were doing here at the dance. Susi each year was participating in a Christmas play, and each year Rosa went with Thekla to see it and to applaud. Then she remembered also her own roles in nativity plays when she could not be Mary. Rosa was content to watch Susi play Mary or the Christmas angel, despite her own history in that matter.

Then came a time where Rosa's fragile inner peace was badly shaken. One evening in January Liz sat by the wood-burning stove freezing so badly that her hands shook.

"Are you that cold?" Thekla asked. Liz just nodded her head. Thekla became concerned.

Jakob urged Liz to lie down on the couch. Rosa watched her mother. Liz was covered with her top cover from her bed and told to sleep here in the Stube as it was warm. The next morning Liz was dangerously ill and almost unresponsive to her siblings' queries. Kon ran to the pub, as it had the only telephone in the village. The family physician came within the half-hour. He diagnosed Liz with pneumonia, with both lungs affected. Liz was closer to death than life. She was carried to her bed, which was warmed up with hot water bottles before. The bedroom door was kept open to let warmth drift in.

"If you want a priest," the doctor said to Jakob, "you should do this soon. Otherwise call me late afternoon in my practice. For now I have done everything I can. Now we need to wait and see. I'll come back after practice time."

And so it was that the local priest came. This horrified Rosa.

"Thekla, she is not going to die, is she?" Rosa wailed.

"The priest is just a precaution, Rosa. The doctor said he is confident."

This was not much consolation to Rosa. She was devastated. It had never occurred to her that she could lose her mother. Thekla tried to reassure her niece but with little success. But Thekla was a veteran of horrors and suffering. Even though she was also extremely concerned about her sister, she did not forget to take care of practical things. Being also concerned about Rosa's state of mind, she tried to get her niece to engage in work that needed to be done.

"Rosa, stay with me. We both need to cook lunch today. Go and help Kon now with the milking. You have to take over part of your mother's chores in the shed. When you are finished we have to start cooking the meal."

"Thekla, I don't know how to cook! I never had to do it!" Rosa said.

"Yes, I know, you have been let off that hook. But don't worry, I am here. We will do this together."

Thekla and Rosa worked well together in matters of preparing meals for the next three to four weeks. During that time Thekla confirmed what she had known about Rosa for years: she did not enjoy cooking at all. Whenever Rosa saw a chance to get out of the kitchen she did so gladly and promptly. She listened and made an effort to learn from her aunt. But she never tried to acquire more knowledge about fine cooking than absolutely necessary. *This is not good for you, my dear niece*, Thekla thought.

Liz recovered, although it took a long time to regain her strength to take over her chores such as the cooking. When she was finally well and strong again and cooked the family meals, Rosa never went to the kitchen to assist. Everything was as before. She felt relieved that she did not have to cook.

When Hans left for Passau after Christmas and New Year's holidays Rosa felt quite sad. She was crucially aware that he would always only be there for brief visits. He would never come back home for good. And during summer break of 1956 he would even move to Munich to live there. That surely was for good. Now Susi was subject to the same issue, which stuck out like a sore thumb. What was she going to do? She could not stay here for her education. But for her it was not time yet. *I am not going to think about this*, Rosa decided. For a long time now she had kept her balance by ignoring, suppressing, and plain not thinking about painful issues. There were still two years for Susi here.

At that time Rosa did not know yet what Jakob had in mind and how he would provide for social life to come right into the Stube. One day in late autumn of 1956 Rosa came back in from watching the cows on the meadow. Immediately when she entered the cozily warm Stube she saw that the radio was gone. Instead, another much bigger apparatus stood in its place.

"What is that?' she exclaimed, even though she knew exactly what it was.

"I bought a TV," Jakob answered with a grin on his face. Kon and Anselm watched Rosa.

"We don't need it," Liz remarked. Later she watched TV all the same.

Thus Rosa's family owned one of two TV sets in the village at the time. It was a sensation! The news was circled in the Sunday pub scene. Soon it brought visitors to the house.

When the next international soccer match was shown, Rosa had a lot of company to watch it. Anselm brought a group of men with him from the pub. Uncle Jakob would tell Rosa to bring more chairs and an additional bench into the Stube. Suddenly the room would be filled with the hum of voices. Cigarette smoke soon would hang in the air.

Everybody cheered or lamented as the goals were shot or missed. It was a new spectacular way of a soccer experience. Rosa loved it with the exception that her cats fled the place.

Eventually people came to watch other sports events. Figure skating seemed to be a favorite for men, women and children. Rosa was looking forward to such events. She loved to have a house full of lively visitors, every one of them from the village. Some of the mostly younger men extended compliments to Rosa or made other verbal advances by way of teasing her. She enjoyed it but was otherwise oblivious to them. And if need be, she would put those in their places as she once did during the world championships in figure skating.

"Man, are these great, good-looking women," one unhappy man remarked once. Rosa sat up straight and turned to him while speaking to all:

"These are also great men and you guys are not," she hissed. There was a brief silence in the Stube until everybody started to laugh. But Rosa looked stern.

"Did you hear that? Rosa, don't be so touchy and mean," one man said to her. He surely expressed what others thought. What had happened to that shy girl? She attacked like a snake had bitten someone.

One August day in 1958, Susi had to leave for a boarding school in Munich. On the day of her departure she tearfully said goodbye to her uncles and Liz. She did not want to leave, but Thekla had repeatedly explained to her that there was no other choice.

"Not to worry," her mother tried to comfort her. "In three weeks you can come home for the weekend. Hans is going to pick you up at the school and bring you."

Rosa, however, was not present to see Susi off. Kon hollered her name. She came around the barn looking distressed. She did manage to shake Susi's hand, saying:

"Why can you leave and I have to stay here?"

"I would like to stay, but I can't," Susi answered.

"Be off," Rosa said roughly, "but be back in three weeks!"

Every family member had witnessed that exchange, although nobody mentioned it again.

Despite her occasional sharp verbal attacks, Rosa was content with her life. She liked the village events and the social life available to her. Moreover, Berta, her sister Theresa, and Mal stayed close friends. They still discussed issues as before. They shared her single status, which comforted Rosa a lot. Together they joined an exercise group that met once a week on the dance floor of the local Inn. When a Tree and Gardening Club was formed Rosa together with her friends became a member. Rosa already had taken over the vegetable garden from her mother. With Liz's advice she produced a considerable variety of vegetables successfully. Her products fed her family with the freshest greenery. Simultaneously her knowledge about horticulture improved by leaps and bounds. The Tree and Gardening Club was mostly a welcome activity and reason to get together with friends and neighbors.

However, Rosa got more and more ambitious in her gardening activities. She enjoyed the competitive aspect of it. Eventually the Tree and Gardening Club awarded her first prize for the flowers hanging from every one of the twelve windows of her home. She had never won a price in anything and was astounded that she should have won over all the others. She kept that ceramic trophy all her life in a glass cabinet.

However, in the middle of her regular and content life, two events were approaching that would change that peacefulness drastically.

***

Hans had not lived in a nuclear family since the bombings of Passau and his father's death. He was fed up with living in a single rented room as a subtenant in the city. He wanted the family life back he once had enjoyed as a boy. He also was aware that his sister Susi had always lived in the extended family of their mother, save for a few months as an infant. Quietly he had investigated the market in Munich. One day he presented his mother with the flat he had found, thinking that this was the right place for her, his sister and himself. The building that was housing that flat, however, was still under construction. Its completion date was set for summer 1960.

"Oh, come on, I don't believe it," Liz exclaimed when her sister informed her about the pending move. Fifteen years of residence on the farm threatened to come to an end.

"And I don't believe it either," Rosa said. Her statement, however, was not as firm as her mother's.

"You have been here for all these fifteen years since the war. Why would you want to leave now? Susi is already gone and at the right places for her further education. And Hans is doing fine in Munich. Do they need you still?"

In this fashion Rosa kept arguing, trying to change her aunt's mind. Finally, Thekla put a stop to it, lest she indeed would have had second thoughts.

"Rosa, listen, we are only going to Munich. We are reachable any time. You can come and visit anytime. You have visited us in Munich before when Hans was a baby. We are not out of this world."

Rosa finally realized that she had lost her case. She reacted with sadness and anger. Thekla had been her mentor and supporter often. When her mother was cross or tried to hold her close to home, Thekla put in a word for her. She had been her safe place when she felt the pains her life had put her way. That was not going to be so readily available any more. Rosa was not a brave traveler anymore. The thought of travelling to Munich frightened her.

Yet, when the moving van came and drove out of the farmyard and Thekla and Susi said their goodbyes, Rosa was prepared. She put on a controlled face. Her eyes were swimming in tears.

"We will be back for a visit in two or three weeks," Thekla promised, to make light of the issue.

Indeed, all three of the "Munich branch" showed up after three weeks. They stayed for the whole day. It was almost like nothing had changed, at least for the day. When they left in the evening Rosa felt better. It looked like her loss was not going to be as huge as she had feared. However, the two-to-three week intervals did not quite materialize over the next two years. Their visits were spaced further apart. But they did come for sure. This continuity of sorts appeased Rosa a lot. She was not going to be dropped and forgotten by people she loved.

***

The family was concerned about Liz. Since she had recovered from pneumonia she had resumed her usual chores of cooking and milking. But over the last few years it became apparent that she never got her full strength back. Generally, she seemed to be short of energy and tired easily. Worse, her cough had not abated. Liz tried hard to hide her suffering. She went to church as she had always done before, even though her coughing had sounded very loud during mass. It also was an effort for her to kneel but she refused to "demonstrate" weakness by sitting instead.

One Sunday in January 1962 on her short way to church, she slipped on some ice and broke her hip. For days she resisted her admission to hospital. But the family physician visiting her at home became very stern when he realized how badly she was injured and how it was sapping her energy trying to clear her chest lying down. He called the ambulance and had her taken to hospital with the permission of the family. But Liz was very sick already. Before two weeks were over she passed away.

In Munich Thekla received a card with two short sentences from Rosa:

> *My mother has died in hospital. Please come to her funeral.*

It was followed by the date of church services. Thekla was acutely aware that Rosa called Liz "my mother" in her note.

The next day Thekla and Susi, now seventeen-and-a-half years old, took the train to the farm. They found the men in a somber, but calm mood. Rosa, however, was shaken by crying spells throughout the day. Her eyes appeared huge and haunted. In addition to her grief she was extremely frightened. Bit by bit over the next few days Thekla learned about Rosa's realization that she was expected to take over her mother's cooking and household duties. For this, however, she was ill-prepared as she never had shown an interest in such domestic chores. Especially cooking, which she had not been called for and had always avoided. She was always an outdoors person. Her anxiety of taking care of her three uncles by way of taking over from her mother was sky high.

"I can't do this, Aunt Thekla, I can't," she shouted. Thekla and Susi stayed on for almost a whole week to ease Rosa into her new responsibilities. Rosa's grief about the loss of her mother had given way to severe anxiety. One more time Rosa was reminded of the circumstances of her birth and existence. With great bitterness she shared her feelings with her aunt.

"How did you like the priest's eulogy at the grave?" Rosa asked without waiting for an answer from Thekla. "It was good, wasn't it? He said that she was a selfless mother to her siblings for all her adult life, and that she had worked hard without complaining. But he avoided mentioning me, her daughter, totally. It was as if I did not exist! Still a sinner, wasn't she? But then, why am I so disturbed about it? It is true I should not have been here in the first place." Rosa's face was distorted with pain.

Thekla, hiding her anger at the priest, tried her best to console Rosa.

"He cannot help it, Rosa. He is a priest. He might not even think this way deep down in his own heart. None of the other people there feels this way nowadays. And we, your family, have always wanted and loved you. You must know that, don't you?"

Rosa did not answer but her tears, indicating her feelings of rejection and disappointment, started to subside. She brought up the subject a few more times with Susi and Hans and then no more. It was another issue she buried in the depth of her soul.

For the next year Thekla visited the farm often to help her niece to adjust to life without Liz. She taught, assisted, and supported Rosa as much as possible. But she also impressed upon her brothers to refrain from criticizing their niece and to be patient with her. Kon especially showed much understanding and when possible helped Rosa with the preparation of lunch, their main meal of the day.

A few months later Rosa's shock of losing her mother also raised fears she might lose one or two of her uncles. The first time ever she considered that Anselm or Kon could get married. She was particularly afraid Kon might leave the house that way. Anselm had affairs but Kon showed no signs of a woman in his life. Rosa was not brave enough to ask Kon about marriage plans. Anselm was easier to approach in that matter.

"Me, how could I get married?" Anselm asked. "I have not learned anything proper. I spent eight years in foreign land fighting for my life. I did not have time to get a diploma from anywhere. How do you think I should support a family? I am ashamed of myself. So don't ask me about this crap again, Rosa. I've had enough of leaving home!"

From that alone Rosa concluded that she had three uncles to take care of, as it was the custom in those days. Her anxiety of not living up to that job stayed on, albeit with lessening terror. Again she was badly needed in her family. Only this time she felt ambiguous about it.

Over the years Rosa got the hang of running a large household in addition to her work with the animals and the outdoors work of planting and harvesting. But she never developed a love for cooking. Whenever Thekla came to visit she would ask her immediately to take over the kitchen. Thekla always agreed and Rosa was out the door at the end of Thekla's "yes, I will."

Eventually Rosa was asked by her friends and other women of the village how she liked being the lady of the house. It caused her to think about the answer. How indeed did she feel about it?

Actually, it is not bad. I am somebody, I am important. I have some money now, Rosa thought. She realized that she had an elevated status in the eyes of her peers. That felt real good. She was more of an equal to other women. So she actually could join them when they took those bus trips in the summer, could she not?

Rosa's immediate neighbor, a woman with a small household, one day tried to persuade her to take a trip with them. And Rosa gladly did. Kon assured her there was not too much to do right now and he would cook for his brothers. One Wednesday morning a large bus stopped in the square in front of the farm gate. Most women had been waiting there for thirty minutes already. Rosa was very excited when she boarded the bus.

"Come, Rosa, sit with me," her neighbor shouted. And off they went to a big lake in the Alps. They were gone all day and came back after dark. Kon started to get nervous. Never had Rosa been gone for so long on her own. This was a first. He stood outside waiting for the bus to arrive. When he saw Rosa walking up to the entrance he was aware of the big grin on her face.

"It was so great," Rosa said. "I did not even want to come back yet," she explained.

"Well, you better do," Kon laughed.

Many trips were to follow this one. Every summer and into the fall Rosa joined every trip of the three per season the women organized.

Thekla kept up her visits to the farm, albeit now in irregular intervals. She had become one of Rosa's anchors. Susi was busy with her education and did not accompany her mother every time. This annoyed Rosa, for she closely watched her cousin's development. She still felt jealous at times that Susi could pursue education with the goal of a professional career. But she still loved Susi and thus was also vigilant that her cousin did not make the same mistakes that she herself had made. Or at least, it appeared to Rosa that way looking back. So one time when Susi came along for a visit again Rosa asked her:

"Susi, have you been kissed already?" Susi hesitated to answer.

"What is it to you, Rosa?" Susi said.

"Well, not much really. But I think you should be aware that you are already twenty years old. Don't you have a boyfriend?"

"Rosa, quit that," Susi said in a louder voice. "I surely don't have to be in a hurry! I want to finish my studies."

"Your studies? Well, do that. But I am telling you that between twenty and thirty you have to get married. After thirty no man wants you anymore," Rosa threatened.

"Rosa, are you kidding me? I don't believe that!"

"You mark my words, Susi – don't miss it. Without a husband you have little value; with one you have more status in life." Rosa said.

"Don't worry, I won't. I might not want to get married at all."

"You will wind up a spinster! Look at me, and Berta, and Mal!" Rosa said and walked off.

In the summer of 1965 Rosa learned that Berta's feared spinster life would end after harvest time. She had connected with a much older widower. After meeting him and looking at his property, Berta accepted the proposal.

She would live in another county, too far away for a casual bike trip on Sundays for a visit. It was going to be a very small wedding at her new village and neither Mal nor Rosa was invited to a traditional wedding celebration. In October a small van drove into her farmyard. Berta's relatively few belongings were loaded in a few hours and the van drove off. Berta came with red-rimmed eyes and a handkerchief in her hand to say goodbye to her friend and neighbor since they were in first grade.

Berta's sister still came most Sundays to that neighborly gathering on the bank under the nut tree in front of Rosa's farm gate. That was very good because the numbers of people appearing for a chat had dwindled. News about Berta was spread that way. Rosa listened eagerly. Mal also contributed her part to gossip. Her source was the village inn. She had started working there Fridays, Saturdays and Sundays. There Mal also learned that Elke, a physical therapist, was offering an exercise evening for women working primarily physically to counterbalance potential damage to their bodies. It was to take place every Wednesday evening on the dance floor of the inn. Quite a few women liked the idea a lot and signed up. In the end and with Mal's urging Rosa joined as well. She soon loved the activity and the get-together for a refreshing beer after exercising a lot.

Rosa developed a closer friendship with the wife of a farmer who had his farm a bit further away. The wife came to the village mostly to attend church services or to shop for groceries at the village store. Now she had become a regular for that Wednesday evening exercise group. Usually she had a cool drink with the other women after the exercises before she went home. However, one Wednesday Rosa came home spitting mad at that woman. Aunt Thekla and Susi were on the farm for a visit. As soon as Rosa entered the Stube she started to tell Thekla in a most animated and agitated fashion what just had happened to her in the inn.

"She is so stupid," Rosa started out, sitting at the large family table. Her three uncles had not come home from the inn yet.

"What did she do?" Thekla asked.

Rosa tilted her head to one side and tried to emulate her friend.

"She said, 'I have to ask a kind of a dumb question.'" Rosa acted. "'Who actually is your father?' the dumb idiot asked me!"

"How tactless," Thekla exclaimed.

"I said to her that this was indeed a really dumb question to ask," Rosa hissed. "I said that it has not mattered for all these decades and it does not matter now. She did not know what to say and just looked dumb. And nobody else asked either," Rosa said in triumph.

She had put everybody in their place and the matter to rest. She was actually proud of herself for speaking up in a loud voice. No more shame, and no more humiliation!

***

After that incident in her exercise group Rosa applied the method of her success more often. She was much more willing to be confrontational, to state her opinion in no uncertain terms, and to be in verbal attack or defense mode whenever the case required. At times she could be quite charming about it. Even her formerly shy ways in dealing with authorities Rosa seemed to have overcome. She proved that with an unsuspecting victim much to the pleasure of her family.

It happened when the third and smallest of the three buildings that made up the farm had to be demolished and rebuilt. One man from the building permit office in Traunstein had come by, bringing with him another man from the Monument Protection agency. It was their job to make sure that something of architectural or historical value was not demolished. They inspected the building, a very old shed for chickens, pigs, and firewood, inside and out thoroughly. Rosa had to stay with them. Gradually, though, she lost her patience with them. "How long will they still take?" she asked.

The man from the building permit office tried to explain the importance of their job and thus to calm Rosa.

"This man," he said, pointing at the guy from the Monument Protection agency, "he came from Munich for this." Rosa, unimpressed, answered promptly:

"Yeah, that's what he looks like, too!"

***

On the surface Rosa appeared settled and at peace with her life. She was no longer afraid that one or both of her uncles were contemplating marriage. No, they would stay and thus Rosa felt protected and connected. She knew that they loved and appreciated her in their own ways. And at long last, Rosa had mastered being the one running the household, standing her ground against three men. She enjoyed her social status. Taking care of the farm's animals was still the essence of her life. She loved them all: cows large and newborn, chickens, lambs and her cats. But whenever there was a bus trip scheduled from the rural women's group, or from a neighboring village, she turned her duties over to Kon for the day and off she went. Actually she went along with many excursions, being to check into a health spa for a day or any other trip that would go for a day. She loved to go south into the Alps.

"Every time I have to leave the mountains I am sad," she confessed.

She lived one day at a time and avoided to think about her future.

"What good does it do?" was her defense when Thekla or even Jakob raised the issue. "Can't change anything anyways. Best not to think about it and make yourself scared."

While this philosophy of hers worked well most of the time, it did not stay unchallenged. Life itself disturbed her peace time and again.

It took her breath away when Anselm came home from the inn one Sunday evening with the news that Siegi was going to marry Mal.

"What?" Rosa asked back. She knew that Anselm sometimes came home a bit drunk.

"You heard me," he said to Rosa, "I am sober, believe me."

Indeed it was true. Rosa went at once to Mal's place. She lived alone there now as her parents had passed away and her brother had long before moved out.

"Yes, I am going to marry him. Are you jealous?" Mal snapped defensively.

"But what do you want with him? He is a widower and he is too old for marriage and he sits in the pub every evening."

"Because it is better with him than without him. I don't want to discuss this, Rosa!"

Well, suit yourself then, Rosa thought. *At least he is moving in with her here. That means she is going to stay. That's good!* The latter fact was calming to Rosa as she would not be the only one of her group to be single. She herself would stay she knew for sure. Never would she marry. She did not even dream about it. Life was good the way it went. It was good that Mal did not even have the slightest celebration outside her family. That also was a good thing, for Rosa was saved from having to attend another wedding.

***

For the next nine years Rosa lived the regular, quiet, undisturbed life she had set up for herself. There was the farm work, her animals, her gardening and her exercise groups, the regular trips into the Alps, and her soccer interest, which she shared with many in the village. But the challenges for her to adjust to new situations came in her way again.

In summer of 1979 Jakob, the owner of the farm and blacksmith workshop, died unexpectedly. Rosa was shocked. A pillar of her life's structure had gone. Kon, Anselm and Thekla all grieved with her. She was not alone. It was a huge funeral. Jakob had been liked and respected in the area. Rosa felt proud that her uncle's funeral was drew such a large crowd of people from near and further away. It even was reported in the newspaper.

However, there was another big surprise that initially she found hard to believe: Jakob had left the farm to her and Kon. Anselm had to receive financial compensation.

It took Rosa a bit of time to see herself as land and property owner. She had never owned anything of substance. Now she was a woman of some means. Rosa felt pride and dignity rising in her self-understanding. Being part owner of the farm now told Rosa that Jakob had loved and appreciated her work on his farm. She held her head high. Not only had she proved that she had been important to him, but he also changed her into somebody to be reckoned with.

However, for Rosa there was one more issue that changed with Jakob's death. She was acutely aware that her family size was declining. A few times she vented her fears to Kon and Thekla, only to suppress the issue again as was her habit with things she did not like. Yet, challenges were ahead and did not let the subject rest.

In early spring of 1983 Anselm started to have problems with dizziness, speech and comprehension. He also got easily angry at his brother or Rosa. Things were not right. He finally experienced a massive stroke from which he did not recover. For the last weeks of his life he was placed in a special palliative care unit. Rosa felt guilty about not taking care of him herself. But she visited the home and watched over him fiercely.

"You treat him kindly," she said firmly to the nursing staff, facing them head on. "I don't want to hear a thing. This man spent four years in the war and four years in a POW camp." Tears were streaming down her face without her noticing. Indeed, she was to be reckoned with. The shy girl had vanished.

Three canon shots were fired during his funeral. Rosa cried for Anselm's tragic life and, again, remembering her male school mates who did not even come back home to be buried. Worse, Alois had vanished in Russia without a funeral at all. But Rosa had only a year to understand that Anselm, an uncle she had known all her life, was no more.

A year later Thekla passed away. She went to Munich with a female neighbor for the funeral. Another anchor and support in her life was gone. But this time Rosa worried about Susi the most. Her attempts to consol Susi were meant well, but seeing a fourth member of her family being buried in rapid succession made her worry. She again was acutely aware that the family was decreasing in size, and family was a sanctuary for Rosa. One had to have a family. Her hopes focused on Susi, who was now married.

"Susi," she once approached her cousin, "aren't you ever getting pregnant? Is our family going to die out?"

"Why don't you talk to Hans as well?" Susi said with a bit of vigor. Rosa did just that.

Life did not provide a break for Rosa. A few months later she learned that Lisa had died in her sleep from a heart attack. For this Rosa was not prepared either. In utter shock she ran to Mal to bring her the news.

"But she was not old at all, Mal." Rosa lamented.

"Well, what can I say?" Mal answered helplessly.

The next loss and major change Rosa had to deal with followed almost immediately.

"Rosa, we two alone can't run this farm," Kon approached her one day. "I am too old for it and I want to retire."

Rosa knew instantly that he was right about this. That thought had entered her mind as well. But, as was her habit, she pushed it aside and went on in her routine. She could not deny, however, that she herself was not as agile and strong anymore as before. Her youth had passed too.

"What do you mean?" Rosa asked Kon.

"Well, what do you think about closing our business and leasing the land to another farmer?"

Rosa saw that he looked distressed as he proposed this. She tried to be strong but was not successful. She could not stem the flood of her tears.

"Let me sleep over this," she asked her uncle.

He agreed and actually welcomed putting the issue off for no more than a night.

In the afternoon of the next day they discussed the practical side of it. Kon said he had talked to another farmer further away from the village who was keenly interested in taking over their livestock and leasing their farm land. Rosa knew him as well and felt comfortable about him. In fact, both had known the owner of the Langerst farm since they were little kids. He would treat her cows and calves, each one of whom Rosa had helped raise, with kindness. If it had to be, then this farmer was a good choice.

Indeed, the next day Rosa and Kon agreed to close the milk business and turn over their entire livestock to the Langerst farm. They also signed a lease agreement. It took a few more weeks to organize the transaction legally and logistically. Rosa dreaded the whole process but knew that she and Kon had no other choice.

When the day had arrived for the animals to be taken away, Rosa was pale. Watching her little calves walk up the ramp into the truck made her finally break down. She ran behind the barn and cried and cried that her body shook. The loss of her animals and her lifestyle was too great a pain to bear. Kon had his own grief but he eventually got Rosa to come back into the house when everything was over. Rosa fixed an evening snack but neither had any appetite. They went to bed early. The next day would be a new day and a new life. Rosa knew that this adjustment would take some time.

Over the next days and months Rosa went to the Langerst farm repeatedly to check on her cows and little calves. It helped her to pet and love them still. She also, of course, saw that the animals were in a nice stable and treated properly. Having gained a bit more peace in her heart that way, she gradually adjusted to the life of a retired farmer. There still were the chicken and the egg business, the gardening and the orchard. Together with Kon they both took good care of their property. Rosa also engaged in her crafts even more as she had more time to attend to such work. She also went on many bus trips with people in the village, enjoying the Alps very much.

For ten years Rosa and Kon lived a peaceful existence in their home they had known since birth. The work was manageable and they both enjoyed it.

***

Basically, Rosa and Kon had always been very healthy people. But now one of them occasionally had an issue with doctor's visits. Rosa had to have both of her eye lenses exchanged in two successive operations. This, so the doctor guessed, was a result of having lived for so long with heavy smokers. From then on she no longer needed glasses for the rest of her life. She always had a happy grin on her face when people asked her how she could read the menu in a restaurant without glasses.

However, when Kon developed lung problems and had to be hospitalized, Rosa's anxiety level skyrocketed. Now there was no more Thekla to talk to and to be calmed by. She turned to Susi to come to the farm for a bit. Rosa had grown up in a large family and had never been by herself. She was scared. And that fear for Kon's health was with her for the following two years. Kon was a heavy smoker and Rosa did not like it at all.

"But I don't bother him about it," she explained to Susi. "He has been in the war for all the six years and cigarettes kept him sane. No, I won't try to stop him."

Eventually Rosa accepted Kon's health issues. After all, he still mowed the garden and split firewood logs in winter. He was eighty years old. What more could one expect? Moreover, he still was there to listen when she had been upset by something. Rosa still could rely on Kon for emotional venting.

It was a religious ceremony on All Saints' Day where the villagers stood by their family graves. For that occasion family members from far away came to be there. It was tradition year after year. Rosa was happy and relieved that Kon still stood at their family grave with her. They had buried so many in this grave. She did not have to stand there alone. The grave was close to the walkway around the church building. Rosa liked that location as she could watch so many people come, people one otherwise did not see for at least a year or more. She did not trust her eyes when she saw an old, slightly stooped-over man walk by whom she recognized almost immediately as Sepp. Her heart seemed to have stopped. It forced her to take a deep breath, but then the past rose in her memory vigorously. With it she felt the old pain and humiliation rising. Now she was a woman of means and confidence. And she lashed out:

"Hey, Sepp, you are an old man now! You can't even walk upright anymore," Rosa shouted at him, forgetting Kon and other people next to her. *Oh, that felt good!*

Later, when she and Kon had their evening meal, Rosa brought up the subject.

"I am sorry," she said to Kon. "It got away from me." But Kon, as always, understood and calmed his niece with an understanding smile.

"Let it be, Rosa. Don't trouble yourself. Put it out of your mind again. It all was a long time ago."

***

Rosa and Kon lived on through their quiet life. They had lived together in the same family for roughly seven decades, minus the war years. To stress the significance of this fact, she told people that this was longer than any married couple who had been together as far as she knew. Later she would often say that these were "the most beautiful years." Those years came to a sudden end one morning in 1993 when Rosa found Kon dead in his bed. She was horrified.

"How come I did not hear him at all?" she asked Susi and Hans interchangeably. Guilt had a firm grip on her. *What if I could have saved him?*

At the funeral she stood by his open coffin and gently moved her hand over his head, saying, "You should have stayed a little longer."

She had called Susi early in the morning that day to bring the terrible news. One sentence she added and said over and over again over the next few days: "Susi, I am alone now!" Susi's reassurance that she and her brother Hans were still with her, although not living on the farm, fell on deaf ears. At the end of the funeral anger of having been left alone surfaced.

"Now I have nobody to bury anymore. I have buried them all. I am finished with this!"

Rosa cried on and off for days. She had never lived alone as a single person in her life. Sometimes she would reassure herself by mumbling to herself, "It will work, it will go okay."

She was seventy years old at that time.

She survived her last and most favorite uncle by twenty years. He had turned over his part ownership of the family farm to her. That fact slowly gained attention in Rosa's life. Now she was the sole owner of substantial property, the property she did not have to get married to Sepp. Sometimes it seemed that she was dumbfounded by that turn of events. Later she adjusted quite well to her new status. With pleasure and laughter she told Susi and Hans how the village people had changed their approach to her. She greatly enjoyed her newfound power of ownership. The municipality asked for a strip of her land to widen a street. Farmers came to enquire about her intentions in terms of selling land or forest. She was asked for various permissions, which gave her a chance to be difficult.

"I am the lady of the house," she even told Hans and his wife.

With the farm also came obligations and paperwork for insurances and such. For a while she mastered it all well. But when she passed her eightieth birthday she asked for more and more assistance. Steadily she turned worse in her forgetfulness and simultaneously lost her independence. She became anxiety-ridden and needy. Her mood became depressive as well as aggressive.

"What do I have to do to get over to the other side?" she questioned.

"What do you mean?" Susi asked her, suspecting what her answer was going to be.

"I mean going to my people, to where they are. All the people who have loved me are there," she said.

When her dementia had progressed to the point that she needed round-the-clock care, Rosa was put in a palliative care home. There, in the very beginning, she still would look when soccer games were on TV. When Susi or Hans visited her she would ask time and again how her mother was doing and who was milking the cows now. But eventually nothing reached her brain anymore. She became unresponsive and apparently no longer recognized Susi or Hans.

Rosa died quietly in her bed. She was a few days short of her ninetieth birthday.

It was said that two weeks later Sepp followed her.

***

About a month after Rosa's death Hans and Susi and their respective spouses were reminiscing. This became a very frequent thing for Susi and Hans, and is still ongoing. Hans loved to tell and retell about the times when he was living on the farm during the last year of the war.

"Rosa and I watched the bombing of the city from the forest. We had no idea how stupid we were. And we climbed on the left-behind tanks in our forests, exploring and looking for things we could use. We were crazy."

One subject also resurfaced regularly between them, and Susi retold the story as she had heard it repeatedly from Rosa. She had loved to tell Susi about the time in her youth prior to the war when she went with her peers to dancing lessons at Lisa's farm. The closing sentence of her tale was always the same: "It was so beautiful a time!"

About the Author

Isolde Martin was born in Passau, Germany, a small town right on the border of Austria and on the banks of the Danube. She spent her entire childhood and youth on the northern edge of the Alps. In 1972 she started her university studies in the United States, finishing with a Bachelor's degree in Psychology at the George Washington University in Washington, D.C. Her Master in Behavioral Sciences – Major Psychology followed in 1981 in Houston, Texas. She has worked in psychology and art psychotherapy in five different countries around the world. She now lives again in Germany.

She published her first book *Far Away from the Brewery*, which reflects on her life as an expatriate in seven different countries and in five continents. Following this, she published *Notes from the 48th North*.

Also by Isolde Martin ...

This book is not fiction.

This is the story of Isolde Martin's life as an expatriate, and takes the reader on a journey through five continents and seven countries.

In her frequent moves from country to country and from continent to continent, Isolde invites the reader to share the pleasures, the richness, the personal gains, and the high emotional costs of such a nomadic lifestyle for her and her family.

Isolde details her struggles to adjust as she learns to live in each culture, experiencing both blunders and successes. She explores her journey towards integrity and inner balance, and shares her growth as a person. This is a story about the psychological, social and cultural effects of a modern nomadic life. Isolde's own story illustrates and clarifies the psychological processes at work. Those who have lived under such circumstances or those who are embarking in it now can learn to understand and perhaps even anticipate their own responses better and thus master the stress of international life more successfully.

Isolde Martin returned to her home of Germany after more than three decades of life as an expatriate, which saw her live on five continents and in six countries. Additional travels included short stays in many more countries and trips around the globe in either direction three times.

After settling, at long last, in Germany, Isolde keenly and painfully felt the loss of the many friends and acquaintances now scattered across the world. Her efforts to stay in touch eventually resulted in poignant, charming, and often witty notes, an attempt to stay connected to friends in distant places – friends she appreciated and loved, and refused to lose to this very day, seven years later.

Now compiled into this single collection, Notes from the 48th North, offers a stream of consciousness that has been written in moods that range the emotional gamut, reflecting her feelings of loss, isolation, and confusion, whilst also exploring issues that have compelled her to write. One could say that the Notes continue a conversation that can no longer be held in person over a cup of tea.

Notes from the 48th North is a must-read for anybody who has traveled, felt the pangs of friendships long separated, or simply enjoys the poetic nature of observation.

www.ingramcontent.com/pod-product-compliance
Lightning Source LLC
Chambersburg PA
CBHW021058080526
44587CB00010B/296